Servants and Servitude in Colonial America

Servants and Servitude in Colonial America

Russell M. Lawson

PRAEGER™

An Imprint of ABC-CLIO, LLC
Santa Barbara, California • Denver, Colorado

Library of Congress Cataloging in Publication Control Number: 2017050144

ISBN: 978-1-4408-4179-8 (print)
      978-1-4408-4180-4 (ebook)

22 21 20 19 18   1 2 3 4 5

This book is also available as an eBook.

Praeger
An Imprint of ABC-CLIO, LLC

ABC-CLIO, LLC
130 Cremona Drive, P.O. Box 1911
Santa Barbara, California 93116-1911
www.abc-clio.com

This book is printed on acid-free paper ∞

Manufactured in the United States of America

In Memory of Laura Susan Lawson, 1964–2005

Sir, they are a race of convicts, and ought to be thankful for anything we allow them short of hanging.

—Samuel Johnson in 1769, referring to the American colonists, in Boswell, *Life of Johnson*

Contents

Prologue: Human Bondage   xi

Acknowledgments   xvii

Chapter 1:   The Children of Jamestown   1

Chapter 2:   Indian Bondage   19

Chapter 3:   The Captives of New France   31

Chapter 4:   English Town by the Sea   41

Chapter 5:   The Dutch Servants of New Netherland and New York   55

Chapter 6:   Daniel Defoe's London   67

Chapter 7:   The Voyage of the Free-Willers   81

Chapter 8:   *Infortunate* Servants   93

Chapter 9:   Oglethorpe's Dream   103

Chapter 10:   The Prisoners of Culloden   113

Chapter 11:   John Harrower and Servitude in the Colonial South   123

Chapter 12:   New England Apprentices   135

Chapter 13:   Servants and the American Revolution   145

Afterword   157

Appendix: Documents in the History of Colonial American Servitude   159

Sources Consulted   185

Index   199

Prologue

Human Bondage

The binding of one person to another, servant to master, has a long history in human affairs. Ancient peoples bought and sold humans, worked and exploited them for material gain, out of vengeance, or for personal status. Warriors in the ancient world lay siege to enemy cities knowing that when the siege was broken and the city fell there would be, after the initial blood-lust was satisfied, hundreds, even thousands of women and their children to capture as booty, to use, work, and sell at will. Bondage as a fact of life, the product of war, purchase, trade, or birth, was the experience of countless peoples of all ages and places for centuries.

Africans enslaved Africans long before 15th-century Portuguese sailed along the coast of West Africa seeking slaves. Africans, like Europeans, Asians, and Americans, captured enemy men, women, and children in battle; some captives were made ritual sacrifices; some were retained as personal slaves; some were sold to others. Besides war captives, there existed a lively trade throughout Africa of buying and selling slaves for labor, agriculture, war, and harems; some kingdoms demanded tribute in slaves from subordinate peoples; some people were enslaved for debt or crime. Notwithstanding religious beliefs—Muslim, Christian, or African polytheism—slavery was matter-of-fact, a present way of life, whether in South Africa, along the shores of the Mediterranean, or in sub-Saharan Africa.

Likewise, the indigenous inhabitants of North America enslaved people through war for centuries before the arrival of the Europeans in the late 15th and early 16th centuries. Indians used war captives for ceremonial purposes, resulting in torture and sacrifice, other times to adopt into the family or clan to replace a lost member, or as outcast laborers. Indian masters traded captive slaves to other tribes and, beginning in the 16th century, to European settlers in North America.

Western European traders began purchasing African slaves in West Africa and transporting them to America beginning in the 16th century and, once

colonies were established in America in the 16th and 17th centuries, purchased American Indian slaves from Indian tribes. The enslavement of war
captives was consistent with the European Christian mind-set, for Christians had long interpreted their religion, according to the tenets of "just war,"
as enabling the attack upon, killing of, imprisoning of, and capture of peoples for the sake of defensive or valid offensive war. The Spanish enslaved
captives in America beginning in the late 15th century, as did the French
and English in the 16th and 17th centuries. The English of the Tudor and
Stuart periods were willing to put their own people into bondage because of
birth, status, and crime, and they were willing to extend this system to
others—the Irish and Scotch, Europeans, Africans, and American Indians.
Like many cultures of the time and during previous centuries, bondage often
came about through war. The English put people—prisoners of war—in
bondage because of domestic and foreign conflicts.

Human bondage was well known in America for centuries, then, involving Indians, Africans, and whites. Few people among the different races of
America seemed to have troubled themselves with its validity or morality
before the 18th-century Enlightenment and its ideals of the rights of humans
and human equality and the inherent liberty and freedom of each individual.
By this time, it was beginning to be realized that those in bondage were dispossessed of their inherent human rights.

People who by their actions wittingly or unwittingly were bound in service to another were dispossessed of liberty, rights, and self-respect. The dispossessed servants of America included thousands of people—English,
Europeans, Germans, French, Africans, Indians, adults, children, sane,
insane, peaceful, violent, condemned criminals, disabled—who were indentured, apprenticed, transported as political prisoners or felons, or kidnapped
or served as redemptioners; some, already in America, such as Indians,
Freedmen, and poor whites, placed themselves into the service of others for
food, clothing, shelter, and security. The numbers of voluntary and involuntarily immigrants in bondage are presently indeterminable. Perhaps over
50,000 convicts and prisoners of war arrived in the colonies during the 17th
and 18th centuries. Perhaps 200,000 people voluntarily bound themselves
in service to cross the Atlantic Ocean.[1]

The numbers hardly matter compared to the individual experiences of
these dispossessed people who served, either voluntarily or involuntarily,
as agricultural, domestic, skilled, and unskilled laborers in the northern,
middle, and southern British American colonies as well as British Caribbean colonies and Canada before and after 1763. Poverty—in Europe, England, and America—drove people to this desperate act. Poverty in colonial
America was relentless, and servitude was the voluntary and involuntary
means by which the poor adapted, or tried to adapt, to their miserable
conditions.

There have always been dispossessed. Those in America today—the underprivileged, minorities, poor, children, and immigrants—were the same people 400, 300, and 200 years ago.

These were people who lost what they had the God-given right to possess, the basic sense of dignity, wellness, security, and freedom to have sufficient food to ward off hunger, shelter to stave off cold, clothing for protection from the elements, security in knowing that their daily needs would be met, inner contentment in knowing that they could live and thrive without feeling insufficient and a failure, able to live appropriately because the future is not a recurring question mark. The dispossessed in colonial America were most frequently servants, people who through an act of desperation gave up their freedom of movement, decision making, and choice, to bind themselves to another, a master, who would thenceforth, during a time specified by contract, have almost total power over them.

Humans live in society, not in the state of nature; society dispossesses by means of institutions, class structure, presuppositions and assumptions, failed morality, distorted sense of humanness, and a distorted understanding of Christian morality. Expediency, not love, drove people to acquire wealth at the expense of the poor. The Christian principles of love, mercy, and forgiveness were rarely extended to the poor and servants, those who comprised the lower class in colonial America. They were the product of the Enclosure Movement (enclosure of farm and grazing land in England), which displaced the English agricultural population, resulting in impoverishment; wars, such as the Thirty Years War in Europe and the Wars for Empire in America, which displaced people, leading to poverty and desperation; famine, the result of periods of climatic change, war, and crop failures, and the inadequate response of society, which led to hunger, malnourishment, and starvation; changes in family and community, which led to orphans without adequate care, widows and widowers with no one to help, the disabled, physically and mentally ill—and unconditional impoverishment became their fate, binding themselves into service their only option, brought by circumstances within or outside of their control.

Humans—children, women, men, young, strong, weak, sick, disabled, immigrants, migrants, elderly, widowed, orphaned, ignorant, unemployed, hungry, foreign, imprisoned, weary, meek, insane, conquered, enslaved, exploited—became dispossessed by chance, by the unfortunate choice of occupation of their father or grandfather, the unavoidable racial, ethnic, or social condition of their birth, their want of education, their lack of money, their particular beliefs, and the political, social, and religious institutions to which they were born and raised.

Who were they? Impoverished people of England, Scotland, Wales, and Ireland who immigrated to all 13 of the British colonies as well as British Caribbean colonies. Many were children, as described in Chapter 1, "The

Children of Jamestown." These 17th-century newcomers to America joined those already serving as slaves and servants to others. Chapter 2, "Indian Bondage," describes Indians, those who as white settlement increased in the 13 colonies, and in the wake of colonial wars (such as the Pequot War and King Philip's War), were forced into servitude as prisoners of war, for security or to pay off indebtedness. The wars for empire of the 17th and 18th century, particularly those fought between the French and English, featured raids and counterraids by the Indians against British settlements and the experience of captivity for English men, women, and children in New France, where they joined French *engagés*, as described in Chapter 3, "The Captives of New France." Those seeking a new life, either the deserving or undeserving poor—poor because of their own fault or another's—signed contracts, or indentures, agreeing to work in the colonies for a term of years in return for transportation to America. Those in a particular town in colonial America, Portsmouth, New Hampshire, are described in Chapter 4, "English Town by the Sea." That many early modern European countries, such as the Netherlands, adopted the system of using dispossessed people to further imperialistic goals of empire, is the topic of Chapter 5, "The Dutch Servants of New Netherland and New York."

Not everyone agreed or volunteered to emigrate to America. Press gangs in England roamed city streets looking for the intoxicated wayfarer or the hapless orphan who could add to a ship's complement of bodies. Spirits, so-called, advertised the wonders of America and chances for wealth to credulous, hungry people looking for a way out. Poverty was such in Tudor-Stuart England that Elizabeth and her successors tried to legislate an answer, the English Poor Laws, which largely failed, leading to desperation among the poor. Many were like Moll Flanders depicted in Daniel Defoe's novel or James Revel, who put his life to verse and became a *Poor Unhappy Transported Felon* who penned a sorrowful *Account of His Fourteen Years Transportation at Virginia in America*. In the wake of increasing poverty and crime, the English penal law system amassed a staggering list of 160 capital crimes that could result in execution by hanging at the gibbet. Some felons learned to claim the "benefit of the clergy," which resulted in the judge providing them the option of transportation to the colonies. Such are those portrayed in Chapter 6, "Daniel Defoe's London."

Impoverished Europeans (mostly German, French, Dutch), or those seeking a new life because of the ravages of war, emigrated from Europe as free people only to discover upon their arrival in America that to pay their passage they had to bind themselves as servants: these people are described in Chapter 7, "The Voyage of the Free-Willers." Those who arrived in America to become subject to the master's whims in work, food, shelter, and punishment had usually brought it on themselves, or at least had made the decision by their own free will. "Free will" was the phrase thrown in the face of the complainers, those from the Netherlands, France, particularly the Rhine-land, who had left their homeland based on the vague promises of the Neu-lander, who neglected to tell these credulous pawns that when whatever funds they had ran out (which usually was the case) on the voyage they would be forced into servitude in the colonies. And so the free-willers endured the voyage to America uncertain of their fate. After a harrowing voyage across the Atlantic, sometimes lasting several months, in crowded conditions among the sick and suffering, few arrivals were prepared for what awaited them. Landing at ports up and down the American coast, from New York to Philadelphia to Charleston to Port Royal, the servants, felons, and free-willers were auctioned to masters who took them away to work for 4, 7, or 14 years on farms and plantations or in towns. Servants discovered that their legal rights depended upon each colony and the whim of the master, who had the right to buy and sell, punish, and work days and hours according to his desire.

Indebtedness in America came in a variety of forms. Arrivals from across the Atlantic, to pay the debt incurred on crossing, followed whoever purchased their indenture: to the plantation, the village, the farm, the ship. Chapter 8, "*Infortunate* Servants," tells the story of one such pauper, William Moraley, who arrived in Philadelphia in 1729. Around the same time, Englishman James Oglethorpe decided upon a benevolent scheme to help the paupers of England start a new life. Chapter 9, "Oglethorpe's Dream," describes the experience of these Georgia immigrants. Some of the impoverished of the British Isles who came to America by force were political prisoners of the wars of England against the Scottish and the Irish. Their experience is described in Chapter 10, "The Prisoners of Culloden." English servants, whether brought to America by choice or force, in the colonial South worked alongside African American slaves. This is the story of Chapter 11, "John Harrower and Servitude in the Colonial South."

There were many indebted in America who had never been on a ship, who were native born to Africans, Europeans, or English who had immigrated voluntarily or involuntarily to America, and who never could escape poverty. Children of servants, once released from bondage, often in desperation bound themselves out to labor for a certain number of years in return for food and shelter. This was often the only choice for American Indians, free blacks, and the *engagés* of English Canada. Servants in New England served as whalers and fishers; in colonial towns many served as tutors and teachers; throughout the colonies they served as man-servants, ladies-in-waiting, or nurses to the wealthy; on farms and plantations in the southern colonies they labored in rice, cotton, sugar, or tobacco fields. Children of paupers, in return for learning a skill, were bound in apprenticeship to a master to serve until maturity. Their story is told in Chapter 12, "New England Apprentices."

All were bound to the system of labor, servants as well as masters. Servants of all ethnic and racial groups engaged in all types of work. In Dutch New Netherland and, after 1664, English New York, Dutch and English worked as servants to pay off indebtedness. In the Middle Colonies, white servants from all places, particularly the Rhineland, joined blacks, Mulattoes, and Indians working the large plantations of the South and Caribbean throughout the 1600s and 1700s until the growing demand for slaves replaced them. The conditions were such that many tried to escape, sometimes successfully; but those who were caught faced corporeal punishment and additional time of service. Those who lived to be released from bondage were given something euphemistically called "Freedom Dues," consisting of money, clothing, or land, depending upon the ability and willingness of the master. Sometimes freedom was its own reward. Masters were bound to the system as well. Some gloried in it and thrived at the expense of others; those of a more sensitive moral nature, as it were, became trapped in a system of exploitation for the sake of profit. Servants and masters alike experienced "the times that try men's souls" during the latter half of the 18th century, when in America a revolutionary movement occurred that tested the idea of human bondage and the limits of human freedom: this is the subject of Chapter 13, "Servants and the American Revolution."

Poverty is, like war, difficult to understand, seemingly ubiquitous throughout time and place, impossible to eradicate, a plague upon humankind yet a phenomenon that often brings out the best responses from humans. In this book these stories are told: of suffering and triumph; of untimely death and survival; of sorrow; and, even at the worst of times, contentment.

Note

1. Estimates found in Christopher Tomlins, *Freedom Bound: Law, Labor, and Civic Identity in Colonizing English America, 1580–1865* (New York: Cambridge University Press, 2010), 35.

Acknowledgments

The debts that I have incurred in the writing of this book go back many years. I first conceived of the desire to trace and recover the lives of indentured servants when I was a graduate student at Oklahoma State University. Under the tutelage of Professor H. James Henderson, I researched indentured servitude and presented a paper at a social scientific conference in 1981 and English poor relief during the Tudor, Stuart, Commonwealth, Orange, and Hanover periods and had an article included in a modest peer-reviewed publication. At the University of New Hampshire, under the tutelage of Professor Charles E. Clark, I researched poor relief in northern New England. Since those years during the 1980s, I have continued my interest in the experiences of everyday people who lived in colonial America and who endured the journey from England and Europe to America. Librarians at various institutions have assisted in my research, especially those at Oklahoma State University and the University of New Hampshire back in the days of card catalogs and painstaking research without electronic devices. Other librarians at the Massachusetts Historical Society, New Hampshire Historical Society, and Portsmouth Public Library have assisted with handwritten manuscripts. I have particularly benefited from the efforts of the many historians and antiquarians of the 17th, 18th, 19th, and early 20th centuries, whose work, especially in local history, has provided a fundamental basis for my research. I wish to also thank Bacone College for continuing support of my research and writing. My wife, Linda, always provides fundamental help and support.

My family, and ancestors, are and were the kind of everyday people portrayed in this book. The commonsense values of family, work, faith, perseverance, and love for freedom that are portrayed in this book are the same values of my personal and ancestral past. This book is dedicated to the spirit of such people.

CHAPTER ONE

The Children of Jamestown

She had golden hair, brightened by the sun on fine days after the early-morning fog lifted in the wake of the west wind blowing from the mountains to the sea. She was but 14 and parentless, her mother and father having either died in England or forsaken her to labor in the New World. She was pretty, in her way, with fair skin, blue eyes, and small features. She pulled her long hair back under a simple coif revealing a broad forehead and thin eyebrows. Her pink lips matched an attractive, dainty nose.

Born in the waning years of Queen Elizabeth's reign, she was destined for a short life, living in squalor in England, one of the millions of impoverished who thronged the streets of cities such as London. Her story is hardly known, fitting the lives and experiences of the poor of England and elsewhere over the centuries. All that remains of her brief beautiful life are bones from an ancient cellar, where her remains had been hastily deposited one day during the winter of 1609–1610, after she died of hunger or disease during a period of privation and want at Jamestown.[1]

How did she end her life so young in the small village of Jamestown on the James River in the New World? She was likely one of the many who were removed from the streets of London and taken to a place called bridewell, a "hospital," like a temporary place of incarceration, for the homeless in London and other 17th-century English cities. Here, she and others languished, waiting for a determination to be made of their fates. The infant colony of the Virginia Company was struggling to survive and make a profit; workers were needed. What better than to send the desperate poor to America to work? Perhaps, it was reasoned, she and others could make a new life in a New World.

This girl—her name is unknown, perhaps Elizabeth, Mary, Margaret, or Jane—and others joined ships that set sail from London for Jamestown during the spring of 1609. Her ship and six others arrived in August. They came to a small, struggling fort where many had already died in the previous two years of settlement. The people on board the vessels were hungry, as were the settlers of Jamestown. Yet under the leadership of Captain John Smith, who had served as president of the colony since September 1608, the colony had become better ordered. Smith had explored the environs of the James River valley and Chesapeake Bay and tributaries, had come to know and interact with the varied Algonquian tribes of the region, had established trade with the Algonquians, had instilled discipline among the colonists, had solidified defenses, and had put everyone to work for the good of the whole. Shortly after the arrival of the girl in August, Captain Smith was horribly injured in an accident and was forced to return to England. With him went the stolidity of uncompromising leadership; the people of the colony as a result suffered during the ensuing winter—the starving time.

Smith learned during his slow recovery after his return to England of the trials the colony endured—brought upon them by themselves—how in his absence all frugality and concern for the future vanished in the wake of hubris and concern for the immediate present. The stores that they had at the beginning of winter were quickly consumed, and the tools they had to provide food lay unused. Of the 500 men and women of Jamestown when Smith left for England in October, "within 6 months after there remained not many more than 60. most miserable and poore creatures."[2]

It did not have to be this way; Smith knew that with proper management and dedicated occupation the colony could survive, even thrive. During the ensuing years, he kept this faith in England's colonial ventures in his heart, yearning to return to America, to establish a proper colony with the knowledge he had gained at Jamestown. Although Smith never returned to Virginia, in 1614 he did sail once again to America, to the lands of the north. He journeyed along the coast, christening the land New England; he kept a journal of his experiences, which he turned into a small book, the *Description of New England*.

When the *Description of New England* appeared in 1616, Smith was 36 years old, a man of humble roots still seeking his fortune. Having been raised by yeomen farmers in Lincolnshire in the 1580s, Smith had decided when he was a teenager to seek his fortune in the military, fighting in the European religious wars. Courage and ability with the sword enabled him to rise above the condition that most other people in 16th- and 17th-century Europe and England experienced—utter poverty.

During the years that Smith was growing up, when Elizabeth I was queen, England continued to be dominantly agricultural; farm productivity increased in the wake of privatization of public lands. Many English farmers, such as George Smith, John's father, were tenants of larger landowners; others were not so fortunate and had to labor on farms for set wages regulated by parish justices. Unemployment, low wages, and limited manufacturing meant that millions of English men, women, and children lived in poverty. War led to disrupted trade, and bad weather resulted in poor harvests, which pushed people close to famine—sometimes over the edge to starvation. Smith escaped the fate of many English villeins and yeomen, agricultural laborers and tenant farmers, by serving as a mercenary soldier. By the time he returned, in 1606, from years of adventure in Europe, poverty had worsened in England (during the reign of James I), and crime was increasing. Wandering beggars and petty thieves spilled across England; laws were rigorous and punishments were harsh; often panhandlers and thieves were placed in institutions that went by the names of "hospital," "workhouse," or "house of correction," where they learned dependence and never-ending hopelessness, which were not solutions, rather causes for more problems.

John Smith's experience in Jamestown from 1607 to 1609 and sailing along the New England coast in 1614 convinced him that the solution to dependence and poverty—the increasing prevalence in England of the able poor, the sturdy beggar—was not the institutionalization of the poor rather their employment in an activity that would fuel an independent, hopeful mind-set. As Smith coasted the shores of Maine, New Hampshire, and Massachusetts from May to July 1614, as he fished the waters and traded with the indigenous inhabitants, he came to know the plenty of the land, where with but a little work it would be difficult to starve, and with much work it would be easy to thrive. "So freely," he wrote in *Description of New England*, "hath God and his majesty bestowed those blessings on them that will attempt to obtaine them, as here every man may be master and owner of his owne labour and land; . . . if hee have nothing but his hands, he may set up this trade; and by industrie quickly grow rich; spending but halfe that time wel[l], which in *England* we abuse in idlenes[s], worse or as ill." Smith believed that God made available a land yet barely touched by the native inhabitants, and King James I encouraged his people to go forth and make a living, benefiting themselves and England. The native inhabitants "compare their store in the Sea, to the haires of their heads: and surely there are an incredible abundance upon this Coast." What Englishman would not wish to spend days "fishing before your doors" and "every night sleep[ing] quietly a shore with good cheare and what fires you will: or when you please [fish], with your wives and familie." Boys and girls can be put to work: boys fishing for cod, mullet, and salmon and, girls spinning fishing lines. New England, he argued, offers everything the poor of England would wish for: all that is needed is labor and desire. "All these and diverse other good things do heere, for want of use, still increase, and decrease with little diminution; whereby they growe to that abundance you shall scarce finde any Baye, shallow shore, or Cove of sand, where you may not take many Clams, or Lobsters, or both at your pleasure; and in many places lode your boat if you please: nor Iles where you finde not fruits, birds, crabs, and mussels, or all of them for taking, at a lowe water. And in the harbors we frequented, a little boye might take of Cunners . . . and such delicate fish, at the ships sterne, more then sixe or tenne can eate in a daie; but with a casting net, thousands when wee pleased: and scarce any place, but Cod, Cuske, Halibut, Mackerell, Skate, or such like, a man may take with a hooke or line what he will. And in divers sandy Baies, a man may draw with a net great store of Mullets, Ba[s]ses, and divers other sorts of such excellent fish, as many as his Net can drawe on shore." There is "no River where there is not plentie of Sturgeon, or Salmon, or both."[3]

In short, Smith proclaimed, "worthy is that person to starve that heere cannot live; if he have sense, strength, and health: for, there is no such penury of these blessings in any place, but that a hundred men may, in one houre or two, make their provisions for a day." Indeed, "who can desire more content, that hath small meanes; or but only his merit to advance his fortune, then to tread, and plant that ground hee hath purchased by the hazard of his life? If he have but the taste of virtue and magnanimitie, what to such a minde can bee more pleasant, then planting and building a foundation for his Posteritie, gotte from the rude earth, by Gods blessing and his owne industrie, without prejudice to any?" At the same time, Smith argued, the humble activities of the English in America will bring Christianity to the native inhabitants and "gaine to our Native mother-countrie a kingdom to attend her: finde employment for those that are idle, because they know not what to doe: so farre from wronging any, as to cause Posteritie to remember thee; and remembring thee, ever honour that remembrance with praise?" It was a win-win proposition, this colonizing of New England.[4]

Smith could see how his own life as a child would have been bettered. He condemned English parents who were unwilling to help their children make something of themselves but rather allowed them to live lives of sloth and idleness. But they had as their example the idle rich of England, aristocrats who constantly waited upon the king for favors. Embracing laziness and ignorance, the English closed their eyes to the means to relieve themselves from the burden of poverty: "wee either so neglect, or oppresse and discourage the present, as wee spoile all in the making, crop all in the blooming; and building upon faire sand, rather then rough rockes, judge that wee knowe not, governe that wee have not, feare that which is not; and for feare some should doe too well, force such against their willes to be idle or as ill." It was not Smith's wish "to persuade children from their parents" or "servants from their masters: onely, such as with free consent may be spared." Youths, the orphaned, the newly married, "heere," in America, "by their labour may live exceeding well."[5]

John Smith was a member of the Church of England who took to heart the precepts of the Book of Common Prayer, the theological, liturgical basis for the Anglican Church. During Smith's time, King James I commissioned the

King James Version of the Old Testament and New Testament. In the opening note, "The Translators to the Reader," the Jacobean men who put together this English Bible justified their work, "for the behoof and edifying of the unlearned" who by means of this translation into English "hear *Christ* speaking unto them in their mother tongue, not by the voice of their minister only, but also by the written word translated." Even little children could discover the love of God in this Bible: "Then were there brought unto him little children, that he should put *his* hands on them, and pray: and the disciples rebuked them. But Jesus said, 'Suffer little children, and forbid them not, to come unto me: for of such is the kingdom of heaven.' And he laid *his* hands on them, and departed thence."[6]

Likewise the Book of Common Prayer provided blessings for English children, in the *Letanie* [Litany]: "That it may please thee to preserve all that travell by land or by water, all women labouring of childe, all sicke persons, and yong children, and to shewe thy pitie upon all prisoners and captives. . . . That it may please thee to defend and provide for the fatherlesse children and widowes, and all that bee desolate and oppressed. We beseech thee to heare us good Lord."[7]

Notwithstanding what the Book of Common Prayer and King James Bible said about the love and welfare of children, the English during King James's reign treated children with neglect and brutality. Throughout history, children have been, after all, the poorest of the poor, the most defenseless members of any society. Such was the case during the Tudor years in England and the Stuart years in England and America.

Children in England during the Tudor years of the 16th century had little opportunity for education, unless their parents were yeomen farmers or of higher wealth and status; poor children were, along with their parents, laborers. During the early years of Elizabeth's reign, there was an attempt to legislate the relationship between laborers and their employers, including children working as laborers or as apprentices. Because the economy was based on agriculture, many children worked as farm laborers often by annual contract as servants to masters; these children would not live at home but rather with the master. Likewise, no child could work at anything other than agriculture unless apprenticed to a skilled craftsman to learn a trade. The Statute of Artificers, landmark legislation relating to labor, in 1563, declared that there were many laws that had been passed over the years to regulate relationships and wages between "apprentices, servants and labourers" and their masters and employers, yet these laws had set wages that did not keep up with inflation, to the despair of the workers. The statute sought by regulating wages to "banish idleness, advance husbandry and yield unto the hired person both in the time of scarcity and in the time of plenty a convenient proportion of wages," so long as servants and masters realized that both had to be fully committed to their mutual tasks and obligations during the term of contract.

The obligation of the masters was primarily to conform to the annual ruling of the justices of the peace as to the legitimate and fair wages to be paid to workers. The obligation of the workers was to engage in their task. During the corn and hay harvest, justices of the peace and constables would require and enforce, upon pain of punishment, workers "to serve by the day for the mowing . . . or inning of corn, grain, and hay, and that none of the said persons shall refuse so to do, upon pain to suffer imprisonment in the stocks, by the space of two days and one night." The statute also required unmarried girls 12 years of age and up to work for wages and boys to work as agricultural apprentices, upon pain, if refusing, of having their movements and freedom restricted by the parish. Apprentices served until age 24 for boys and 21 for girls. The statute provided for the protection of apprentices from the abuse of masters and the protection of masters from the unwillingness to work of apprentices.[8]

Although the English by Elizabeth's reign had embraced ideas of the essential freedom and rights of the English people, there continued to be an attitude toward the poor that resembled the medieval past, when the vast majority of the English population was bound to servitude in the system of serfdom, or villeinage. The streets of London, for example, in 1569, and many times thereafter, were cleansed of human refuse, as it were, and the poor of all ages and conditions were sent to one of four bridewells, or hospitals, which was a euphemism for a place where the incarcerated poor would languish and stay out of the way. A law passed in Elizabeth's 14th year (1572) provided for corporeal punishment: vagabonds of at least age 14 would be, stated the law, "grievously whipped and burned through the gristle of the right ear with a hot iron of the compass of an inch unless some credible person will take him into service for a year." Four years later, legislation provided that idle youths were to be supervised in their work by parish officials; poor children and adults who refused to work would be incarcerated in the parish workhouse or house of correction, where said recalcitrants would produce iron, flax, hemp, and wool for the benefit of the parish. Workhouses often had something akin to a training school to teach youths the values of work. Officials called "wardens" and "censors" supervised the poor in these houses. In the wake of crop failures and famine from 1594 to 1597, Elizabeth and her ministers developed a sophisticated poor relief system that included overseers in each parish administering monies raised by the poor tax for outright relief to the deserving poor or incarceration in houses of correction, workhouses, or hospitals for the undeserving poor. The overseers were also charged with putting poor children to work or apprenticing them to a master. When public means of poor relief and solving the problem of vagrancy failed, which usually happened, private charity might fill the gap. There were schemes in many parishes to erect private almshouses and workhouses to engage the poor more charitably than their public counterparts. Often public workhouses, initiated with an intent to help and employ the poor, became more coercive houses of correction.[9]

Under Elizabeth, the undeserving poor and vagrants, young and old, lost their rights as freeborn English. Authorities categorized the poor according to three types: "poore by impotency and defect," those who were ill, aged, disabled, orphaned, or insane; "poore by casualty," those who were poor by chance, suffering disasters that rendered them dependent; and "thriftlesse poore," those who essentially chose to be poor by indolence and extravagance. All three types of poor in England were subject to institutionalization, in a hospital, workhouse, or house of correction. To what end, however, was never clear. As the 18th-century social commentator Frederic Eden wrote, "Never were severe laws issued in greater abundance nor executed more rigorously; and never did the unrelenting vengeance of justice prove more ineffectual." Indeed, the numbers of the poor never quite declined notwithstanding the variety of measures deployed. William Harrison, who wrote a book describing England in 1577, claimed that there were thousands of vagrants loose upon the highways; 25 years later, there were 30,000 impoverished people in London. And these poor souls, wrote Phillip Stubbes in 1583, "lie in the streets upon pallets of straw" or, worse, "mire and dirt," whereupon they "are suffered to die in the streets like dogs or beasts without any mercy or compassion."[10]

The old manorial system, where, generation after generation, families were connected to the land, had this one advantage: even the lowest serf felt connected to the product of his or her labor; the more work done, the more food at the serf's table. But when the manorial system collapsed during the 14th, 15th, and 16th centuries, the English laborer no longer had a stake in a particular property, in the land. The English Reformation likewise freed people from dependency on the Roman Catholic Church for land and charity. The freeborn English men and women increasingly had to find their own path in farm work or trade and manufacturing; freedom from dependence on the lord was its own challenge. Inability to find work led to consequences; privation often led many such unfortunates to bind themselves to a master for a period of time, to work for food and security—almost a return to the experience of serfdom. For others who felt put upon to work for another, the state intervened, requiring work on pain of losing one's liberty.[11]

The 18th-century writer Joshua Gee summed up what many English religious, social, and political leaders thought about the disparity between rich and poor: "Hunger and Cold will make People work to supply their Necessities." Such a callous approach to life explains the behavior of the English toward the poor, particularly poor children, during the 16th and 17th centuries. Magistrates incarcerated children, male and female, next to the most hardened criminals in gaols such as Newgate, Bridewell, and Marshalsea. Elizabethan English such as Thomas Anguish, founder of the Norwich

Children's Hospital, were as concerned with idle children as they were with idle adults. Anguish created a place for the "keeping, bringing up, and teaching of young and very poor children," notably those who "lie in the streets, vaults, doors, and windows," whereupon they "fall into great and grievous diseases and lamenesses, as that they are not fit for profession, ever after." This was the rub: a sick child was a dependent child, and dependent, poor children were very commonplace, and becoming more so. English society depended upon the work of children as much as adults. Orphans were placed in institutions for their health, their maintenance, and to work, as were children of parents still living. Magistrates, shipmasters, and kidnappers were often complicit with parents who allowed their children to be removed from their family to other places and institutions, whether in England or overseas in America.[12]

Notwithstanding the Elizabethan poor laws, which James I, who ascended to the throne in 1603, adopted, there continued to be poverty and crime, particularly in cities such as London. The state continued to force the freeborn English man and woman to work or be incarcerated. The poor, understandably, thought that the rich were to blame, especially the great landowners who were enclosing land and displacing small freeholders. Bands of armed "rogues" marched through the land threatening the contented rich. Organized actions, such as the Midland Revolt of 1607, a brief expression of unrest, led by "levellers" who wished to see increasing equality, accomplished little of substance, and the poor continued to be always present. James and his Privy Council determined that rogues and vagabonds caused much of the unrest and proclaimed that "incorrigible or dangerous rogues . . . shall be branded in the left shoulder with a hot burning iron of the breadth of an English shilling, with a great Roman R upon the iron, and the branding upon the shoulder to be so thoroughly burned and set upon the skin and flesh that the letter R be seen and remain for a perpetual mark upon such rogue during his or her life." That such punishment scarcely worked was shown by the increasing numbers of the poor. The author of a pamphlet published in 1622, *Grievous Groans for the Poor*, stated the case: "Though the number of the poor do daily increase, there hath been no collection for them, no, not these seven years, in many parishes of this land, especially in county towns; but many of those parishes turneth forth their poor, yea and their lusty labourers that will not work, or for any misdemeanor want work, to beg, filch, and steal for their maintenance, so that the country is pitifully pestered with them." One solution, besides branding, incarceration, and hanging, was to rid the realm of them. The Spanish minister to England, Don Alfonso, recognized as much in 1611, writing: "Their principal reason for colonizing these parts is to give an outlet to so many idle and wretched people as they have in England." The Crown identified "places or partes to which such incorrigible or dangerous rogues shall be banished: The New found Lande, the East and West Indies,

Fraunce, Germanie, Spayne, and the Lowe Countries." The Lord Mayor and the various merchant and trade companies of London agreed with this solution and, in 1609, went so far as to raise hundreds of pounds upon the scheme, never realized, of founding a colony in America for the poor and vagrants.[13]

Virginia, therefore, became the destination for the poor of London and elsewhere in England. In 1610, for example, 300 disorderly vagrants were shipped to Virginia, which caused the governor and Council of Virginia to complain to their superiors at the London Company that those hitherto shipped to labor in Virginia "drop forth by year after year . . . ill provided for before they come, and worse governed when they are here, men of such distempered bodies and infected minds, whom no examples dayly before their eyes, either of goodness or punishment, can deter from their habitual impieties, or terrify from a shameful death. . . . But as a necessary quantity of provisions for a year at least must be carefully sent with men, so likewise must be the same care for men of quality . . . chosen out." Nevertheless, in ensuing years, judicial authorities in England reprieved felons for transportation to Virginia. Such were the likes of John Fyerbrasse, convicted of stabbing another; John Peircy, convicted of "housebreaking & stealing"; "Stephen Rogers, convicted of a killing and reprieved, ordered to be sent to Virginia . . . because he is a carpenter"; and "Joseph Johnson, an incorrigible rogue." Upon arriving, they found other ne'er-do-well servants serving as an example of what to expect when committing such infractions as "impudence and neglect": "Thomas Garnetts, servant to Captain William Powell, was pilloried"—put in the stocks—as a consequence of his ill behavior.[14]

Vagrant children were also shipped to Virginia. In August 1618, "William Laratt, vagrant brought in from Fleet Street, a little boy born in Hounsditch who says his mother dwells in the country at Westminster," who was incarcerated in the local bridewell, learned he was bound for Virginia. Joining William that autumn were scores of other children, boys and girls (called "wenches"), picked up off the streets of London, where they bivouacked in places such as Cripplegate, Bishopsgate, St. Sepulchre, Smithfield, Cornhill, near the Tower, and along the Thames. In October 1618, "Captain Andrews and Jacob Braems, merchant in the *Silver Falcon*" planned "to ship to Virginia 100 young boys and girls who lie starving in the streets" of London. The terror felt by children at such a plan, as detailed in London records, was such that 40 "maidens" fled the city and were sought by their concerned parents upon news that one Owen Evans had a commission to transport them to the New World. Every month more youngsters were brought to bridewells where they awaited their uncertain fate. These included "Thomas Walsingham, William Charter, Francis Wilson, William Makepeace and John Tainter," who were "vagrant boys and young rogues . . . to be kept at work until they are sent to Virginia."[15]

The transcripts of the Virginia Company of London at this time reveal the cold calculations of knights, noblemen, merchants, and the king to exploit the suffering of children for the sake of profit in Virginia. The treasurer, that is, executive officer of the company in 1619, Edwin Sandys, outlined his conception of how to use the poor to ensure success in the colony. He proposed in a November meeting that 300 men be sent as tenants to work on behalf of the company and king; accompanying them "for their ease and comodiousnes there be 100 young persons sent to be their Apprentices." Moreover, to bring stability to the disorderly rabble that made up Virginia and prevent those already sent from cultivating plans to return to England, Sandys advised that the company ship "one hundred young Maides—young and uncorrupt—to become wifes; that wifes, children and familie might make them lesse movable and settle them, together with their Posteritie in that Soile." These 500 people, he proposed, would be sent by the cheapest route via "ships trading to Newfoundland, and so to transport them at six pounds a person."[16]

To accomplish these ends, the company wrote a letter to the Lord Mayor of London, dated November 17, 1619, in which the company thanked the Lord Mayor for his past assistance in rounding up and sending 100 children to Virginia, where, "by the goodnes of God, ther safely arrived (save such as dyed in the waie)"; they requested his assistance again, in sending another 100 early in the year 1620. "Our desire" for these children, the company wrote: "is that we may have them of 12 yeares old & upward, with allowance of Three pound a peec for their transportacon, and forty shillings a pees for their apparell, as was formerly granted. They shall be apprentizes; the boys till they come to 21 years of age; the girles till like age, or till they be marryed, and afterward they shall be placed as Tennants upon the publique lands, with best condicons, where they shall have houses with stocke of corne and cattle to begin with, and afterward the moyty [moiety] of all increase and profit whatsoever."[17]

The children would be shipped out to Virginia with hardened convicts, euphemistically called "tenants." King James had demanded the company proceed with as many ships as possible to bring as many poor rogues away from England as possible; men of the company thought that at least four ships must sail, such a flotilla being the means to prevent mutiny by the hard cases on board. The idea of transportation to Virginia was not popular to the "superfluous multitude," as Sandys referred to the poor of London; indeed, the 100 children selected to go were not at all happy, notwithstanding that Sandys believed that "under severe masters in Virginia" they "may be brought to goodness." The king desired that the London Company select the ne'er-do-wells and impoverished to go, keeping them at bridewells as they awaited ships to be made ready for the voyage. The company granted parcels of land in Virginia to those merchants willing to supply funds to ship the poor to

America. Planters who took a boy as a servant were to pay 20 pounds of tobacco, a bargain compared to the 120 pounds charged, a year later, for young maids to take to wife. The company sent "twelve lustie youths" to a plantation along the James River called Martin's Hundred; "fourty more" soon followed. The company sent others to Virginia besides English. "Two French youths," in September 1621, joined "one Miles Prickett" on a voyage across the ocean to serve the planters. Prickett's servitude, wage-free, which was to be until "Allhollantide," that is, October 31, of 1622, was in return for his transport to Virginia and "apparrell given him." Prickett was a salt maker.[18]

Although the managers and investors of the London Company recognized that marriage between two people proceeds "according to the law of nature," the company encouraged the leaders of the colony in Virginia to be as fathers to the maids sent there, receiving them with "the same Christian pietie and charitie as they were sent from hence"—as fathers, they were to make sure the maids marry "freemen or tenants as have meanes to maintaine them" rather than other servants. These women were to be wives, not servants. Accordingly they were to be as marriageable as possible: "We have used extraordinary care and dilligence in the choise of them, and have received none of whom we have not had good testimony of theire honest life and cariadge, wch together wth their names, we send there inclosed for the sattisfaction of such as shall marry them; for whose further encoradgement we desire you to give publique notice that the next spring we purpose to send over as many youths for apprentices to those that shall now marry any of them and make us due sattisfaccon." Those men who took them to wife would in turn be sent servants to help them establish a proper household. The typical head-rights, land granted to those who sponsored immigrants, would not be granted for these wives. The maids who were not married, or chose not to be, were to be put in service, the masters to pay the tobacco for their servitude. Meanwhile, unlike females, male servants could not marry freely.[19]

The maids who arrived in Virginia were treated well, at least according to a report from Martin's Hundred, where the inhabitants "doe willinglie and lovinglie receave the new comers who also shall have from us all lawfull aide and assistance in all things."[20] Besides the challenge of adapting to a new environment of work and marriage, and the different (from England) climate of the Virginia tidewater, these young women also endured the dreadful attack on James River settlements by the local (Powhatan) Algonquians on March 22, 1622. Half of the inhabitants of Martin's Hundred died, while one-fourth of the English colonists of Virginia lost their lives.

The Indian attack on the English settlements was the brainchild of Opechancanough, who had taken control of the loose confederacy of Algonquians once ruled by his brother, Wahunsenacawh, whose title was Powhatan. According to John Smith, Opechancanough had from the start, in 1607, opposed the English, and after taking control upon his brother's death in 1618, sought to avenge the brutal invasion of his lands in the James River valley. The interaction between the English and the Indians from 1607 to 1622 had been mixed—at times cordial and friendly, at other times aggressive and intimidating. Both sides committed violence against the other. The English brought their notions of civilizing the Indians by Christianizing them, which found mixed reactions among the Indians. One young man whose name was Chanco (or Chauco), and who was associated with William Perry, most likely as his servant, was told of the impending attack the night before. He was an Indian who had been converted by the English to Christianity, and he felt particularly close to his master/employer Perry. According to John Smith, "Perrys Indian," or Chanco, informed the English of the planned attack; "thus them that escaped was saved by this one converted Infidell," Smith wrote. "And though three hundred fortie seven were slaine, yet thousands of ours were by the meanes of this alone thus preserved; for which Gods name be praised for ever and ever."[21]

As seen in Chanco's example, the London Company had formed the benevolent design of bringing Christianity to young Indians; a school at Henrico had even been proposed for the purpose.[22] The English believed that part of the philosophical basis for founding colonies in the New World was a religious one, that is, to fulfill the Great Commission, wherein Christ commanded all His disciples to bring the Gospel to all people, worldwide. Yet competing with these religious scruples were the other overwhelming desires of the English for power and wealth. The poor children of England, already Christian, were considered commodities to buy and sell and upon whom to force labor for, ostensibly, their own good of reforming their impoverished, lazy characters.

Unfortunately for these young immigrants, life in America was especially hard. The colonists of Virginia overwhelmingly died of sicknesses of all sorts. Merchants packed their ships to the brink, and, during the voyage to America, poor nutrition, despair, and illness prevailed, so that those who arrived at the James River were weak, hungry, and ill. Inhabitants of the James River valley referred to the first few months of residence as the time of "seasoning," when newcomers would either adapt and live or fail to adjust to the climate and conditions of labor and die. The Dutch writer David Pietersz de Vries, in *Voyages from Holland to America*, learned from the English that "during the months of June, July, and August, it is very unhealthy; that their people, who have then lately arrived from England, die during these months, like cats and dogs, whence they call it the (sickly) season. When they have this sickness, they want to sleep all the time, but they must be prevented from sleeping by force, as they die if they get asleep. This sickness, they think arises from the extreme heat that exists there." The London Company received a report in 1622 that "divers old Planters and others . . . allure and beguile divers young person and others (ignorant and unskillful in such matters) to serve them upon intollerable and unchristianlike condicons upon promises of such rewards and recompense, as they were no wayes able to performe nor ever meant." Such duplicity led George Thorpe, a leader of the colony, to write that "more doe die here of the disease of their minde then of their body by having this countrey victualles over-praised unto them in England and by not knowinge they shall drinke water here."[23]

This despair felt by the immigrant in Virginia resulted either because the young man or woman arrived in Virginia completely against their will, separated from home, friends, and family, or because they had been convinced in England that America would easily supply all of their needs and help them to prosper. There were many tracts written by promoters of colonization who sincerely believed that the impoverished of England could thrive in this new land. John Hammond, for example, in *Leah and Rachel, or the Two Fruitfull Sisters, Virginia and Mary-Land*, wrote of his astonishment that so many impoverished in England, "rather then they remove themselves [to America], live here a base, slavish, penurious life; as if there were a necessity to live and to live so choosing rather then they will forsake *England* to stuff *New-Gate, Bridewell,* and other Jayles with their carkessies, nay cleave to tyburne it selfe; and so bring confusion to their souls horror and infamie to their kindred or posteritie, others itch out their wearisom lives in reliance of other mens charities, an uncertaine and unmanly expectation; some more abhorring such courses betake themselve to almost perpetuall and restlesse toyle and druggeries out of which (whilst their strength lasteth) they (observing hard diets, earlie and late houres) make hard shift to subsist from hand to mouth, untill age or sicknesse takes them off from labour and directs them the way to beggerie, and such indeed are to be pittied, relieved and provided for." There was an alternative: America. "Those servants that will be industrious may in their time of service gain a competent estate before their Freedomes, which is usually done by many, and they gaine esteeme and assistance that appear so industrious: There is no Master almost but will allow his Servant a parcell of clear ground to plant some Tobacco in for himself, which he may husband at those many idle times he hath allowed him and not prejudice, but rejoyce his Master to see it, which in time of Shipping he may lay out for commodities, and in Summer sell them again with advantage, and get a Sow-Pig, or two, which anybody almost will give him, and his Master suffer him to keep them with his own, which will be no charge to his Master, and with one years increase of them may purchase a Cow Calf or two, and by that time he is for himself; he may have Cattle, Hogs, and Tobacco of his own, and come to live gallantly; but this must be gained (as I said) by industry and affability, not by sloth nor churlish behaviour." So well did Virginians, free and servile, succeed, according to Hammond, that "children increase and thrive so well there, that they themselves will sufficiently supply the defect of Servants."[24]

William Bullock, on the other hand, wrote a more sober account, *Virginia Impartially Examined*, in which he noted the great demand among the English during Charles I's time for people to settle the new "plantations" in America and at the same time the great loss of life and property that had resulted thereupon. Bullock argued that the New World offered much potential for the impoverished of England, but only if they went about it the right way. The wrong way was to listen to voices in books, in pamphlets, in broadsides, and on the streets proclaiming the "best place" to go in America. There was competition among planters, promoters, and merchants for trade of goods and people, and many lies were spread to encourage the credulous and gullible to cast their fortune upon a particular scheme.[25]

There were in England and Europe, during the 17th and 18th centuries, tradesmen, craftsmen, ladies, and gentlemen, who moonlighted, as it were, selling America to the most desperate people, encouraging them to allow others to "spirit" them away to the paradise of the New World. In England, those who sold America were called "spirits," and they were either good or evil, some making a living sincerely by encouraging the poor to emigrate and others using any means to solicit, cajole, even kidnap people, young and old, to provide bodies for labor-starved Southern plantations. Spirits preyed upon "the idle, lazie, simple people they can intice, such as have professed idlenesse, and will rather beg than work; who are perswaded by these *Spirits*, they shall goe into a place where food shall drop into their mouthes; and being thus deluded, they take courage, and are transported."[26] Children—homeless, abandoned, neglected—were particularly subject to the wiles of the dishonest spirit. Such was the fear based on the reality of spirits "stealing, selling, buying, inveigling, purloyning, conveying, or receiving Children so stolne" that Parliament passed laws against spirits, and justices were on the lookout for adults participating in the nefarious practice. In 1660, for example, the authorities received word that "barbarous and inhumane" spirits had, "at this tyme," put on board ships bound for America "sundry . . . Children and Servants of severall Parents and Masters, so deceived and inticed away Cryinge and Mourninge for Redemption from their Slavery."[27] The abuse of the rights of children reached such a pitch by 1670 that Parliament passed a law making illegal spiriting a capital crime requiring death. Toward the end of Charles II's reign (1660–1685), however, the demand among merchants for white human cargo had declined, and, indeed, mercantilists, those who had directed British colonial policy, came to believe that it was in the best interests of England to keep its impoverished labor force at home rather than sending it abroad.[28]

The children of Jamestown were not slaves rather servants, though the distinction between these two forms of bound labor was not clearly apparent in the early 17th century. Slavery was introduced to Jamestown about the same time as children were brought to the colony in great numbers from the streets of London. The demands of labor in Jamestown and its environs compelled people to buy and sell children and others—white adults and felons, Negroes, and Indians. Exploitation of one person for material gain by another was a way of life in America, from the beginning of the European colonies in the 15th, 16th, and 17th centuries, continuing throughout the British colonial period to American independence, and into the future of the United States.

Notes

1. "Forensic Analysis of 17th-Century Human Remains at Jamestown, VA., Reveals Evidence of Survival Cannibalism," *Smithsonian Insider*, May 2013. http:// smithsonianscience.si.edu/2013/05/forensic-analysis-of-17th-century-human -remains-at-jamestown-va-reveal-evidence-of-cannibalism/

2. John Smith, *The Proceedings of the English Colonie in Virginia* (Oxford: J. Barnes, 1612; reprint ed., *Works: 1608–1631*, ed. Edward Arber, 2 vols. (Birmingham: printed by author, 1884)), 170.

3. John Smith, *Description of New England* (London: Robert Clerke, 1616; reprint ed., *Works: 1608–1631*, ed. Edward Arber, 2 vols. (Birmingham: printed by author, 1884)), 196, 198, 199, 207–208. For a full account of John Smith's activities in New England, see Russell M. Lawson, *The Sea Mark: Captain John Smith's Voyage to New England* (Hanover, NH: University Press of New England, 2015).

4. "Description," 208–209.

5. Ibid., 215.

6. *King James Bible*, lix; Matthew 19, 13–15; *Book of Common Prayer* (London, 1604).

7. *Book of Common Prayer.*

8. David W. Galenson, "The Rise and Fall of Indentured Servitude in the Americas," *The Journal of Economic History* 44 (1984): 3; A. E. Bland, P. A. Brown, and R. H. Tawney, eds. *English Economic History: Select Documents* (New York: Macmillan, 1919). Philip A. Bruce, in *Economic History of Virginia in the Seventeenth Century* (New York: Macmillan, 1907), 578, writes that parish justices, by setting wages low, not only increased poverty but also caused more parish revenues to be spent on the poor.

9. Frederic Eden, *The State of the Poor*, 3 vols. (London: Davis, 1797), 125, 128; Richard Burn, *History of the Poor Laws with Observations* (London: Woodfall and Strahan, 1764), 85, 91; George Nicholls, *History of the English Poor Law*, 2 vols. (London: Murray, 1854), 158, 166–168, 177; E. M. Leonard, *The Early History of English Poor Law Relief* (Cambridge: University Press, 1900), viii, 217, 227.

10. Eden, *State of the Poor*, 111; Leonard, *English Poor Law*, 139–140; William Harrison, *The Description of Britain* (London: John Harrison, 1577); Ian Mortimer, *The Time Traveler's Guide to Elizabethan England* (New York: Penguin, 2012), 45, 47 (quoting Stubbes), 48 (quoting the law of 1572). Oscar and Mary Handlin, *Origins of the Southern Labor System* (Indianapolis: Bobbs-Merrill, 1957), write

(201): "The essential attributes of villeinage were fastened on many men not through heredity and ancient custom, as in the case of the villein, but through poverty, crime or mischance."

11. Thomas Mackay, *The English Poor: A Sketch of Their Social and Economic History* (London: Murray, 1889), viii, 119; Samuel McKee, *Labor in Colonial New York, 1664–1776* (Port Washington: Friedman, 1965), 98; Nicholls, *Poor Laws*, 194; Leonard, *English Poor Law*, 14–15. Dorothy Marshall, *English People in the 18th Century* (London: Longmans, 1965) writes (21): "Parliament was quite willing that a great proportion of the people should live not much above subsistence level, since it was argued that only by the compelling fear of hunger could the poor be freed to undertake long hours and arduous work that the export market demanded." Wilhelm Hasbach writes in *A History of the English Agricultural Labourer* (London: P. S. King, 1908), 38: "The enclosures . . . almost always resulted in an increase in the number of free proletarians; that is to say of men possessing nothing but their labour power," which "proletarization went on at such a rate that many could find no work at all, and the problem of pauperism becomes a serious one for the English nation from this time forward."

12. Joshua Gee, *The Trade and Navigation of Great Britain Considered* (London: Buckley, 1730), 37; Walter H. Blumenthal, *Brides from Bridewell: Female Felons Sent to Colonial America* (Rutland, VT: C. E. Tuttle, 1962), 19, 64–65. Anguish is quoted in Margaret Pelling, *The Common Lot: Sickness, Medical Occupations and the Urban Poor in Early Modern England* (New York: Routledge, 2014), 112.

13. Nicholls, *Poor Laws*, 226–227; C. J. Ribton-Turner, *A History of Vagrants and Vagrancy, and Beggars and Begging* (London: Chapman and Hall, 1887), 133–134, 141. The quote from "Grievous Groans for the Poor" is reproduced in George L. Craik and Charles Macfarlane, *The Pictorial History of England*, vol. 3 (London: Charles Knight, 1840), 660. The quote from Don Alfonso is found in Alexander Brown, *The Genesis of the United States*, vol. 1 (Boston: Houghton Mifflin, 1890), 456.

14. Peter W. Coldham, *The Complete Book of Emigrants, 1607–1660* (Baltimore: Genealogical Publishing, 1987), 8, 11–13.

15. Edward D. Neill, *History of the Virginia Company of London* (Albany: Joel Munsell, 1869), 45–46; Coldham, *Complete Book of Emigrants*, 3, 8–11.

16. Neill, *Virginia Company*, 157–159.

17. Ibid., 161–162.

18. Ibid., 160–161, 237, 249.

19. Ibid., 246; James C. Ballagh, *White Servitude in the Colony of Virginia: A Study of the System of Indentured Labor in the American Colonies* (Baltimore: Johns Hopkins, 1895), 31.

20. Neill, *Virginia Company*, 278.

21. John Smith, "The General History of Virginia" (1624; reprint ed., *Works: 1608–1631*, ed. Edward Arber, 2 vols. (Birmingham: printed by author, 1884)), 578; Neill, *Virginia Company*, 320.

22. Neill, *Virginia Company*, 137.

23. David Pietersz De Vries, *Voyages from Holland to America*, trans. Henry C. Murphy (New York: Billin and Brothers, 1853), 54. Abbot Emerson Smith,

Colonists in Bondage: White Servitude and Convict Labor in America, 1607–1776 (New York: W. W. Norton, 1947), 67–68. George Thorpe is quoted in Carl Bridenbaugh, *Jamestown, 1544–1699* (New York: Oxford University Press, 1980), 48.

24. John Hammond, *Leah and Rachel, or the Two Fruitfull Sisters, Virginia and Mary-Land* (London: T. Mabb, 1656; reprint ed.); Peter Force, ed., *Tracts and Other Papers*, vol. 3 (Washington, DC: Force, 1846), 14–20.

25. William Bullock, *Virginia Impartially Examined, and Left to Publick View, to Be Considered by All Judicious and Honest Men* (London: John Hammond, 1649).

26. Smith, *Colonists in Bondage*, 68–69.

27. Ibid., 71–72.

28. Ballagh, *White Servitude in the Colony of Virginia*, 38–39, 41–42.

CHAPTER TWO

Indian Bondage

The indigenous inhabitants of America—long before Columbus reached the shores of America—captured, enslaved, and forced into bound labor those who through chance or necessity fell into the hands of their enemies. Indians practiced slavery as a product of war and vengeance. Raiders often took away not only livestock but children, women, and sometimes male warriors; these captives were brought back to live and die among the captors: some were tortured and sacrificed; others were adopted into families to replace a loved one; and some were bartered away to other tribes. When the English arrived in the late 1500s and early 1600s, they adopted the practice that they found among the native inhabitants of enslaving one another. Indian captives of the English were sometimes executed, but more often they were transported to other colonies as slaves or given a term of years of service upon which there was a vague promise of freedom.

Such was the experience of a young Indian boy, a native of the Montauk tribe of Long Island, who was made captive by the invading English during the Pequot War. The Pequots were a warlike Algonquian tribe of southern New England, who after the English began to explore and settle the coastline in the early 1600s into the 1620s and 1630s, tried to resist encroachment upon their lands and ways. English expansion from Massachusetts into Rhode Island and Connecticut in the 1630s and Dutch settlements along the Connecticut River valley put many tribes on the defensive. As in other wars before and since, each side during the Pequot War of 1637–1638 committed aggression and savagery upon the other. The deaths of some English traders at the hands of the Pequot resulted in an aggressive response by the English, including the attack on Block Island by the English under John Endicott. The Pequot responded, laying siege to the English fort at Saybrook on the Connecticut River. The English avenged this attack with one of their own on the

Pequot fort at Mystic; the English surrounded the fort and set it on fire, kill-ing all who tried to escape. Hundreds of people died. Thereupon the weak-ened Pequot attempted to avenge their deaths of hundreds, but they were ultimately destroyed.[1]

A young Indian male from the Montauk tribe of Long Island, of unknown age and name, later called Cockenoe, who had journeyed across Long Island Sound to southern New England, trading with or otherwise visiting the Pequot, was captured at some point during the war. As he was not Pequot, he did not suffer the fate of most male Pequot warriors: execution or enslave-ment in the West Indies; rather, Cockenoe became a servant to Richard Calli-cott of Dorchester, Massachusetts. Callicott had participated in the Pequot War as a militia sergeant and had been granted the Indian servant as part of the spoils of war. Callicott was a tailor by trade, a town leader, a deputy in the Massachusetts General Court, and after the Pequot War received tribute on behalf of Massachusetts from the surviving Pequots and other defeated Indians; he was also a fur trader with the Indians. In this endeavor, he was undoubtedly aided by his servant, Cockenoe, who was described as "inge-nious," able to read and speak English.[2]

The English colonists of New England engaged on numerous occasions in this practice of bonding prisoners of war into forced labor. The Indian youths—male and female—who after the Pequot War became servants in New England, typically served until the age of about 25, though their status was very unclear, being prisoners of war, and masters could equivocate on any societal standards. The Puritans of Massachusetts, Rhode Island, and Con-necticut considered Cockenoe and others like him—those who ended up as servants in New England or those who were sent as slaves to the Caribbean—as legitimate prisoners taken in a "just war" fought against the enemies of Christendom for defensive purposes. It was therefore legal and moral to put them into bondage. As the Massachusetts Body of Liberties proclaimed in 1641: "There shall never be any bond slaverie, villinage or Captivitie amongst us unles it be lawfull Captives taken in just warres." Those taken in just wars would enjoy the benefit of being introduced to Christianity. At the same time, they were in bondage and corporeal punishment could be used against them for recalcitrancy, to prevent them from escaping, or as a punishment upon recapture.[3]

The enslavement of prisoners of war was not a novel idea introduced by the English to North America or the Spanish to Central and South America. Africans practiced slavery against each other on a broad scale. As Captain John Smith found out in 1602 and 1603, Muslims enslaved Christians in North Africa and Eastern Europe. New Englanders did not enslave American Indians in great numbers; and, although there were some instances of it in the aftermath of King Philip's War, the English after the Restoration of the Crown in 1660 typically looked upon the Indians as subjects of the British

Empire, not fit to enslave, though they could be held in bondage as servants. The status of Indian servants and slaves in 17th- and 18th-century New England was never clear legally or morally.[4]

Powerful Puritan leaders, such as John Winthrop and his son John Winthrop Jr., played a dominant role in trading and employing servants. Even before the Pequot War, the Winthrop's used American Indian servants. Puritan ministers bought and sold, owned and used, slaves and servants as well. One such minister was John Eliot of Roxbury, Massachusetts, who was a leading 17th-century Puritan missionary to the American Indians. Like Roger Williams, who came to know the Narragansett Indians of Rhode Island, and who also used Indian captive servants, Eliot was one of a number of European and American scientists who were fascinated by the Native Americans, their customs, and their origins. Of the many speculations on the origins of the American Indians, some of the more sophisticated were ruminations of Williams published in *A Key into the Language of North America* (1643), in which he argued that the language and customs of the Indians bespoke a heritage not unlike the ancient Hebrews. "First," he wrote, "others (and my selfe) have conceived some of their words to hold affinities with the *Hebrew*. Secondly, they constantly *annoint* their *heads* as the *Jewes* did. Thirdly, they give *Dowries* for their wives, as the *Jewes* did. Fourthly (and which I have not so observed amongst other *Nations* as amongst the *Jewes*, and *these*:) they constantly separate their Women (during the time of their monthly sicknesse) in a little house along by themselves foure or five dayes."[5] Eliot generally agreed with Williams's speculations, believing some Algonquian dialects were so like Hebrew that it made sense to teach these people the Hebrew Bible. In time, he changed his opinion, opting instead to embrace the onerous project of learning the Algonquian language so that he could perform religious services, preach, and translate the Bible for the conversion of Algonquians. The problem was that Algonquian had no syllabary and no systematic grammar, and it was a spoken language, concrete rather than abstract. To help him learn Algonquian, Eliot relied on Indian assistants, the first of whom was Cockenoe, Richard Callicott's servant. Cockenoe "was," Eliot wrote, "the first that I made use of to teach me words, and to be my interpreter." Cockenoe knew how to read English when Eliot first met him; Eliot "taught him to write, which he quickly learnt." Eliot later recalled how he formed a design "to teach" Indians "to know Christ, and to bring them into his kingdome," when "presently I found out, (by Gods wise providence) a pregnant witted young man, who had been a servant in an English house, who pretty well understood our Language, better than he could speak it, and well understood his own Language, and hath a clear pronunciation; Him I made my Interpreter."[6]

With Cockenoe's help Eliot learned the local (Massachusetts) Algonquian dialect. He met with the Massachusetts Indians on numerous occasions, with Cockenoe at his side, speaking, preaching, and teaching in their tongue. The first time Eliot was joined by three others as well as Cockenoe; it was October 28, 1646, along the Charles River. He met with "men[,] women, children, gathered together from all quarters round about, according to appointment, to meet with us, and learne of us." The sachem, Waaubon, had expressed a desire to learn Christianity, and indeed had sent his son to an English school in Dedham, Massachusetts, for said purpose. Eliot prayed with them in English, "being not so farre acquainted with the *Indian* language as to expresse our hearts herein before God or them." Afterward, the missionaries taught them the Ten Commandments, spoke of the significance of Jesus the Messiah, and taught them the rudiments of prayer. The English missionaries often relied on Cockenoe's help: "borrowing now and then some small helpe from the Interpreter whom wee brought with us, and who could oftentimes expresse our minds more distinctly than any of us could."[7]

John Eliot believed like most English missionaries that embracing Christianity was insufficient without also embracing the civilized accoutrements that accompanied the faith. He believed that the way of Jesuit and Franciscan missionaries—to live among the Indians and adopt their ways as a stimulus to conversion—was inappropriate. "I find it absolutely necessary to carry on civility with religion," he wrote. He sought true and committed converts, which included "strict observance of the Sabbath, family prayer, grace at meals, Bible-reading, a conviction of their sinful and lost state, spiritual experience of renewal, and a sincere purpose to lead a godly, consistent life."[8]

Eliot followed in the wake of his missionary forebears in journeying to reach distant peoples to bring the message of the Gospel. Hearing of the great sachem of the Penacooks, Passaconaway, a shaman who reputedly had mastered the dark arts (in Eliot's mind) to convince his people of his great power over nature, Eliot traveled up the Merrimack River in 1647, and again in 1648, and met with Passaconaway. Some traditions claim that the great leader converted, though perhaps not. The Penacook Confederation was at this time, in the mid-17th century, caught between expanding English power in northern New England, expanding French power in the St. Lawrence River valley and tributaries to the south, and the power of Mohawks (Iroquois) to the west—south and east of Lake Ontario. Passaconaway and his son and successor Wannalancet tried to negotiate with all of the competing forces to preserve their power along the Merrimack River. In this they failed, and Wannalancet took his people upriver to the Pemigewasset River, and eventually further north of the White Mountains of New Hampshire. Reputedly, he was a Christian by this time, converted by John Eliot. If Eliot had any success with Passaconaway and Wannalancet, it was in part because of the efforts of his interpreter, Cockenoe.[9]

Eliot was part of a missionary society inspired by Englishmen such as the scientist Robert Boyle and chartered in the 1660s in New England: hence its name, the New England Company, initially called the Society for Propagation of the Gospel in New England. Like most such societies it collected and invested funds, from which it supported and paid missionaries and schoolteachers and supplied them with books, sermons, and Bibles by which to convert and teach the Indians. They believed that conversion was necessarily long and drawn out because of the inability of the Indians to read the Scripture. To remedy this, Eliot worked closely with Cockenoe, resulting in the formal process of developing a vocabulary and grammar based on the English alphabet to teach the Indians how to read and write. "By his help, I diligently marked the difference of their grammar from ours; when I found the way of them, I would pursue a Word, a Noun, a Verb, through all the variations I could think of." *The Indian Grammar Begun: Or, an Essay to Bring the Indian Language into Rules,* published in 1666, and dedicated to chemist Robert Boyle, was the result. Perhaps reflecting on Cockenoe's influence among both the Indians and the English, Eliot wrote: "Because the *English Language* is the first, and most attainable Language which the *Indians* learn, he is a learned man among them, who can *Speak, Reade and Write the English Tongue.*" Eliot used his growing knowledge of Algonquian as the means by which, with the help of Cockenoe and other Indian assistants, and with monies from the New England Company and Commissioners of the United Colonies of New England (New England Confederation), he published an interlinear English Algonquian version of the Gospel of Matthew followed by the entire New Testament (1661) and the book of Genesis followed by the entire Old Testament (1663). He published *The Indian Primer, or, the Way of Training Up of Our Indian Youth in the Good Knowledge of God, in the Knowledge of the Scriptures, and in an Ability to Reade,* in 1669.[10]

Cockenoe left Massachusetts for Long Island in 1649—perhaps his term of service came to a conclusion. Eliot replaced Cockenoe with other "praying Indians," such as John Sassamon and Job Nesutan, who, Eliot wrote, "can write, so that I can read his writing well, and he (with some paines and teaching) can read mine." Daniel Gookin, who like Eliot formed a close relationship with the Christian Indians of Massachusetts, wrote of Nesutan: "He was a very good linguist in the English tongue, and was Mr. Eliot's assistant and interpreter in his translations of the Bible, and other books of the Indian language." These two men died in King Philip's War.[11]

War is a burden on all people, whether they are victorious or defeated. The emotional consequences of war are as horrendous as the material consequences. During King Philip's War, the violence of the struggle and the hatred that was expressed and fueled on both sides created a horrible burden on all people involved. English colonists—up to 2,500—died, including Captain William Turner, whose widow, Mary, petitioned the governor and Council of Massachusetts in 1676 for aid—not material aid, but that her two servants, John Sawdy and Samuel Buckman, who had marched with Captain

Turner, be released from service to return home and help the widow. Mary Turner referred to the Indians as "Barbarious & Cruell Heathen the Enemy," and indeed many of the English considered all Indians, even the Christian, "praying Indians," to be of the same character. King Philip's War involved many of the praying Indians—some of whom were servants—being involved in fighting against King Philip, the sachem of the Wampanoags and his allies the Narragansetts and Nipmucs. During the course of the conflict, however, the British Americans, in the wake of the horror of war, came to view the Indians as being one and the same, equally liable to be treated harshly. As the conflict progressed, the praying Indians were suspected of helping the enemy; one writer at the time joked that they were "preying Indians." The indiscriminate view toward Indians led to mistreatment, captivity, and enslavement. The colonies of Massachusetts Bay and Plymouth treated captive Indians harshly, often enslaving them or, at the very least, condemning them to an indefinite term of service.[12]

Suspicion even toward friends and Christians resulted from the devastation of Massachusetts and Rhode Island during King Philip's War. The Narragansetts, Nipmucs, and Wampanoags destroyed numerous English towns; in Rhode Island, only a handful of places were not partially or utterly destroyed. The inhabitants of Providence generally fled the onslaught; though some English defenders refused to depart. One of these stalwarts was William Hawkins, who was one among the first English settlers of Rhode Island. William, by trade a glove maker, had sailed from England in 1634 bound for St. Christopher (St. Kitts); also on board the unnamed ship was Margaret Harwood of Devon. Whether the two already knew each other, or romance blossomed on board, William and Margaret married and, it appears, relocated to New England. William and Margaret were among those who in 1638 received lots of land in the new Baptist settlement of Providence, founded and headed by Roger Williams. The new town was on the western side of a hill on a broad peninsula bordered by the Seekonk River to the east and Great Salt River, or Providence River, to the west. William's land was at the southern edge of the peninsula, or neck, near Mile End Cove. William, in 1640, along with his neighbors, signed an agreement to form a government.[13]

Roger Williams had initially befriended and negotiated with the Narragansetts and was for decades a champion of the rights of freedom of conscience and fair dealing with the American Indians. After the Pequot War, relations between the English of Massachusetts, Plymouth, Connecticut, and Providence and the Indians, such as the Narragansetts, were tenuous. After years of potential conflict, war arrived in 1675. In December of that year, the English attacked the professedly neutral Narragansetts, who joined forces with the Wampanoags and Nipmucs in King Philip's War; intense warfare in and about Providence followed. Many of the Rhode Islanders fled, but not William Hawkins and his family. He helped to man the garrison in

Providence, despite the destruction all around. After the defeat of the Indians, the colony awarded Hawkins with land in the region once occupied by the Narragansetts. Also, he and other veterans were entitled to the use of Indian servants.[14] Hawkins's already considerable land holdings and, it can be assumed, servants were therefore augmented by his valiant behavior during the war; his wealth resulted in political status as well, as he was elected to represent Providence in the General Assembly in 1677 and 1678. Although many Rhode Islanders during the 17th century were opposed to slavery, even demanding (in 1652) that African slaves serve only a term of 10 years, "as the manner is with the English servants," Hawkins was not one of them, and indeed many Rhode Islanders were active in slavery and the slave trade.[15] Even so, in 1699, Hawkins, now an old man, signed a document that would release from slavery "a certaine Negro man of about twenty yeares of Age, Named Jack," in 26 years, 1725.[16]

Generally, however, the people of Rhode Island, perhaps because of the moderating influence of Roger Williams, and because of a significant presence of Quakers in the colony, refused to enslave Indian captives in the wake of King Philip's War. In Providence, a committee of five citizens determined the fate of captive Indians, who could be sold, for example, but only for a term of years, the length depending upon the age of the adult or child. In Portsmouth, a committee of three citizens were "by publick Authority appointed and Impowered to dispose of and place out Indians as apprentices in the Said Town." The records of the town of Portsmouth preserve an indenture, signed on April 27, 1678, binding a six-year-old "Indian girl . . . who is Daughter of one meecquapew an Indian woman late of pocaset as an apprentice unto William Wodell of Portsmouth." The girl, named Hannah, was to serve 15 years, during which time she was to "well and faithfully Serve her Said master William Wodell." In return, Wodell was to provide "Said appl[r] entice Sufficient food and Rayment and other necessaries"; after the 15 years, Hannah was to be granted her freedom, nothing more. At the same time, Hannah's mother, Meequapew, was bound to Wodell as an apprentice qua servant for a little over two years, when she would be granted her freedom.[17]

Other New England colonies followed Rhode Island's lead in replacing slavery with servitude. Indian servitude for the remainder of the colonial period mirrored white servitude in England and the British colonies: Indians, like whites, could be put into bondage for a term of years for debt, criminal behavior, and poverty. And, as many white servants experienced abuse in this system of bondage, so did Indian servants. As British American settlements expanded and Native American settlements declined, Indians came into increasing contact with British Americans, as workers, customers, debtors, and thieves. They experienced a natural disadvantage, of course, not being citizens and considered a different, often inferior race; hence, Indians were taken advantage of and their rights frequently abused, in unlawful or extensive servitude. White courts and masters considered Indian labor less valuable than white labor; hence, the terms of service of Indian servants often increased, and whites bought and sold Indian labor, that is, people serving terms of service, regularly and without hesitation. Indians frequently were condemned to years of service for debt. Like the free-willers, or redemptioners, who came from Germany to Pennsylvania in the 1700s, Indian parents often sold their children into service to satisfy debt. Such a case happened in 1703, when "Jefrey Indian" of Connecticut, because of debt, had to sell his daughter into long-term servitude. Missionary Gideon Hawley discovered during the mid-18th century that the Mashpee tribe of southern New England had such debt to the English that "there is scarcely an Indian Boy among us not indented to an English Master." This had been going on for decades. In 1700, for example, the Mashpees had petitioned the Massachusetts General Court for relief from debt servitude brought about by "Ignorance of the Law, weaknes[s], foolishness, & Inconsideration."[18]

The native peoples of eastern North America—between the Mississippi River and Atlantic Ocean—were intimately involved in the major military contests that occurred for over a century between France and England. The varied Indian tribes of what is today New England—such as the Abenaki, Passamaquoddy, Penobscot, Penacook, Piscataqua, Sokokis, Mi'kmaq, Pequod, Pequawket, Norridgewock, Massachusett, Nipmuc, Wampanoag, Nauset, Narragansett, Pequot, Mohegan, and Massabesic, all part of the Algonquian language family of the northeast Atlantic coast—had since time immemorial been at war with each other in raids and counterraids, taking scalps, children, and women in an endless cycle of retribution and bloodletting. The arrival of the French and English in the 1500s and 1600s presented further incentives for the already warlike Algonquian tribes to pursue their ambitions for trophies and conquest. The Catholic French, in particular, befriended, lived with, taught, and converted the Indians, encouraging their distrust and hatred of the arrogant Protestant English. As a consequence, European conflicts erupted in New England. The first great war, spawned by the Glorious Revolution in England, called King William's War in the colonies, was a violent conflict between the French and their Indian allies and the settlers of coastal and inland New England. King William's War lasted from 1689 to 1697. The second of these conflicts, Queen Anne's War, began in 1703 and lasted for 10 years. Shortly thereafter was Dummer's War from 1722 to 1725, followed by King George's War (the Cape Breton War) from 1744 to 1749, then the greatest and last of these wars, the French-Indian War (1755–1763).

These conflicts—spanning the history of New England from King Philip's War to the end of the French-Indian War, and beyond—featured whites and Indians in raids and counterraids, atrocities and war crimes, kidnapping and enslavement. The English and British Americans continued their 17th-century policy of capturing Indians for long-term bondage.

At the outbreak of the French-Indian War, the Massachusetts General Court responded to the hostilities against British Americans by supporting English raiders attacking hostile Indians and their French allies on the northern frontier. In 1755, for example, Massachusetts lieutenant governor Spencer Phips issued a proclamation, specifically directed to the Indians of the Penobscot River valley in Maine, requiring "his Majesty's Subjects of this Province to Embrace all opportunities of pursuing, captivating, killing and Destroying all and every of the aforesaid Indians." To encourage English soldiers, Phips offered the following war subsidy beyond their typical pay: "For every Male Penobscot Indian above the Age of twelve years that shall be taken within the Time aforesaid and brought to Boston Fifty Pounds. For every scalp of a Male Penobscot Indian above the age aforesaid brought in as evidence of their being killed as aforesaid Forty Pounds. For every Female Penobscot Indian taken and brought in as aforesaid and for Every Male Indian Prisoner under the age of twelve Years taken and brought in as aforesaid Twenty five Pounds. For every Scalp of such Female Indian or Male Indian under the Age of twelve years that Shall be killed and brought in as Evidence of their being killed as aforesaid, Twenty pounds." Based on the higher reward for scalps over captives, Phips appeared to encourage dead rather than captive Indians. At the same time, however, Phips expanded his proclamation to include citizen-soldiers currently not part of the provincial forces: "Resolved That there shall be allowed and paid out of the Public Treasury to any Number of the Inhabitants of this province, not in the pay of the Government, Who shall be disposed to go in quest of the Indian enemy, & shall before they go signify in Writing to the Chief Military Officer of Yt. [that] part of the Province from which they shall go, their Intentions, with their names the following Bounty . . . . . For every Indian Enemy that they shall kill and produce the Scalp to the Gov. & Council in Evidence, the Sum of three hundred Pounds. For Every Indian Enemy they shall Captivate & deliver to the Governor & council, the Sum of Three hundred and Twenty pounds." Here, then, the captured Indian was considered more valuable than the dead Indian.[19]

Phips's proclamation came at the beginning of the French-Indian War, which generally involved contests between the British and French over possession of the Connecticut River, Lake Champlain, and the frontiers of New York and Pennsylvania. Many forts were built in Maine immediately before and during the French-Indian War. Fort Pownall, named for the governor of Massachusetts, was constructed in 1759 at the mouth of the Penobscot River to protect against French and Indian incursions. According to historian Joseph Whipple, Governor Pownall "repaired in person to the Penobscot, and completed his work without opposition. He sent to the [Penobscot] tribe of Indians to inform them of his purpose, and invited them to defend their land if they intended it. He told them that should they kill an Englishman in future, they should be forced to fly from the country, which he would sweep from one end to the other, and hunt them all out. That he sought not their favor, but pitied their distress, and if they would become English, and live near the fort, he would protect them, assign them planting ground, and permit them to hunt as usual." The Penobscots, as well as other Maine tribes, weakened by years of warfare, had by this time become insignificant in the face of English power. Few challenged the power of England; hence, few became captives of war experiencing the variety of statuses that others of the 17th and 18th centuries had experienced, ranging from lifelong slavery (sometimes euphemistically called "servitude"), to temporary enslavement/ servitude until redeemed, to servitude according to a set or variable number of years.

The long history of the wars for empire in North America featured attacks and counterattacks, parties of French and their Indian allies attacking British settlements, and British American militia and citizen-soldiers responding in kind, or taking the offensive to gain the advantage. The pages of history for these years tell the story of bloodshed, requited and unrequited, time and again, vengeance being the primary motivation for war with the chance to earn money for scalps or captives being a secondary consideration. Story after story reads like the following, based on the pages of one of the best histories of these wars for empire, Jeremy Belknap's *History of New-Hampshire*:

In the uneasy final year of King Philip's War when British and Indian relations were difficult, and the English, particularly of Massachusetts, still sought to arrest Indians who had fought with the defeated Philip, militia companies were sent to the New England eastern frontier in search of the enemy. They came into a region that had enjoyed peace since the previous winter of 1675–1676. During the fall of 1675, tribes of New Hampshire and Maine had committed a number of deprecations on the towns and villages of the Piscataqua valley. But when an early winter hit the region, and famine began to reign, these warriors decided to go for help. They came to the home and garrison of Major Richard Waldron, and sued for peace, which the major granted, to the joy of the British-American inhabitants of northern New England. The peace was disrupted, however, when Indians from southern and western New England—often referred to by the English as the "strange Indians"— journeyed north and east to mix with the Penacook of the Merrimack River and the Pequawket of the Saco River. As they were on the run from militia sent by the Province of Massachusetts, 400 of them surrounded the garrison at Dover, New Hampshire, appealing to the garrison commander Major Waldron, of whom they conceived as their friend, for protection. Waldron, however, respecting English authority more than the friendship of Indians, devised a stratagem to avoid bloodshed yet diffuse the power of the enemy. Two militia companies arrived, led by Captain Joseph Syll and Captain William Hawthorne, who wanted to engage immediately the Indians. Waldron, however, persuaded them to wait, while he convinced the 400 Indians to join in an apparent military exercise with the English. Waldron convinced the Indians in this "sham fight" to fire their weapons first, which then enabled the militia troops to surround and capture them. Waldron allowed the Penacooks under Wonalancet to depart, but the 200 "strange Indians" from the south were taken to Boston, then "sold into slavery in foreign parts," generally meaning that they were sent as captive prisoners to the islands of the Caribbean. They returned many years later to seek vengeance against Major Waldron. Either these Indians were slaves who escaped, or servants who returned to New England at the expiration of their term of servitude. Whatever the cause, they arrived again at the Piscataqua valley and looked for a chance to avenge themselves.[20]

Notes

1. Charles Orr, ed., *History of the Pequot War: The Contemporary Accounts of Mason, Underhill, Vincent and Gardener* (Cleveland: Helman-Taylor, 1897).

2. William W. Tooker, *John Eliot's First Indian Teacher and Interpreter: Cockenoe-De-Long Island and The Story of His Career from the Early Records* (New York: Francis P. Harper, 1896), 11.

3. Ibid.; Alice Morse Earle, *Margaret Winthrop* (New York: Charles Scribner's Sons, 1895), 197; Alan Gallay, ed., *Indian Slavery in Colonial America* (Lincoln: University of Nebraska Press, 2009), 36–38. Alan Gallay, in the introductory essay to the book, writes (15): "The basic rationale employed by Europeans, Africans, and Native Americans: slavery was the just desserts of war captives. All considered that sparing the captive's life entitled the captor to keep the individual as a slave. Slavery, then, was a by-product of war." See *The Liberties of the Massachusets Collonie in New England, 1641: Old South Leaflets* (Boston: Directors of the Old South Work, n.d.). http://history.hanover.edu/texts/masslib.html

4. Gallay, *Indian Slavery*, 20, 38. For a general discussion of Indian servitude in colonial New England, see Margaret Ellen Newell, *Brethren by Nature: New England Indians, Colonists, and the Origins of American Slavery* (Ithaca, NY: Cornell University Press, 2015).

5. Roger Williams, *A Key into the Language of North America* (1643; reprint ed., Bedford, MA: Applewood Books, 1987).

6. Earle, *Margaret Winthrop*, 196; Tooker, *John Eliot's First Indian Teacher*, 12–13.

7. John Eliot, *The Day-Breaking if Not the Sun-Rising of the Gospell with the Indians in New-England* (London: Fulk Clinton, 1647), 1, 2, 4.

8. Justin Winsor, *The Memorial History of Boston*, vol. 1 (Boston: Osgood, 1881), 263, 265.

9. See Russell M. Lawson, *Passaconaway's Realm: Captain John Evans and the Exploration of Mount Washington* (Hanover, NH: University Press of New England, 2002).

10. Tooker, *John Eliot's First Indian Teacher*, 13; John Eliot, *The Indian Grammar Begun: Or, an Essay to Bring the Indian Language into Rules* (Cambridge: Marmaduke Johnson, 1666; revised ed., Boston: Phelps and Farnham, 1822), 27. William Kellaway, *The New England Company, 1649–1776: Missionary Society to the American Indians* (New York: Barnes and Noble, 1961). John Eliot, *The Indian Primer, or, the Way of Training up of our Indian Youth in the Good Knowledge of God, in the Knowledge of the Scriptures, and in an Ability to Reade* (1669; reprint ed., Edinburgh, Scotland: Andrew Elliot, 1880).

11. Tooker, *John Eliot's First Indian Teacher*, 16–17.

12. John M. Bodge, *Soldiers in King Philip's War: Being a Critical Account of That War, with a Concise History of the Indian Wars of New England, 1620–1677* (Boston: printed by author, 1906), 248; Frederick W. Gookin, *Daniel Gookin, 1612–1687: Assistant and Major General of the Massachusetts Bay Colony* (Chicago: printed by author, 1912), 150; Almon W. Lauber, *Indian Slavery in the Colonial Times within the Present Limits of the United States* (PhD dissertation, Columbia University, 1913), 126–128.

13. Peter W. Coldham, *The Complete Book of Emigrants, 1607–1660* (Baltimore: Genealogical Publishing, 1987); Charles Hopkins, *The Home Lots of Early Settlers of the Providence Plantation* (Baltimore: Clearfield, 2009).

14. Emily W. Leavitt, *Palmer Groups: John Melvin of Charlestown, and Concord, Mass. and His Descendants* (Boston: David Clapp and Son, 1901–1905), 402.

15. John R. Bartlett, ed., *The Colony of Rhode Island and Providence Plantations, in New England: 1636–1663* (Providence: A. C. Greene, 1856), 243.

16. Horatio Rogers et al., eds., *The Early Records of the Town of Providence*, vol. 4 (Providence: Snow and Farnham, 1893), 71–72.

17. Lauber, *Indian Slavery*, 128–130; *Early Records of the Town of Portsmouth* (Portsmouth, RI: E. L. Freeman and Sons, 1901), 432–433.

18. Gallay, *Indian Slavery*, 51–56.

19. "A Proclamation," *Sprague's Journal of Maine History* 7 (1919): 47–48.

20. Jeremy Belknap, *The History of New-Hampshire*, vol. 1 (Dover, NH: Stevens and Ela and Wadleigh, 1831), 74–76.

CHAPTER THREE

The Captives of New France

In 1689, when England and France went to war, in what was called in America, King William's War, the French, allied with the Abenaki of Maine and Penacook of New Hampshire, waged war against the British settlements in northern New England. The Indians who in 1676 had been forsaken by Major Waldron and taken to Boston and sold into servitude had found their way back to New England, thanks in part to the efforts of John Eliot, Robert Boyle, and other members of the New England Company. Once back in New England, these former servants determined to take revenge on the English militia leader major Richard Waldron. The major was utterly surprised. He had forgotten, or hoped others had forgotten, the episode and was on good terms with the native inhabitants of the Piscataqua valley. Although he was given warning of a possible surprise attack, he ignored the warning, believing that he knew the Indians too well to suspect anything. The weather being rainy one June night in 1689, Waldron allowed some Indian women to stay within the gates of the garrison on the Cochecho River, saying, "Let the poor Creatures Lodge by the Fire!" Late that night, the women opened the gates to the waiting attackers, who rushed in, and after a brief fight with the sword-wielding Major Waldron, tortured and killed him. According to one account, the Indians "kill'd them all" in the garrison. They attacked other places in Dover as well; overall, they killed 22, and captured another 29, many of whom were brought north to the St. John's River, and on to Quebec.[1]

New France in 1689, from its base along the St. Lawrence River, and the settlements of Quebec and Montreal, was expanding into the hinterland—the Great Lakes and the Mississippi River and tributaries—because of the efforts of explorers such as René-Robert Cavelier, Sieur de La Salle, governors such as Louis de Buade, Comte de Frontenac, and adventurers such as the Baron de St. Castin. The French in America established a lucrative fur trade, built forts and trading posts throughout North America, converted to

Christianity the members of dozens of Indian tribes, had good trade and diplomatic relations with tribes throughout America, and created a large, if poorly administered, empire stretching from Newfoundland, Labrador, and Acadia south and west to the Great Lakes and the Mississippi River valley. The harsh climate of Canadian winters and seclusion made it difficult to attract immigrants to New France. Hence, to bolster the labor force, the French, like the English, relied on indentured servants, called *"engagés"* in New France.

The system was very similar to British servitude, with desperate people in France in search of opportunity, an institution or master willing to pay for the transport, and a ship captain available and willing to carry people across the Atlantic to America. The French indenture was, according to Canadian historian Clare Pentland, like "that of an apprentice, but the servant usually was an adult who made his own contract and possessed already whatever skill he would ever have. Economically, the indentured servant accepted the position of a slave—a slave with a termination date to his servitude, but a slave, nevertheless. The master likewise assumed the rights and duties of a slave-owner."[2]

During the decades-long political and military contest with England for control of North America, the French did everything they could to populate New France with strong and able laborers. The French government passed laws in the early 18th century to require ship captains to have on board at least three to six *engagés*. The conditions of transport and servitude were, according to Quebec historian Alice Lunn, that "the men had to be between the ages of eighteen and forty, not less than 4'4" tall, and in a condition to work. They must serve some master in the colony for three years, in return for which they were to be fed, housed, clothed and paid a small wage by their employers. At the end of three years, they were free to return to France or to settle in the colony." Upon the conclusion of their term of service, colonial officials and masters encouraged them to stay and would not pay for their passage back to France. In lieu of free laborers, the French followed the English model of transporting felons to New France to serve for a period of five years. Also, as in the British American colonies, blacks and Indians (called Panis) were indentured, though their terms of service were not, officially, lifelong. Panis and black servants were typically unskilled and worked as domestics for the upper class in New France. The French, like the English, transported some Panis and blacks to their West Indian colonies for service. And the French, increasingly at the end of the 17th century and beginning of the 18th century, received white war captives from New England and bound them to terms of service.[3]

One of those captives was Sarah Gerrish, the granddaughter of Major Waldron, who was captured on the night that her grandfather died. She, along with many others, were taken to New France. Sarah was only seven years old. Historian Jeremy Belknap referred to her as "remarkably fine," meaning that she was not the type, at least physically, to survive such an ordeal. But she did. She was passed from master to master on the journey. Once she was left behind in a snow storm and awoke covered with snow; somehow she was able to find the others, already on the trail. Upon arriving at Quebec, the wife of the intendant of New France (the administrator under Governor Frontenac) purchased Sarah and had her educated in Catholicism and French in a convent; eventually she was rescued by William Phips when he invaded Quebec in 1690, and she returned to New England.[4]

Among the captives was a three-month-old baby, Margaret Otis. Her father, a brother, and a sister were killed that June night in Dover, but Margaret and her mother survived the attack as well as the journey to Quebec. Margaret was sold, baptized, and raised in a convent. When she was 16, she married and had children. Upon her husband's death in 1713, Margaret wished to return to New England. When in 1715 Captain Thomas Baker arrived in Quebec to redeem captives, she was purchased. Baker himself had been captured at Deerfield in 1704 and carried to New France, from which he escaped. Ten years later, now in Quebec, he was able to gain her release but not that of her children. When she arrived in New England, she and Captain Baker married and had children. Eventually, she returned to Dover with her husband, from where she journeyed to Quebec to redeem her children, but without success.[5]

During the journey to New France, Sarah Gerrish, Margaret Otis, and the other captives from Dover were united briefly with another group of captives from Pemaquid. Among those captives was a nine-year-old boy, John Gyles. Captured in the same year, 1689, Gyles was a captive servant for half a dozen years before his release. In time, he became an interpreter for the English and a captain of St. Georges Fort during Dummer's War. Toward the end of his life, he decided to record his experiences and observations. John Gyles's *Memoirs of Odd Adventures, Strange Deliverances, &c. in the Captivity of John Gyles, Esq., Commander of the Garrison on St. George's River*, published in 1736, is a fascinating account of a captive boy's experiences in Maine and New France during King William's War.

Of the many places on the Maine coast that feature good harbors and dramatic views, few are as appealing as Pemaquid. The coast between Portland and Penobscot is one of jutting peninsulas and narrow inlets. Pemaquid is one of these narrow pincer points of land, boasting a secure harbor next to rising land that appears perfect for defense. In the 1620s, the English first established fishing and trading at Pemaquid, mooring their sloops and shallops in Pemaquid Harbor at the mouth of Pemaquid River. Today's visitor to Colonial Pemaquid State Historic Site can appreciate not only the beauty of the place but its strategic significance at a time when colonial outposts of fishing and trade were supremely important for the economies of competing empires. Indeed, although the English first settled Pemaquid, the French found the site equally appealing—conflict inevitably erupted between the two imperial powers. The English constructed Fort Charles at Pemaquid Harbor in 1677 because of the sporadic attacks and counterattacks of King Phillip's War. The economic attractions now made apparently secure by a fort and cannon inspired such settlers as Thomas Gyles to move to Pemaquid in the 1680s. Gyles, who had lived for a time at Merrymeeting Bay on the Kennebec River, was a landowner—sufficiently wealthy and respected to be appointed chief justice of the settlement. His son John remembered the father to have been a "strict Sabbatizer" with a stern sense of duty. Gyles was a farmer with a wife, family, and servants under his authority who like all the inhabitants of the coast of Maine sought only to thrive and enjoy his domestic situation without the distractions of violent conflict. The territorial ambitions and dynastic pretensions of the English and French, however, ensured continued raids, kidnappings, torture, and terror. The Duke of York, King James II, having been granted title to the lands of the Maine coast at the Restoration of the English Crown (1660), assumed that his title extended north to include the Penobscot region, which was in contrast to the French view, held by the Baron de St. Castine, that the region from the Penobscot north to Nova Scotia was French. As a result, both sides lumbered into war. The European War of the League of Augsburg, which began in 1688, spilled over into the colonies in 1689; both sides used the European conflict as a pretext for their own territorial ambitions and acts of vengeance for past wrongs.

Years later John Gyles recalled the August day in 1689, on the farm of his father Thomas Gyles near Pemaquid Falls, when warriors attacked the town and fort. Many were killed, including Thomas Gyles, and captured, such as the young John Gyles, who was nine years old. Others in the family, including his brother, two sisters, and mother, were captured as well. The Indians took young Gyles and other captives by birch bark canoe to Penobscot fort, held by the French. On the way, the canoe Gyles was in came alongside another canoe carrying his mother. "She asked me, How I did? I think I said, Pretty well, (tho' my Heart was full of Grief). Then she said, O, my Child! how joyful & pleasant it would be, if we were going to *Old England*, to see your Uncle, . . . and other Friends there?—Poor Babe! we are going into the wilderness, the Lord knows where!—She burst into Tears, and the Canoes parted!" A few days later, when a French Catholic, a "Jesuit," considered purchasing Gyles, his mother said "Oh! my dear Child! if it were GOD's Will, I had rather follow you to your Grave! or never see you more in this World, than you should be Sold to a Jesuit: for a Jesuit will ruin you Body & Soul!" Her prayers were answered, for a time, as Gyles stayed with an Indian master.[6]

The young captive John Gyles with his new Indian master went up Penobscot River to the Indian village of Madawamkee, where he experienced a strange ceremony whereby a captive was placed at the discretion of the tribe's squaws over whom to bicker in a way that seemed like torture. But Gyles's Indian master bartered his release with payments of corn. The Indians and their captives proceeded east to Medoctack Fort on St. John's River. Here Gyles saw "five or six poor Captives, who had been taken some Months before from Quechecho [Dover], at the same time when Major Waldein [sic] was most barbarously butchered." His captors forced young Gyles to join the Cochecho captives; "we look'd on each other with a sorrowful Countenance," knowing they were about to be "tortured," that is, mostly humiliated by the squaws. Young Gyles himself experienced the terrifying ceremony that he had seen the Cochecho captives endure; luckily his master bought his release with a bag of maize. A squaw separated Gyles from the others; when he returned, he saw "one of my Fellow-Captives, who gave me a melancholly Account of their Sufferings, after I left them."[7]

From here his Indian master took him up St. John's River to a village called Medockscenscasis, where they lived on fish, wild grapes, and roots. When winter came so did privation. Many days the band of 10 Indians and John Gyles were without food. They lived off the land, moving constantly so to find food. Two warriors had guns, which they unfortunately rarely used, as game was hard to come by. A moose kill was a great accomplishment. Sometimes the band of wandering Indians discovered a bear emerging briefly from its winter den. The Indians told Gyles that if the bear went fat into the den at the beginning of winter, it emerged fat (as did its cubs) at the end of winter, and, if thin, then thin accordingly. Indians feasted when a kill was made then fasted until the next kill. Squaws danced outside the wigwam before the feast saying: "Wegage Oh Nelo Who!" which Gyles translated as "Fat is my eating!" in praise of the feast. The captive Gyles had to wait outside the wigwam until the warriors had their fill before he was able to eat.[8]

During his first year as a captive, Gyles was continually at a loss as to what was the purpose of his captivity. He performed no visible work and was an extra mouth to feed; perhaps the Indians wanted to have an extra male on hand for the hunt. Over the course of his many years of captivity, Gyles was indeed employed by his Indian master on various tasks and errands. Although Gyles suffered, he also learned and had experiences he otherwise would not have had. Gyles learned, for example, about the moose: "A Moose is a find [sic] lofty Creature about eight Feet high, with a long Head and Nose like a Horse: with Horns very large and strong (Some of them are above six feet, from the Extremity of one Horn to that of the other) shaped and shed every Year like the Horns of a Deer: likewise their Feet are cloven like Deers Feet. Their hind Legs are long and fore Legs short like a Rabbit. They resemble a Rabbit also in the length of their Ears and shortness of their Tail: The Female have two dogs like a Mare tho' they sometimes bring three young ones, at a foaling: they foal but once a Year, and at one Season, viz. When the

Trees put out Leaves, for them. There are a sort of Moose that have a Main [*sic*] like a Horse." Gyles noted that some "naturalists" believe the moose bears an "Unform'd Embryo, and lick their Litter into Shape:—a gross Mistake! I have seen their Fœtus of all Sizes, taken out of the Matrix, by the Indians, and they are as much, and as well Shap'd as the Young of any Animal."[9]

The small band kept on the move until winter's end, where they were beyond the head of St. John's River by the "Lady Mountains." Returning to the St. John's at the beginning of spring, they halted to make "Canoes of Moose Hides sewing three or four together, and pitching the Seams with Charcoal beaten and mixt with balsam." Thereupon they proceeded downriver to the Indian village of Madawescok, then to falls in the river called Checanekepeag, then on to the Medoctack Fort. Over the summer they planted corn, fished, harvested the corn, and stored some of it in pits, then prepared to go upriver for another winter hunt. Gyles learned that "when the Corn is in the Milk they gather a large Kettle full and boil it on the Ears until it is pretty hard, and then they take it up and shell it of the Cobb with Clam-Shells, and dry it on Bark in the Sun; and when it's thro'ly dryed, a Kernel is no bigger than a Pea, and keep Years—and boil'd again it swells as large, and tastes incomparably sweeter than other Corn."[10]

The next several years Gyles experienced the same seasonal routine, the wandering, the want followed by plenty, the periodic humiliation and terror intermixed with compassion and companionship. One winter Gyles's master ordered his captive and a young Indian warrior to march through the woods to retrieve a moose that had been killed and deposited on a hunt. When they arrived at the spot it was night and snow was falling. The next day they wandered back to the tribe; Gyles was wet and cold and near death. Upon arrival to the wigwam "the Indians cry'd out, *The Captive is froze to Death!*" The Indians immediately set to helping Gyles. They "cut off my Shoes, and stripped the Clouts from my Feet, which were as void of feeling as any frozen Flesh could be." Gyles's feet were frostbitten, and he soon lost the ends of his toes. The Indians thought he would die yet told him anyway to apply a salve of "fir-balsam," which he did. The Indians also contrived snowshoes for him to allow him to walk on his heels. He suffered terribly yet slowly recovered.[11]

The Abenaki, being allied to the French, were converts to Catholicism, ministered to by Franciscan priests, who told them to moderate their abuses to the captives or God would punish them. The Indians were nevertheless very superstitious and devoted to old pagan rites. To determine the success of a pending hunt, pagan medicine men, "powaws," made a small hut of skins within which were hot stones, which they poured water upon, making tremendous steam, from which they believed they could determine the future. Gyles witnessed Abenaki marriage rites and mourning practices and wrote about them in detail in his *Memoirs*. He discussed in detail their preparations for war, including an odd ceremony whereby the warrior seeking strength in battle would kill a dog by splitting open its skull, grasping its brains, and eating them on the spot.

Gyles was impressed by the natural knowledge of the Indians and their ability to survive in the most extreme conditions. They taught Gyles to hunt for tortoise eggs by thrusting a stick in sand next to a stream. When discovering a gooey substance on the stick, if one dug into the sand about a foot, up to 150 tortoise eggs were discovered, which were superior eating. Fishing for salmon was best done in the summer in shoal water of the river or stream; the hunter armed with a pitch torch at night could see the salmon lying partway out of the water, where they could be easily speared. The Abenaki with whom Gyles traveled were skilled with the fire drill. They boiled food in earthen or stone kettles. If caught in the forest without proper utensils, they knew how to fashion a birch bark bowl that was sturdy enough to hold water and food, which was cooked by progressively heating the water to a boil with hot stones.

Notwithstanding the sufferings of captivity, Gyles experienced much during these years. He learned of and related a fascinating account of Indian attempts to ascend the highest Maine mountain, Katahdin. "I have heard an Indian say, that he lived by the River at the foot of the *Teddon*, and in his Wigwam, seeing the top of it thro' the Hole left in the top of the Wigwam, for the passing of Smoke, he was tempted to travel to it: accordingly he set out early on a Summer's Morning, and laboured hard in ascending the Hill all Day, and the top seem'd as distant from the Place where he lodged at Night, as from the Wigwam whence he began his Journey: and concluding that Spirits were there, never dare make a second Attempt." Gyles also learned of others who made a similar attempt, in particular "three young Men" who tried to ascend the *Teddon* over the space of "three Days and a half, and then began to be strangely disordered & delirious, and when their Imagination was clear, and they could recollect where they were, and had been; they found themselves return'd one Days Journey: how they came down so far, they can't guess, unless the Genii of the Place convey'd them! These White Hills at the head of *Penobscot River*, are, by the Indians, said to be much higher than those, call'd *Agiockochock*, above *Saco*."[12]

Gyles grew to have a regard for his Indian masters, who various times saved the captive from suffering and, perhaps, death. One summer, Mi'kmaq Indians from Nova Scotia arrived at the St. John's and wanted to avenge themselves against the English, so they chose Gyles and another captive upon whom to vent their anger. After being ruffed up, Gyles escaped and hid in a swamp, aided by his master, who apparently had no influence over the Mi'kmaq. Many years later, on two occasions, Gyles and his first (of two) Indian master reunited, the final time when Gyles was stationed at the garrison on the St. George's River. Here, Gyles "made him very welcome."[13]

After six years of captivity among the Abenaki, Gyles was sold to a French merchant who traded on St. John's River. This Frenchman and his wife also were good to Gyles; the mistress made an ozenbrig shirt, cap, and coat for Gyles. Gyles had become fluent in many Abenaki dialects and helped his master trade with the natives; in time the servant learned French as well. Gyles gained his master's trust and assumed much responsibility in his trading business. At the conclusion of King William's War, John Gyles obtained his freedom and returned to New England, where he was reunited with surviving members of his family. Having lived with the Indians for nine years, and knowing the Abenaki and Mi'kmaq tongues (as well as French), he found employment as an interpreter for merchants and soldiers who traveled to Penobscot Bay and other points along the Maine coast to trade or exchange prisoners. During Queen Anne's War, Gyles was granted a commission as a captain and served on military expeditions to the east and Canada and at garrisons along the Maine coast. At the end of the war, Captain Gyles was ordered to construct Fort George at Pejepscot. During Dummer's War, Captain Gyles commanded the garrison, served as an interpreter for the Penobscot and other tribes, and led rangers up rivers and even to the White Mountains of New Hampshire in search of Indian raiders. He finished his military career serving as commander of the fort at St. Georges River. In 1736, he published his *Memoirs* to honor the request of family and friends to memorialize his parents and to show the many blessings he had received at God's hands.

Gyles's experience as an Indian captive and French servant across the St. Johns River in Canada was illustrative of the experiences of hundreds of people kidnapped, enslaved for a time, and taken to Quebec as a consequence of the wars for empire between the French and English. Many other women joined John Gyles's mother in being forced to travel north to Canada, suffering privation and the desperate fear of their children's fate. Hannah Swarton of Casco Bay, captured in 1692, journeyed "over steep and hideous Mountains one while and another while over Swamps and Thickets of Fallen Trees, lying one, two, three foot from the ground, which I have stepped on, from one to another, nigh a thousand in a day; carrying a great Burden on my Back."[14] Swarton, who of her husband and three children was the only one to survive or be freed from captivity, believed that she deserved it: "I must justifie the Lord in all that has befallen me," realizing that "he hath punish'd me less than my Iniquities deserved."[15]

Samuel Whitney, of Brunswick, Maine, suffered capture during a time of supposed peace, between King George's War and the French-Indian War, in July 1751. In a petition to the Massachusetts General Court the following December, Whitney recalled "that your Memorialist and his son Samuel with five more of Inhabitants while at work together mowing their hay, on Wednesday ye 24th day of July last about two o'clock in the afternoon were surrounded and surprised by Nineteen Indians and one Frenchman, who were all armed and in an hostile manner did seize upon and by force of arms obliged them to submit their lives into their hands." The raiders killed one young man and several dozen cattle, before taking their captives north. "The said party of Indians were nine of them of Norridewalk [Norridgewock] Tribe, one of whom was well known; the others were Canada Indians." Whitney learned that the Norridgewock, once the dominant force of the Kennebec River valley, were residing in Quebec where they sold the captives for guns and clothes. The English were forced "to sing a Chorus as is their custom of using their Captives." Eventually a kind man, an ex-captive of the English, loaned Whitney the price of freedom, though, Whitney told the General Court, "Your Memorialist's Son yet remaining in Captivity among the Indians with three more that were taken at the same time, and he has a wife & Children under difficult Circumstances by reason of this Misfortune." Whitney petitioned the General Court that "they will in their great Goodness provide for the Redemption of his son & enable him to answer his obligation" for the "Ransom."[16]

At the conclusion of the French-Indian War in 1763, England controlled New France. The British imposed control over the French inhabitants, though by 1774, the Quebec Act allowed the French inhabitants to essentially worship and live their lives as they had prior to British control. During the War for American Independence, Canada did not join the 13 colonies in their revolt against England, and in fact became a refuge for Loyalists seeking to escape from oppression in the 13 colonies. The British established Upper Canada (Ontario) as a place for refugees who came to Canada; these refugees included slaves and servants, though not in any great numbers. That such bondage did exist, and was not entirely agreeable to the British government of Canada, is shown in "An Act," passed in 1793 by the British Parliament, "to prevent the further introduction of SLAVES, and to limit the Term of Contracts for SERVITUDE within this Province" of Canada. Slavery was to be gradually abolished in Canada; those born after 1793 were free; otherwise emancipation was granted at age 25 (hence by 1818 all slavery ended). Indentured servitude increasingly became an alternative to slavery. Henceforth, African servants were indentured. For example, Maria Breckenridge was "an indented black servant girl" in 1826 when her master sought her capture for theft. Upper Canada became a destination for escaped slaves in the 19th century. Here, theoretically, a slave could be free upon crossing the Niagara River. And Scots, who had once fled to the 13 British American colonies in the hopes of redemption and a new life, emigrated to Lower (Quebec) and Upper Canada for land and opportunity. The *British Queen*, for example, arrived at Quebec in August 1790, from the Scottish Highlands, with four servants on board, three men and one woman. As the years passed into the 19th century, thousands of Scots immigrated to western Upper Canada, the peninsular region north of Lake Erie and south of Lake Huron.[17]

Notes

1. Jeremy Belknap, *History of New-Hampshire*, vol. 1 (Dover, NH: Stevens, and Ela and Wadleigh, 1831), 125–129; John Gyles, *Memoirs of the Odd Adventures, Strange Deliverances, &c.* (Boston: Kneeland and Green, 1736), 6–7.

2. H. Clare Pentland, *Labour and Capital in Canada, 1650–1860* (Toronto: James Lorimer, 1981), 8.

3. Alice J. E. Lunn, *Economic Development in New France, 1713–1760* (PhD dissertation, McGill University, 1942), 2, 3, 5, 12–14, 20. According to Junius P. Rodriguez, ed., *The Historical Encyclopedia of World Slavery*, vol. 1 (Santa Barbara: ABC-CLIO, 1997), 122: "The need for labor was such that Canadians sometimes resorted to ransoming English captives of local Amerindians for use as bonded domestic servants until the English could manage to repay the French who had ransomed them."

4. Belknap, *History of New-Hampshire*, 129–130.

5. Ibid., 130; Alonzo Lewis and James R. Newhall, *History of Lynn, Essex County, Massachusetts* (Boston: Shorey, 1865), 117–118.

6. Gyles, *Memoirs*, 4–5.

7. Ibid., 7–8.

8. Ibid., 10, 31.

9. Ibid., 9–10.

10. Ibid., 10–11.

11. Ibid., 16–17.

12. Ibid., 30.

13. Ibid., 34.

14. Quoted in Laurel Thacher Ulrich, *Good Wives: Image and Reality in the Lives of Women in Northern New England, 1650–1750* (New York: Alfred A. Knopf, 198), 206.

15. Quoted in Alden T. Vaughan and Edward W. Clark, eds., *Puritans among the Indians: Accounts of Captivity and Redemption, 1676–1724* (Cambridge: Harvard University Press, 2009), 148.

16. *Sprague's Journal of Maine History* (1915): 141–142.

17. *A Collection of Acts Passed in the Parliament of Great Britain, Particularly Applying to the Province of Upper Canada* (York, Ontario: R. C. Horne, 1818), 30; Lucille H. Campey, *The Scottish Pioneers of Upper Canada, 1784–1855: Glengarry and Beyond* (Toronto: Natural Heritage Books, 2005), 4, 183; David Murray, *Colonial Justice: Justice, Morality, and Crime in the Niagara District, 1791–1849* (Toronto: University of Toronto Press, 2002), 197; Janet Carnochan, *History of Niagara (in Part)* (Toronto: Briggs, 1914), 203–204.

CHAPTER FOUR

English Town by the Sea

As in Virginia, bound labor existed in New England from the beginning of colonization. Indeed, Lord Chief Justice John Popham, one of the most powerful men in England during the early reign of James I and, along with Ferdinando Gorges, responsible for establishing a colony in *northern Virginia* at the same time as Jamestown was founded in *southern Virginia*, sought to found a colony based on bound labor, namely, reprieved convicts. Popham and Gorges sent the ships *Gift of God* and *Mary and John* to the coast of Maine in 1606; they sailed into the mouth of the Kennebec River, at a place called Sagadahoc by the local natives. Whether or not Popham directed that the founders of the colony, his nephew George Popham and Raleigh Gilbert, son of explorer Humfrey Gilbert, use bound labor to build their colony, is indeterminable. There have been arguments back and forth about Popham and his aims for centuries. Regardless of whether transported convicts were part of the crew of the two ships that landed at Sagadahoc in 1607, the colony was abandoned after a harsh winter, so that the first permanent English colony in New England had to wait another 13 years.[1]

The idea of building a colony on the backs of convicts brought forth trepidation from some promoters of colonization. Francis Bacon, for example, essayist, scientist, and one-time Lord Chancellor, wrote, in "Of Plantations": "It is a shameful and unblessed thing to take the scum of people and wicked condemned men to be the people with whom you plant; and not only so, but it spoileth the plantation; for they will ever live like rogues, and not fall to work; but be lazy, and do mischief, and spend victuals, and be quickly weary, and then certify over to their country to the discredit of the plantation." Rather, a new colony, or plantation, should be founded and inhabited by "gardeners, ploughmen, laborers, smiths, carpenters, joiners, fishermen, fowlers, with some few apothecaries, surgeons, cooks, and bakers." Most of these people were skilled, though "laborers," in particular, could be a synonym, as it were, for servants. And indeed the promoters of colonization in New England supplied their colonial ventures with workers both skilled and unskilled, many of whom were "servants."[2]

The character of bound labor from England in America during the first half of the 17th century included adventurers who crossed the Atlantic in the service of employers in England or America who operated companies for profit. Two men, for example, William Stevens and Thomas Fell, contracted with the Plymouth Company, the joint-stock company that sponsored the establishment of the Plymouth Colony in 1620, to serve "as planters for shares and not for wages." They had signed a contract with the Treasurer of the Company to "serve the Company for 5 years" in return for "passage to New England, food, drink and clothing." There were, of course, more lowly servants who came to Plymouth on the *Mayflower.* Jasper Moore, "a servant boy of Gov. Carver, . . . died soon after arriving." But Carver had other servants, such as the boy, William Latham.[3]

Likewise, on board the *Gift of God* in 1606 was a young man, a servant to Ferdinando Gorges named David Thomson. The boy was about 14 years old, having served Gorges at Plymouth Fort in the English West Country since 1605. On the voyage to Sagadahoc, Thomson traveled in the company of Dr. Richard Vines, an apothecary and scientist who was an agent for Ferdinando Gorges. Vines saw America as an endless source for the materials of medicine (*materia medica*) that English physicians and apothecaries relied upon to calm and cure their patients. He had been part of Martin Pring's 1603 voyage to the Piscataqua River of New Hampshire; now, three years later, he traveled with George Popham to Sagadahoc. David Thomson was, apparently, serving as an apprentice to Vines, learning the art of *materia medica.*[4]

Such boys and men were those that John Smith had envisioned on his voyage along the New England coast in 1614. He argued, in books such as *Description of New England* (1616), that men and women, boys and girls, those in want in the streets of London and elsewhere in Jacobean England, were the best fit to begin fishing colonies along the Atlantic coast of America. Here, whether bound or not, people could, through hard work, not only survive but thrive, and make their way into the world with property and wealth. Smith never had the chance to pursue his dream to lead such a colony in New England, yet he inspired others to make the attempt. One group of "merchant adventurers," as they were called, obtained a charter from King James, forming the Council of New England, which had jurisdiction over the trade and fishing in coastal northern New England. James I and later his son Charles I sought to establish colonies to extend the power and wealth of England by means of granting charters to peers and knights who wished to establish New World fiefdoms at the core of which were manors worked by servants. Two of the leaders of the Council were Ferdinando Gorges and

John Mason, to whom James granted sole proprietorship over vast tracts of land ranging from the Merrimack River north to the Kennebec River. At various times their proprietorship was called New Hampshire, Gorgeana, Laconia, and NewSomersetshire. Mason and Gorges never visited America, rather let their agents and employees try to establish trade and a firm colonial foundation. Their chief agent was a Scotsman, David Thomson.

When David Thomson sailed Ferdinand Gorges's ship *Jonathan* into the mouth of the Piscataqua in 1623, he was already a seasoned sailor and explorer. Thomson had followed up the journey to Sagadahoc in 1606 with a journey, accompanying Richard Vines, to the Saco River in 1616, then another to the Piscataqua River and Boston Harbor in 1619. Accompanying Thomson on his new venture aboard the *Jonathan* in 1623 were workers styled "servants": these were men who had signed a contract by which they were to work on behalf of the proprietor for a set number of years in return not for wages but living expenses. According to the records of the Council of New England for December 3, 1622, "Mr. Thomson propoundeth to have order from the Council for transportation of ten persons with the provisions for New England. And the persons so transported to pay the Council for the usual rate for their transportation, after the expiration of two years." This was a type of servitude often found in the initial establishment of colonies in America in which certain individuals felt compelled to bind themselves to a master to work in return for the opportunity to set themselves up as independent landowners.[5]

Thomson employed "a Considerable Company of Servants" in building "a Strong and Large House, enclosed it with a large and high Palizado and mounted Gunns, and being stored extraordinarily with shot and Ammunition was a Terror to the Indians, who at that time were insulting over the poor weake and unfurnished Planters of Plymouth. This house and ffort he built on a Point of Land at the very entrance of Pascatoway River," now called Odiorne's Point. The following year Robert Gorges, the son of the proprietor, arrived with more servants.[6]

Besides Vines and Thomson, other agents working on behalf of the proprietors of northern New England included Captain Walter Neal, who arrived at the Piscataqua valley in 1630 to serve Mason and Gorges as an administrator, soldier, and explorer; Ambrose Gibbons, who took charge of the falls and mills at Newichawannock, or Salmon Falls River; and Humphrey Chadbourne, who after building a "Great House" at Strawberry Banke relocated upriver to South Berwick. The Piscataqua gathered the waters of southern Maine and northern New Hampshire, rivers such as the Squamscot, Lamprey, Cochecho, and Salmon Falls, which supported communities such as Berwick, Dover, Oyster River, and Exeter. Across the mouth of the Piscataqua from Strawberry Banke was the town of Kittery, settled in 1623 and incorporated in 1647. The communities of the Piscataqua in the mid-17th

century were typically called *Pascataqua* by New Englanders. They were fishing, lumbering, and shipbuilding communities that attracted settlers from
southeastern and southwestern England as well as Lowland and Highland
Scotland. Many immigrants made their way to Pascataqua as servants.
Throughout this region, servants lived and worked and found a way to
advance and thrive notwithstanding their humble circumstances.[7]

At Newichawannock, along the upper reaches of the Piscataqua River,
Ambrose Gibbons arrived in 1631 with his wife and daughter and four
men, all or some of whom were servants; three carpenters arrived in 1634.
As steward to John Mason, Gibbons was to employ his servants and workers
to build a saw mill at the falls of the Newichawannock and to collect stores
of pine, oak, and birch boards for shipment back to England. To Mason's
complaints that, before the saw mill was constructed in 1634, little of value
had been returned to England by means of the ship, *Pied Cow*, Gibbons curtly
responded: "You complain of your returnes; you take the coorse to have little.
A plantation must be furnished with cattle and good hire-hands, and
necessaries for them, and not thinke the great looks of men and many words
will be a means to raise a plantation. Those that have been heare this three
year, som[e] of them have neither meat, money nor cloathes—a great
disparagement. I shall not need to speak of this; you shall hear of it by others.
For myself, my wife and child and 4 men, we have but 1/2 a bb. of corne;
beefe and pork I have not had, but on peese this 3 months, nor beare [beer]
this four months, for I have for two and twenty months had but two barrels
of beare and two barrels and four booshel of malt; our number commonly
hath bin ten. I nor the servants have neither money nor clothes."
While Mason was alive, the saw mill cut boards and a grist mill grinded
grain at Newichawannock and the steward, carpenters, and servants barely
made a living. Upon Mason's death, his employees dispersed elsewhere in
the region and the "servants shared the residue of the goods and stock among
them, which was left in that and the other plantations, and possessed themselves of the houses and lands." Early records listing the "stewards and servants" of Mason include the names of six stewards, one "chirurgeon"
[surgeon], 49 other men, some of whom were servants, eight Danes, doubtless also servants who were used "to build mills, to saw timber, and tend
them, and to make potashes," and 22 women, some of whom were servants,
then wives.[8]

One of these servants was Roger Knight, who after the demise of Mason
became a landowner at Strawberry Banke. Knight was originally working for
Thomas Wannerton, one of Mason's stewards, who leased land at Strawberry
Banke to Knight in 1643 "in consideration of his faithful services." Wannerton had four men, including Knight, one boy, and one woman, Knight's wife,
working for him on the southern shore of the Piscataqua in the 1630s. The
ex-servant Knight became a well-known landowner in the Piscataqua region

in the 1640s, 1650s, and 1660s. In old age, he became too feeble to care for himself; the town paid townspeople to care for the old man for six years. The Portsmouth selectmen arranged with Thomas Onyon to care for Knight for four years at a rate of £2.5 per year. Thus Roger Knight, who had once bound himself as a laborer to John Mason and Thomas Wannerton, had at the end of his life someone bound to him.[9]

Labor according to indenture for the means of living or wages occurred in Portsmouth, and throughout America. For people who were incompetent because of age—too young or too old—the town provided a form of institutional indenture with one of their inhabitants. Deacon Samuel Haynes, for example, in June 1678, was bound by the selectmen to care for and raise "Jennets orphan child" for 15 years, as the child was but five years old. The town paid Haynes £12 "to find her with sufficient of meate, drinke, clothing washing and Lodging and to teach her to reade for all which s[ai]d term wee the Selectmen bind her to him."[10]

Also arriving at the Piscataqua, sailing up the broad river in 1631, was a young Scandinavian, Hugh Gunnison. He arrived from England as a single man traveling with several immigrant families. They sailed up the river to Dover Point, which separates the Piscataqua from the Great Bay; here eight years earlier Edward Hilton had established a short-lived colony, though at the time Gunnison arrived there were probably no English settlers; up the Piscataqua to the north was the new settlement at Newichawannock. Gunnison apparently stayed here for a few years, at the most, because by 1634 he lived in Boston, where he was "servant to . . . Richard Bellingham," lately arrived from England. Whether or not Gunnison came to America as a servant, or found by force of necessity that he must bind himself to Bellingham by 1634, is not known. Gunnison was not a servant for long, as he was made a "freeman," or voting citizen, of Boston in 1636. Gunnison had problems with the Massachusetts Bay authorities, however, on the matter of religious belief. He apparently sided with Anne Hutchinson and was reprimanded for it. A "vintner" by trade, in 1642 he kept "an Ordinary with a Cooke's Shop" where he sold beer. An obscure record from 1646 implies that Gunnison also supplied wine for the General Court and that by this time he had his own servants. During the next few years, however, Gunnison fell on hard times and eventually had to give up his beer and wine operations to creditors; he moved back to the Piscataqua in 1651, settling in Kittery. Here, the former servant generally thrived, his business in spirits allowing him to become a representative to the General Court, judge of the Common Pleas, and a significant landowner. In October 23, 1653, "Hugh Gunnison was indicted for allowing his daughter, Sarah Lynn, to stay at home whole months from religious services." He died in 1660.[11]

Other servants of the Piscataqua valley fared well in the 17th century. Francis Champernowne, friend and relative of Ferdinando Gorges and one of the greatest landowners on the northern shores of the Piscataqua, had a servant named Elizabeth Small, who obtained her master's permission to marry, perhaps when her term of service expired. She wedded Thomas Hooper; they had four children. When Champernowne died, he left Elizabeth Hooper dozens of acres of prime land along Spruce Creek in Kittery. One of her neighbors was Thomas Jones, one-time servant of landowner Alexander Shapleigh, who himself obtained land along Spruce Creek. Nearby, one of Ferdinando Gorges's former servants, Christopher Rogers, became a landowner in the region between Kittery and York. A former servant of John Mason, Alexander Jones, became a landowner in Kittery, Portsmouth, and the Isles of Shoals; his son owned land on the western shores of Spruce Creek. Another son of a servant, John Hole, who served John Winter from 1637 to 1640, rose above his father's station to become a freeman and constable of Kittery.[12]

Across the river, on the southern shores of the Piscataqua, by the 1660s, when Samuel Maverick wrote a "Description of New England," "Strawberry Banke" had "many Families, and a Minister & a Meeting House." The town assembly began meeting in the 1640s, during which selectmen were chosen to direct the internal affairs of Portsmouth as well as relations with surrounding settlements. These settlements, like all communities past and present, had rich and poor, young and old, healthy and sickly, able-bodied and disabled, sound of mind and mentally ill. Some people residing in towns such as Portsmouth were newcomers, not possessed with ample material resources to fill the role of citizens. These dependent sorts, particularly the newcomers, were often not welcomed, at least by town authorities. On April 5, 1652, the town "ordered this day that francis Trike is toe clear his hous[e] of goodman greene, and his wife, and children, in a munths time, and for every day that the sayd francis Trike, shall entertain them aboue the sayd time, he is to pay twenty shillings." This custom of "warning out" people who were not wanted because they posed the potential of becoming dependent upon town resources was found throughout New England. The Portsmouth authorities declared therefore to all unwanted visitors and residents that "to keepe the Town harmless from being burthened in way of Charge," only those with security of property or noteworthy friends could remain in the town. Freeholders and inhabitants in the town were ordered not to receive strangers, or else they "shall secure the towne of all such charges at there one cost and damadges allsoe."[13]

The male citizens of the towns of the Piscataqua valley in the 17th century met in assembly and chose "selectmen" to run town affairs "as though," in the words of the recorder of the Portsmouth town records in 1652, "our selves the wholl Towne wear Presente." The selectmen granted land, determined tax rates, considered whether or not to admit "New-Comers," and prepared town defenses. In June 1666, they ordered that "every dweller and liver in this town above the age of sixteen years, whether householder, child, servant, or any other residing in the towne," must help maintain the fort on Great Island (Newcastle), at the mouth of the Piscataqua, which had initially been constructed in 1631. The ideal of the 17th-century New England town was a cohesive unit of people living among and relying on one another. The town expected individuals—men, women, property owners, and servants—to perform duties for the sake of the whole. In return, should a dependent status burden a townsperson as a consequence of living, then those needing care and alms found it among their neighbors.[14]

Portsmouth, being the leading seaport north of Boston, grew in population during the course of the 17th century. By the 1670s and 1680s, some of the original surviving settlers were quite old. Andrew the Dutchman, who had lived at Strawberry Banke for 20 years, was declining in 1689; Daniel Duggins and his wife were paid a pound a month to care for him until he died. Goodman Lucomb and his wife were property owners yet elderly, unable to care for themselves; the town loaned them £5, which turned out to be insufficient; they advanced them £2 more. The selectmen determined then to put the responsibility in the hands of a son and daughter living in Boston; if they failed to care for their parents, the town would auction the Lucomb's property to pay the expenses. Another old-timer, called simply Old Lewis in the town records, too feeble to care for himself, experienced the good will of the selectmen, who found an inhabitant, every year, to care for the old man in return for expenses and a bit more for the trouble.[15]

There was enough mobility up and down the coast and to and from England that every year there were more strangers and newcomers—those with means were welcomed; those without, were not. Nevertheless, even these latter unfortunate ones often found help. In 1692, for example, William Brooking and his wife agreed to care for the cripple, William Champernowne, in return for a suspension of the town tax payment. This notwithstanding that Champernowne had entered the town illegally, and the Brooking's had already opened their home—also an infraction—to him. The number of newcomers sometimes overwhelmed the constables' ability to warn them out, so other measures had to be taken. When John Reed arrived, penniless, the selectmen ordered that he bind himself out as a servant or else be expelled from the town. Binding the poor person to a master as a preventive to the high cost of dependency was increasingly the practice in provincial towns that were growing in the late 17th century, even in the wake of the destruction and dislocation of war: King Philip's and King William's. Some servants were ne'er-do-wells, ranging from sturdy beggars and panhandlers to more serious criminals, as one hapless Piscataqua fisherman discovered when his two servants, in anger, killed their master, took his money, and fled; though eventually they were caught and executed. Provincial legislators, in an attempt to restrict such potential violence by servants, ordered innkeepers, in 1680, not to sell intoxicating beverages to servants on pain of a 10 shilling fine, one-half to be paid to the informant, one-half to the poor.[16]

The costs of caring for deserving and undeserving poor were sometimes too much for the town budget. In 1692, the Portsmouth selectmen decided to sell town land "Lying in Nooks and Corners," the proceeds to be used to maintain the poor. Portsmouth, like other towns in British colonial America, modeled their approach to the poor according to English standards and statutes. When the English, during Elizabeth's reign, found the numbers of the poor becoming overwhelming, they appointed well-to-do parish members to serve as overseers; that is, to regulate how the parish helped the poor by paying others to care for the destitute, by creating and maintaining workhouses, and by keeping parish funds in the black. British American colonial governments also found the necessity of appointing overseers. In 1692, the Provincial assembly of New Hampshire ordered relevant towns to appoint overseers of the poor. These individuals had the right, with the approval of justices of the peace, to bind into apprenticeship poor children; they were to make yearly reports about those bound into service, the budget, and the numbers relieved and employed.[17]

As British American towns grew, the idea of a personal relationship of caregiver and dependent based on indenture dissipated, in part because the familiarity of community members became blended with a host of outsiders, "outlivers," who were anonymous newcomers who lived on the outskirts of the large New England township. Boston was the first city to adopt an institutional solution to the increasing numbers of the poor. Styling it an almshouse, or workhouse, after the English models, the poor were incarcerated regardless of age, gender, guilt, or innocence.[18] Other New England towns followed Boston's lead, thinking it easier and cheaper to put all of the anonymous poor into one institution where it would theoretically not cost so much and they could be put to work to help pay town expenses. Governor Edmund Andros during the Dominion of New England ordered towns to begin the process of building almshouses "for the Imploying or poor and Indigent People."[19]

Institutional poor relief, as well as personal servitude, were both based on bound labor, one to a person, another to an institution. The town of Portsmouth embraced the institutional model of poor relief, beginning the planning of the town almshouse in 1711; it took five years to complete. In the meantime, the town continued to provide for the poor in the old ways, by binding deserving poor to caregivers, and indenturing undeserving poor to masters. In 1706, the indigent infant John Atkinson was bound to Thomas Parker for 21 years. A year later, Richard Davis and his wife were indigent, receiving monies and supplies from the town, until her death, whereupon the town ordered Davis to reimburse Portsmouth or "to chuse his master with whome to live til such money be paid." Interestingly, even after the

Portsmouth almshouse opened, the province passed, in 1718, "An Act for Suppressing and Punishing of Rogues, Vagabonds, Common Beggars, and other Lewd, Idle, and Disorderly Persons, and also for Setting the Poor to Work." Any ne'er-do-well, including fortune-tellers, jugglers, fiddlers, brawlers, and runaway servants, were to join the able-bodied and deserving poor in such an institution. Runaway servants might regret their decision to have escaped their service upon being put in the stocks or feeling the whip of the almshouse keeper. Luckily, the keeper could lay only 10 stripes at a time on the bare back. Overseers could bind to a master youngsters under the age of 21 (men) or 18 (women), in lieu of service and punishment in the almshouse. The goal was not only to save the town from expenses but also to ensure that youth "be brought up or imployed in Some honest Calling which may be profitable to themselves and the Publick."[20] Sometimes American Indians were involved in these decisions; some were indentured servants. In 1729, the town assembly decided to care for "Kate the Indian woman who is Sick," even though 11 months earlier they had voted against helping her. Kate might have been one of those disabled, deserving poor who were kept in the almshouse, it being determined in 1733 that no longer would any private relief be afforded the poor: all would be placed in the almshouse. There are often exceptions to such declarations, the first one being three years later when one Benjamin Miller was given tax relief plus a stipend to care for a relative, Jerry, who was "bereaved of his reason." Five years later the town, concerned by the number of bastards under care of the almshouse, designated Samuel Hart to investigate and whenever he discovered the fathers of such children to prosecute them.[21]

By the time Portsmouth was almost a century old, in the 1730s, the population had grown to such an extent that there were greater numbers of sturdy and deserving poor; town expenses to pay for their upkeep were rising; the almshouse required constant upkeep and repair. Hitherto the town records did not record the name of the overseers of the poor, if there were any, but beginning in 1739 the town began to record the annual overseers of the poor. They were directed "to hire a proper person to see the poor that are able to work Constantly Imployed"; they were to "furnish said poor with Provisions" and to be sure that the poor be "furnished and Provided for In the Alms house and not els[e]where." A few months later, however, the overseers were given "Discretionary power" to determine who should be cared for in the almshouse, and who "to Support, out of the Almes House." By 1747, the town made a subtle change of approach to the poor by determining it was time to construct a workhouse. The question was, how to fund it; perhaps a lottery. In the meantime, once again the townspeople decided that the poor should be kept exclusively in the almshouse only to decide to leave such a decision up to the overseers. Clearly, the almshouse was not effective and too expensive. When in 1750 the three men elected overseers of the poor refused to serve, the discussion turned to constructing a workhouse, the idea being that a workhouse would more efficiently work the poor, helping to defray the cost of their upkeep. A lottery was determined upon, and tickets were sold; in addition, a social library was organized to raise money for the workhouse. Over the course of several years, the townspeople worked for the goal of a workhouse, which was finally erected in 1756 "to Imploy Such Person or Persons there to do Such Business & Servis as Shall be Necessary in Order to the Looking After the People that are or Shall Live there & to Send all Such to Live there as Shall apply to them for Support." Even so, some inhabitants were deemed unfit for the workhouse, and cared for privately. And after several years of the experiment, the workhouse seemed to be not quite working. Hence, the townspeople appealed to the General Assembly to pass a law to solve the problem of "poor Vagrant Persons whether Children or Adults Such as common Beggars & have no visible means of a Livelyhood," that they "be Properly employed that such Children be Obliged to be Sent to Some of the Publick Schools or be Bound Out to Such Buissness as may be most Likely to make them useful to Society and to them Selves." Townspeople apparently discovered that sometimes the old ways, such as indenturing the poor to masters, worked best. The New Hampshire assembly agreed, deciding in 1766 that overseers of the poor were to apprentice poor children whose parents were unable to care for them; in addition, overseers could indenture impoverished adults for up to a year; any wages they earned would go toward their family's upkeep. The same year the town assembly granted to the overseers of the poor in Portsmouth the ability "to purchase Necessaries for the Support of the poor & Purchasing Stock at the Whole Sale and Cheapest Rate to Employ any Poor Person Either in the Work House of Elsewhere in the Town."[22]

Notwithstanding such efforts of binding the poor to individuals and institutions to ensure that habits of "Industry and Good Morals" would replace habits of "Idleness & Vice," the numbers of the idle poor increased during the 1760s and 1770s. More time, money, and effort were put into the institution of the workhouse: children received education; the sick received medical care; the Sabbath was observed; the mentally ill received separate treatment. Yet there was little evident success. Exasperated townspeople in 1769 wondered "w[h]ether it Will not be a saving to said Town to Board out the Poor in the Work House to Householders Living out of the Town Where Provisions are Cheaper." All solutions to the problem remained on the table. The number of participants, however, willing to come to the table to help the town struggle with the increasing numbers of poor was declining. Moreover, the temptations of city life were distracting youths and the humbler sorts from their duties. A petition was sent to the General Assembly in 1773 condemning theatrical performances: "such Exhibitions by exciting the

Curiosity of the poor draw them off from their necessary Labours and induce them to spend that in gratification of their Curiosity which ought to have purchased Bread for themselves and Families." Also, such performances "engage the attention of our youth as greatly to impede their Progress in the most important parts of Learning both in our Schools and among our Handicrafts."[23]

At the same time, Portsmouth and other towns of New England, especially coastal, port towns, were in conflict with England and among themselves over the actions of Parliament—the Sugar Act, Stamp Act, Townsend Acts, and the consequent disruption of trade. Wealthy leaders, typically merchants, of Portsmouth, increasingly refused to serve as selectmen and overseers of the poor. Not only was the town exerting greater pressure on overseers of the poor to solve the problem of impoverishment in the town, but usually the monies supplied by the town for relief of the poor were insufficient, and overseers had to make up the balance. In addition, the insolence of the poor toward the overseers, their supposed betters, became increasingly intolerable. The solution, it appeared at a town meeting in 1771, was to put more pressure on the poor, to build a "house of Correction" in the workhouse yard to enforce the will of the town upon recalcitrant individuals. The town already had a "gaol" for the general criminal, and for those who were imprisoned for debt, so the house of correction was meant specifically for the recalcitrant poor.[24]

Then, a series of events occurred that made the troubles over binding the poor and providing for their needs seem inconsequential. First, in late 1774, Portsmouth patriots such as John Langdon and John Sullivan attacked Fort William and Mary at the mouth of the Piscataqua, making away with powder, shot, arms, and cannon. A few months later, the New England militia attacked the British Redcoats on their return to Boston from bloody victories at Lexington and Concord, Massachusetts. With war came the suspension of trade with England, disrupting the shipbuilding and timber industries of the Piscataqua valley; privation and inflation; fear of attack; and the impoverishment of many people. Portsmouth attracted the poor of surrounding communities. Disorder and chaos threatened, and the townspeople, many of whom were no friends of revolution, were forced to submit to a revolutionary government. War brings out the best and worst in people. Of the latter included those who sought to profit by the suffering of others. The new state of New Hampshire therefore declared that people be on the watch for "Monopolies[,] Extortion & Oppression so predominant in Town & Country by which the Poor, the Widow, the Orphan[,] the Fatherless & many other Classes of People are suffering."[25]

The institutions and ways of binding the poor and setting people to work continued, now darkened by the thunderous clouds of war.

Notes

1. *The Popham Colony: A Discussion of Its Historical Claims* (Boston: K. Wiggin and Lunt, 1866).

2. Francis Bacon, *Essays and New Atlantis* (New York: Walter J. Black, 1942), 142–143.

3. Peter W. Coldham, *English Adventurers and Emigrants, 1609–1660: Abstracts of Examinations* (Baltimore: Clearfield, 1984), 17; Henry Whittemore, *Genealogical Guide to the Early Settlers of America* (Baltimore: Genealogical Publishing, 1967), 315, 374.

4. Ralph E. Thompson and Matthew R. Thompson, *David Thomson 1592–1628, First Yankee* (Portsmouth, NH: Peter E. Randall Publisher, 1997).

5. Samuel Maverick, "Maverick's Description of New England," in *New England Historical and Genealogical Register* 39 (1885): 36; "Indenture of David Thomson," *Proceedings of the Massachusetts Historical Society* (Boston: Massachusetts Historical Society, 1875–1876), 361.

6. "Maverick's Description," 36.

7. Everett S. Stackpole, *Old Kittery and Her Families* (Kittery, ME: Lewiston Journal Company, 1903), 20, 321.

8. Ibid., 21–27; Nathaniel Adams, *Annals of Portsmouth* (Portsmouth, NH: printed by author, 1825), 18–19.

9. Stackpole, *Old Kittery*, 21, 32; *Portsmouth Records, 1645–1656: A Transcript of the First Thirty-Five Pages of the Earliest Town Book, Portsmouth New Hampshire* (Portsmouth, NH: printed by author, 1886), 32; *Portsmouth Town Records* (hereafter, PTR), Typescript, Portsmouth Library, 143A.

10. PTR, 213A–213B.

11. George A. Foxcroft, *A Genealogy of the Descendants of Hugh Gunnison of Boston, Mass.* (Boston: printed by author, 1880), 13–18; Stackpole, *Old Kittery*, 183

12. Stackpole, *Old Kittery*, 35, 37, 61, 107, 536, 537, 558, 701, 716.

13. Ibid.; *Portsmouth Records*, 16; PTR, 46A, 153A.

14. PTR, 1, 117A; Adams, *Annals of Portsmouth*, 19, 49–50.

15. PTR, 214B, 267A, 267B, 274A, 290A.

16. Ibid., 242A, 293A. "Rev. John Eliot's Records of the First Church in Roxbury, Mass.," *The New England Historical and Genealogical Register*, vol. 33 (Boston: Clapp and Son, 1879), 297.

17. *New Hampshire Laws, 1679–1702, Province Period*, vol. 1 (Manchester, NH: John Clarke, 1904), 220, 526.

18. Carl Bridenbaugh, *Cities in the Wilderness: The First Century of Urban Life in America* (New York: Oxford University Press, 1938), 75, says that the Boston almshouse was largely for "unruly servants and slaves."

19. *New Hampshire Laws*, vol. 1, 36, 165.

20. PTR, 365A, 13-F-B; *Laws of New Hampshire, 1702–1745*, vol. 2 (Concord, NH: Rumford Printing, 1913), 266, 267, 269, 342.

21. PTR, 59-F-A, 67-B-B, 80B, 85B-85C, 90B-90C. The town records of neighboring York, Maine, reveal that an Indian servant with the unlikely name,

Portsmouth, died on April 20, 1720: *New England Historical and Genealogical Register,* vol. 46 (Boston: New-England Historic Genealogical Society, 1892), 87.

22. PTR, 91A, 92C, 113A, 122A-B, 123B, 124B, 126A, 129B, 145A, 161B, 188A, 204B; *Laws of New Hampshire, 1745–1774,* vol. 3 (Bristol, NH: Musgrave Printing, 1915), 391.

23. PTR, 219A, 231A, 234B, 241B, 241C, 242A, 250A; *Documents Relating to the Towns in New Hampshire, New London to Wolfeborough,* vol. 13 (Concord, NH: Cogswell, 1884), 276–277.

24. PTR, 252B–252C; Charles Burroughs, *Discourse Delivered in the Chapel of the New Almshouse* (Portsmouth, NH: Foster, 1835), 33; Adams, *Annals of Portsmouth,* 199.

25. *Documents Relating to the Towns in New Hampshire,* 282.

CHAPTER FIVE

The Dutch Servants of New Netherland and New York

On a September morning in 1609, a modest square-rigged sailing vessel with a small crew captained by Englishman Henry Hudson sailed into the Hudson River, a broad tidal river surrounded by steep bluffs and vast inland forests. Hudson sailed up the river, speckled with islands, to near the confluence of the Hudson River, flowing from the mountains to the north, and the Mohawk River, flowing from the west. Employed by the Dutch East India Company, Hudson claimed the land for the Netherlands, which became the basis for the colony of New Netherland. A few years later Hendrick Christiaensen followed up on Hudson's explorations with his own journey, during which he founded a fort on Castle Island in the Hudson River, just below the confluence with the Mohawk. Fort Nassau would later be called Fort Orange, eventually Albany. The Dutch built upon these early voyages, establishing a trading outpost, expanded into a formal colony, centered on the Hudson valley. The colony of New Netherland fell to the English in 1664, thereupon becoming the English colony of New York.

Like the English colonies in North America, Dutch companies out for profit engaged in the initial exploration and settlement of the Hudson River valley. Unlike the English colonies, however, the company—after 1621 the Dutch West Indian Company—maintained extensive control over the colony and its peoples. In 1629, the company issued the Charter of Freedoms and Exemptions, which outlined the system of governance of New Netherland. The charter divided the land into patroonships governed by the patroon, a landowner and magistrate, who had almost unlimited authority over the inhabitants, which the patroon was responsible for transporting to the colony. Most of the inhabitants of New Netherland, as a result, were bound to the company in one way or another. "Free colonists" could own land, as it were, but in return for the land they allowed themselves to be transported to America, where they had to stay for at least six years; all of their produce was sold to the company. They were not free to relocate. At least they had it better than the indentured servants, bound to the company to work the land of its four chief landowners, the patroons; they were transported and held in service for four years. The company, which answered to the Netherlands States General, possessed authoritarian rule and allowed no government participation to the three levels of society: free colonists, indentured workers, and artisans.[1]

Into this atmosphere of company authority came Adriaen van der Donck, a lawyer who became the schout (sheriff and prosecutor) of the patroonship—massive independent estate—of Rensselaerswyck, founded by Killian Van Rensselaer. Van der Donck was the first historian of New Netherland, writing *A Description of New Netherlands* in 1653.[2] His *Description* was the typical promotional literature of the 17th century, describing the land, climate, resources, and people of New Netherland, which the Dutch indulgently considered to stretch from the Delaware River to the upper Hudson River to the Connecticut River. The Dutch, like all European imperialists, believed that they were the first to come to this particular area of North America, which was inhabited by people that they called "wilden," or wild men, a supposition based in part on their paganism.[3] The Dutch, like the English, sought colonies by which to solve social problems at home. Van der Donck, in the *Description*, imagined a conversation between a Netherlander "patriot" and a "New-Netherlander," in which the latter tried to convince the former of the value of the Dutch colony in America. The New-Netherlander argued that, in the home country, "since the peace [of Westphalia, in 1648, ending the Thirty Years' War], there is not much employment, and there are many persons injuriously idle—hence it certainly appears, that it would be of service to the country to settle another Netherland with the excess of our population, which can be easily done, as a sheet-anchor and support to the state." In response to the argument that a colony might depopulate the home country, the New-Netherlander replied that there were many people outside of the Netherlands who were interested in immigrating, so that the population at home was growing; a colony was an investment, as it were, in people and prosperity, to help the mother country in times of need. Indeed, as the population of the colony grew, which it would very quickly, "we could derive formidable assistance from the same in men and means in times of need, which causes all republics to be respected by those who envy their prosperity."[4]

Van der Donck was not only an avid promoter but a landowner of note, who purchased land along the Hudson River on the upper reaches of Manhattan, subsequently named for him (Colendonk, then Yonkers).[5] He had a falling out with Van Rensselaer and came to believe in the rights of the colonists, servants, and artisans in New Netherland; when he returned to the home country, he joined a petition on behalf of the inhabitants against the controlling power of the West India Company. Eventually the power of the company was curtailed, and some rights were granted to the inhabitants: for example, in 1652 the citizens of New Amsterdam were empowered to elect the magistrates of the city.[6]

Van der Donck's apparent concern for the rights of every person in New Netherland was the exception rather than the rule. The tedium of farm labor, working for the company or another person, was the experience of most inhabitants. Nevertheless, the Dutch of Fort Orange, Beverwyck, and Rensselaerswyck contracted with servants for a variety of purposes, honest as well as dishonest. Servants were bound by indenture for a year or more in return for payment in kind or money—sometimes for passage from the Old to the New World. Servants in Dutch New Netherland typically entered into the arrangement voluntarily, to better their economic situation. These servants were men, women, children, blacks, Indians, and whites; most of the latter were Dutch, but there were servants from various European countries, many of whom came to New Netherland, which was Protestant and not subject to New England's Puritan orthodoxy or the Church of England of other colonies, to practice freedom of conscience.[7]

Magistrates of the Dutch courts of New Netherland and, after 1664 and the English victory over the Dutch, New York jealously guarded the rights, privileges, and responsibilities of both parties, servant and master. Quarrels were frequent between the two sides respecting the legal requirements of indentures. Dutch courts usually followed the contract to the letter in decisions. The shortage of applicable laws for many cases often forced magistrates to base their decisions on collected evidence, testimony, traditions, and common sense. Magistrates demanded that a servant faithfully serve the master "or any other master who he may get in the colony, and do their work and obey them in everything." In return, magistrates required masters to pay wages for the work of servants according to contract. Courts also protected the rights of servants whose masters attempted to extend illegally their term of servitude. The tradition in the Netherlands was to treat servants well, which was extended to New Netherland. Evert Pels discovered this in 1648 when he refused to pay servant Claes Tyssen wages of 26 guilders; magistrates demanded payment, which Pels refused, and the director of the colony of Rensselaerswyck, Brant van Slichtenhorst, paid the guilders and demanded that Pels reimburse him for the "loan." In 1678, in the Dutch community of Gravesend, Long Island, one master aimed to pay a debt to another by means of transferring the indenture of servant Elizabeth Burton, but when she successfully convinced the court that her term of servitude had been completed, the court agreed and freed her. Magistrates also protected the rights of masters whose servants had performed their tasks inadequately. In one case from the 1650s, a servant sued the widow of his master, demanding payment of wages for work; the widow, meanwhile, complained of the servant's slanders. The court, perhaps following the biblical injunction, sided with the widow, and even demanded that the servant reimburse her for wages advanced by the deceased master. The court in English Newtown protected a master's rights in 1682 when a servant did such an inadequate job for his master that the court ordered the servant to return part of his freedom dues, that is, wages. On the other hand, the court at Newtown demanded that a master pay a servant's freedom dues, which included livestock, land, and a sword. A year later in Newtown, when a master did not provide adequate medical care for an ill servant, the court demanded that the master provide such care or the servant would be freed.[8]

Magistrates of New Netherland and New York also closely followed Dutch and English law respecting the obligation of servants to meet completely the required terms of service. Adriaen Dircksz discovered this in 1651, when his master, Thomas Chamber, brought him to court for refusing "to serve out the term," and he "wastes and neglects his time, claiming to be free, contrary to the contract signed by him." Dircksz acknowledged the contract but proclaimed his desire to leave the master's service. The magistrates were exasperated, demanding, "for the maintenance of good order and justice and to curb the refractory spirit and intolerable insolence of the indented servants," that Dircksz be incarcerated for a fortnight, and fed bread and water at his own expense; moreover, for the term of his incarceration, since his master had to hire a temporary worker, Dircksz was liable for the debt. After a week of imprisonment, "through the mediation and upon the persistent request of certain petitioners," Dircksz was "graciously released from confinement on condition that he . . . promises to perform his duties faithfully and in all obedience, without in any wise acting sullenly, or opposing his master in whose service he is, and to serve out his bounden time, under penalty of double punishment."[9]

Dircksz did not long enjoy his release from incarceration. He was killed five weeks later. The killer was Evert Nolden (Noldingh), the schoolmaster of Rensselaerswyck since 1648, who was a tailor by trade. In mid-November 1651, for no apparent reason (according to the court records), Nolden struck Dircksz with a pair of tongs (used for the fireplace, or by a smith), "completely smashing his nose and mortally wounding him." Director Brant van Slichtenhorst derided such a "serious crime in a land of justice," which could "not remain unpunished." The schoolmaster lost his position, of course, and was "arbitrarily punished" and fined 300 guilders, which, if he could not pay, was to be satisfied through hard labor—in other words, servitude.[10]

Ultimately, Nolden retained most of his rights: to sue in court, to practice his trade of a tailor, to own land. The next year, in November 1652, he sued Jan van Breeman for back wages and won. A month later, he requested "a lot between the road near Annetgen Bogardus and Machiel, the lademaker. The

Hon. Volckert Jansz and Cornelis Theunisz van Westbroeck are appointed a committee to lay out and convey the said lot and road." But Nolden was unable to give up his violent ways. On May 13, 1658, he drew a knife on Peter Jansen, then two weeks later he drew a knife on Peter Lambersen. By this time, Nolden was himself a servant to a tavern keeper. A felon and servant, nevertheless he served as a witness in court in 1662.[11]

Court records of Dutch New Netherland and English New York are replete with cases involving crimes and other forms of insubordination perpetrated by servants. Servants lied, stole, assaulted, and murdered. Usually the penalties were light: admonishment, fines, or brief incarceration. Two recalcitrants, Claes Andriesz and Dirck Hendricksz, upon refusing to serve their master, were "ordered" by the Rensselaerswyck court in 1649 "to fulfil their contract of service . . . , under penalty, on the next default, of being put on bread and water for eight days at their own expense." These two rogues were constant gadflies to the director Van Slichtenhorst. Claes was a threat with his knife, and once "drew a sheath . . . across the director's body," on another occasion "treated the director insolently on the public road." Claes "begged forgiveness on his knees." A fortnight later, Claes appeared with "his master, Jan Baerentsz Wemp, and his wife," who asked the court for leniency on behalf of their servant. Upon the servant's pledge to obey, the court stipulated that Claes no longer visit taverns, especially on the Sabbath, but rather attend church; that he promise to obey faithfully his master and mistress as well as the patroon and other authorities of Rensslaerswyck; that he treat all people with mutual respect. Otherwise, "he shall be publicly punished for all his previous misdemeanors." Dirck, meanwhile, in July 1649, "unhitched one of the patroon's horses which was tied near the patroon's house and rode it into the Casteels [Castle] island creek, with the result that the horse was drowned under him." Besides this, he "slandered the director" and was a threat with the knife as well. In the spring, 1650, Dirck agreed to pay "two hundred guilders," and "is ordered for the present to go at the first opportunity in the service of the patroon to Katskil, his case to be disposed of some time hereafter according to his conduct." In 1671, a 17-year-old servant, Juriaen Barbatsco, broke into a house and stole some guilders, which he claimed that he needed "to pay for one half-interest in a canoe belonging to Franck, Mr Laval's servant, who advised him to do so." Barbatsco confessed the crime "without torture or irons," and the court condemned him to flogging and banishment. Upon the appeal of some inhabitants, that the young servant would not do so again, and that his sister was weak and with child, the court decided to waive the flogging; nevertheless, Barbatsco was banished "from this jurisdiction" for six years. In 1672, a servant named Mancque Willem wounded Roeloff Jansz, causing Jansz "surgeon's fees, pain and loss of time." In an extraordinary case recorded in the court minutes of Albany in 1675, one Jan Gerritsen, servant to Frederick and Margriet Phillipsen, condemned two Dutch Reformed Church ministers of being "false prophets." Gerritsen had told the two ministers on previous occasions that they "should repent," and he had convinced his mistress that they were disciples of the devil. She believed as well that Gerritsen "was a prophet and imbued with the Spirit of God." Indeed, Gerritsen had told Nicholas van Rensselaer, one of the ministers, "you are the devil, a false teacher and a false prophet," whereas "I am the true prophet." The magistrates of the court decided that such a case had to be considered by the "general Court of Assizes" in New York City. The same year in New York City, one of the most brazen thieves, who was also a servant, Robert Bowman, stole a mulatto slave and cannon, the latter of which must have been difficult to pawn or hide, and after his capture he was given 39 stripes on the back and was returned to his unfortunate master to control and work.[12]

Court and town records of New Netherland and New York reveal that servants as well as masters—in short, humans—made questionable decisions, according to 17th-century Christian standards of morality. A mistress, Ann Sewell, in 1695 was brought before the New York City Court of General Sessions, charged with "keeping in Chains and Irons for several Weeks upon Bread and water only & also for Cruelly beating" her servant, Ann Parsons; the court freed Parsons and made Sewall pay court costs. Up the Hudson River, servant Cornelis Michielse was a baker who served in the house of Abraham Staes. An African American servant also working for Staes, known in the records simply as the "negress," was with child, the father unknown. The magistrates determined to have her questioned "while in the throes of childbirth." During her ordeal, she claimed that "he who is the father of one is also the father of the other." As it was known that Cornelis was father of her previous children, he was arrested for fathering the newborn. But he denied the accusation, and pledged to take an oath to exonerate himself. He did so, and a jury declared him not guilty, though he was admonished by the court for his earlier transgressions with the "negress" and required to pay court costs.[13]

There were plenty of masters in Dutch New Netherland and English New York who ordered their servants to commit illegal activities, for which the master was ultimately responsible. Evert Pels, who decorates the records of Rensselaerswyck with a variety of obstinate, illegal actions, in 1648 was accused not only of committing violence on Thomas Jansz, hitting him on "the head with a piece of wood," but also of ordering his "servant" to "get the canoe of Thomas Jansz without his knowledge or consent." Several years later, under English rule, another master, Jan Clute, employed his servants, driving wagons to his farm, on the Sabbath, which the sheriff suggested to the magistrates at Albany should incur a fine. The magistrates were unconvinced by Clute's ridiculous claim that he did not know that it was illegal for servants to work on Sunday and fined him for "desecration of the Sabbath."[14]

Servants were, of course, dependents, hence, subject to the whims—often violent—of masters. Evert Pels, abusive toward freemen and servants alike, in 1648 beat his servant Claes Tyssen such that the servant was unable to work. Christoffel Davits was a violent sort; not only did he "hit Ryck Rutgersz on the head with a post," and "struck Jan van Bremen on the head with a tankard, making two wounds," but he also beat "his servant black and blue," for all three of which infractions he received a stiff fine. Jan Thysz and his servant Jan Jacobsz had frequent violent encounters; on one occasion in 1668 the schout of Rensselaerswyck charged the master with hitting the servant with a reaper's hook. Thysz admitted it but said it did not injure the servant, who needed the correction for his "abusive language." The following year a servant, Jan Aelberts, brought his master, Aelbert Andriesz Brat, to court, charging him with "beating, cursing, and swearing at" the servant's son, who "complains that he can not live with him that way."[15]

Besides farm labor, Dutch servants in New Netherland worked as masons, wagoners, bakers, carpenters, cooks, tailors, attorneys, tutors, and accountants. The latter included Jacob Sandersz Glen, servant to Jan Bastiaensen Van Gutsenhoven. Friends of Van Gutsenhoven realized the worth of this loyal servant and encouraged Van Gutsenhoven when he wished to travel to the Netherlands, advising that Glen could manage his affairs during the master's absence. Glen, according to the Van Rensselaer family correspondence, is "very careful" in recording transactions "and always properly transfers the accounts, for he is very neat and particular that things do not get mixed up." Glen was so trusted and useful that Van Gutsenhoven, upon his departure, loaned his servant to Van Rensselaer to help the latter manage Van Gutsenhoven's affairs, which included collecting on debts (in beaver pelts) from the inhabitants of Fort Orange. The loan was "on condition that he is to pay his wages and that I am to give him his board." When Van Gutsenhoven died, Glen settled the estate. This involved appearing in court (by this time under the authority of the English) as a plaintiff on behalf of his deceased master against defendants who were unwilling to pay debts in beaver pelts; Glen sued on multiple occasions, always victoriously. Likewise, Matthys van der Heyden, the "servant and attorney of Mr. Corn[elius] Steenwyck," sued, as plaintiff on behalf of his master, multiple defendants in 1677 for debts: in boards and beaver pelts. One of the defendants, Volkie Pieterse, had received "prunes, currants, syrup and other goods" from the plaintiff; she had paid already 18 beaver pelts; the defendant and her husband agreed to settle the issue out of court, as the servant Matthys van der Heyden would shortly return to New York City.[16]

Although servants retained the basic rights of human beings, once they signed an indenture, they could be bought and sold, and their labor transferred from one master to another to satisfy debt. Servitude was sometimes the resort of impoverished people to pay off a debt with work. This was Mary

Van der Ripe's recourse in 1724 New York City. She became ill under the employee of cooper Joost Sooy, who paid physicians for her healing. To pay this debt, "having noe other way to pay or Satisfy the same than by Servitude," she bound herself to Sooy for four years, during the first year of which "under the greatest hardships that ever poor Soul Labour'd," her master refused to clothe her adequately, so that she "went almost Naked and Sildome a Stockinges or Shoes to her feet either winter or Summer . . . besides the other bitter usage which she has received from their hands." After the first year, Sooy bound her out to a John Garra, "a Victualler," who likewise did not adequately provide for her, "so that yr Petitioner must undoubtly perish." Servitude could also be imposed on a person for criminal activity, as happened to freeman Jacob Loockermans in 1657 under Dutch rule. Loockerman "deliberately and without any occasion, shamefully cut Meuwes Hoogenboom with his knife, so that the said Meuwes Hoogenboom will be disfigured all his life, the wound extending from the left side of his forehead to the lower lip and reaching down to the bone." The magistrates at Fort Orange decided that Loockerman, rather than going to prison, would pay a fine of 300 guilders and serve 18 months "in the hardest labor" as a servant.[17]

In the wake of the Dutch settlement and occupation of the Hudson River valley were many conflicts and subsequent peace treaties with the native inhabitants—the various tribes of the Algonquians and Iroquois. The Dutch, especially at Fort Orange, at the confluence of the Mohawk and Hudson Rivers, had frequent interaction, peaceful and otherwise, with the Mohawk and other tribes. On one occasion in late summer of 1678, after the "ringing of the bell," signifying the closing of the gate of the fort, the schout, Gerardt Swart, discovered that Jan Clute "had a savage in his house, in violation of" local laws, which required a fine against Clute. Clute, in his defense, claimed that he had told his servant to demand that the Indian leave, but that the Indian had refused. Masters often asked their servants to interact with Indians. Another example from Albany records was the case, in 1670, of Jan Dirricxsz, servant of Herman van Gansevoort, whom schout Swart had arrested and confined for assault upon an Indian "squaw." Dirricxsz was fortunate in escaping torture or being put in irons because he confessed to the assault, though he in part blamed his master for awakening him "from his sleep" so that "in ill humor he struck a squaw," without provocation, "with a broomstick on the head," though "he did not intend to hurt her so badly." At first Dirricxsz told the story that his master Gansevoort had "ordered him to drive the squaw forcibly out of the yard," but he later changed his story. The court decided that after "arbitrary punishment," probably corporeal in nature, he be released upon posting of bond, which his master willingly paid.[18]

A particularly egregious crime, in the eyes of the magistrates of Fort Orange, was the selling of intoxicating beverages to the Mohawks and other tribes. In an ordinance from 1660, the magistrates made punishable by stiff fine the action of selling, "giving or presenting of wine, brandy, strong liquor or beer to the Indians." In one case from 1658, the schout, Jacob Teunissen, accused servant Mattys Van Beeren of selling brandy to an Indian; the schout had found the Indian with a small casket, which the man claimed he had purchased with beaver pelts at the house of Johannes Withart, whom Mattys Van Beeren served. The defendant denied the charge, demanding proof, which was not forthcoming, apparently; so the court decided that Van Beeren "purge himself by oath of the charge of having sold brandy to the Indians." He did, which convinced the magistrates of his innocence, and they dropped the charge. In 1657, Hans Vos appeared at the court at Fort Orange accused of using his servant, Michiel, to obtain and sell wine and brandy to the Indians, threatening Michiel and others that "if any one denounces me or blabs that I sell, or have sold, any wine to the savages, I shall tie a rope with a stone around his neck and throw him into the kill," the rivulet of Katskill.[19]

Fort Orange magistrates also accused Dutch masters of breaking the law by using their servants as "brokers" to range the forests seeking Indians with beaver pelts to sell. The defense of master Willem Brouwer in 1660 was that it was common practice among the Dutch to range the woods seeking to purchase beaver pelts and that very often masters employed servants for said purpose. Many masters were brought before the court at Fort Orange and this was their common plea. Adriaen Jansen admitted that he sent his servant in search of pelts "but declares that he did not know that every one was free to go into the woods, as the servants of Rutger Jacobsen, Anderies Herpertsen and Philip Pietersen openly went into the woods." He did not convince the magistrates with his specious argument "that one should . . . sin on account of the example of others." So many were the cases brought before magistrates of the misuse of servants relating to the Indians, that the court restated an old ordinance, "That no one, of what nation or quality [free or servant] he may be, shall directly or indirectly send any Christians or Indians as brokers into the woods, either with or without presents, to fetch or entice any Indians, under the penalty of the fine heretofore provided. . . . Secondly, no one shall be allowed to take from the Indians, whether in the woods, without or within the settlements, houses, or places, any beavers, to carry them for the Indians on horses, carts, or on their backs, under penalty of a like fine."[20]

In a case of questionable, perhaps treasonous, interaction with the Indians, from 1669, the schout of Schenectady, Jan van Marcken, accused a "negro" servant, Bastiaen Piters, of journeying up the Mohawk River to solicit the Mohawks to travel to Schenectady to help some of their people, for what reason is unclear from the court records. The schout argued reasonably that "Christians ought to keep out of the doings of the savages" and demanded that Piters's wages be taken from him. Two weeks later the matter came up again before the magistrates; this time Piters was accused of informing the

Mohawks that "their enemies were near" Schenectady. Piters, however, argued that his master, Juffrouw Curlers, ordered him to do it without pay; hence, the servant's money should not be confiscated nor should he be punished for his master's doings.[21]

A fascinating court case that appeared before the English magistrates in Albany in 1683 involved "two young Indian servants," who escaped from their New England masters (in Connecticut). The masters discovered their escaped servants living with the Mohican tribe at Skachkook. The English magistrates were in a quandary, because as servants these two men had no right to escape, but as Indians in New York they were legally free English subjects, and the court could not force their return. The magistrates "strongly recommended" that the servants return with their masters. The tribe thought differently and offered "30 beavers for the two Indians," which was agreeable to the masters. Escaped French servants were not, however, inherently free in the British colonies; hence in 1668 when English authorities heard that four Frenchmen had been seen on the road to Schenectady, court magistrates presumed "that they have run away from their masters"; the schout and four soldiers were sent in pursuit to recapture the supposed escapees.[22]

The experience of indentured servitude in colonial New Netherland and New York reveals that servitude as an economic and social phenomenon, as well as the attributes of servants and masters and their good deeds or lack thereof, did not significantly change with the transition in leadership from the Dutch to the English in 1664. Indeed, the characteristics of servitude in New Netherland and New York were largely mirrored up and down the coast, in the British American colonies, during the 17th and 18th centuries. In short, servants were people in search of something: a new life, a secure living, redemption from their past, release from the harsh economic realities of the early modern period. Some of these people, such as the Dutch who served the patroons of New Netherland, used servitude as a means of crossing the Atlantic and making a living, perhaps securing a foothold in America. Some people found themselves in debt and had little choice but to bind themselves to another for food, shelter, and clothing. Some found their way to servitude as payment for bad decisions, whether economic or moral mistakes. All of these people were dispossessed of something: the right to secure their own happiness; the right to forge their own path and exercise their own will; and the right to a life free from the most utter horrors of want.

Notes

1. A. C. Flick, ed., *History of the State of New York*, vols. 7–8 (Port Washington: New York State Historical Association, 1962), 225–226, 246–248.

2. Adriaen van der Donck, *A Description of New Netherlands*, 2nd ed. (Amsterdam: Evert Nieuenhof, 1656).

3. Ibid., 190.

4. Ibid., 229–230.

5. Van der Donck was apparently known as the Jonker, or Yonker, "a common appellation for a gentleman among the Dutch farmers." Ibid., 127.

6. E. B. O'Callaghan, *History of New Netherland: Or, New York under the Dutch*, vol. 2, 2nd ed. (New York: D. Appleton, 1855), 192.

7. Flick, *History of New York*, 284.

8. A. J. F. Van Laer, ed., *Minutes of the Court of Rensselaerswyck 1648–1652* (Albany: The University of the State of New York, 1922), 122; A. J. F. Van Laer, *Minutes of the Court of Fort Orange and Beverwyck 1657–1660*, vol. 2 (Albany: The University of the State of New York, 1923), 164; Richard B. Morris, *Government and Labor in Early America* (New York: Harper and Row, 1946), 414; *Town Minutes of Newtown, 1653–1734*, 4 vols. (New York: The Historical Records Survey, 1941), 2: 141, 148, 264; Flick, *History of New York*, 190.

9. E. B. O'Callaghan, ed., *Laws and Ordinances of New Netherland 1638–1674* (Albany: Weed, Parsons, 1868), 24; Van Laer, *Minutes of the Court of Rensselaerswyck 1648–1652*, 163–166.

10. Van Laer, *Minutes of the Court of Rensselaerswyck 1648–1652*, 29, 173–174.

11. A. J. F. Van Laer, *Minutes of the Court of Fort Orange and Beverwyck 1652–1656*, vol. 1 (Albany: The University of the State of New York, 1920), 43–44; E. B. O'Callaghan, ed., *Calendar of Historical Manuscripts in the Office of the Secretary of State, Albany, N.Y.* (Albany: Weed, Parsons, 1865), 320; A. J. F. Van Laer, ed., *Early Records of the City and County of Albany and Colony of Rensselaerswyck*, vol. 3 (Albany: The University of the State of New York, 1918), 183–184.

12. Van Laer, *Minutes of the Court of Rensselaerswyck 1648–1652*, 82, 109–112, 115; A. J. F. Van Laer, *Minutes of the Court of Albany, Rensselaerswyck and Schenectady, 1668–1673, 1675–1680, 1680–1685*, 3 vols. (Albany: The University of the State of New York, 1926–1932), 1: 276–278, 299; 2: 9–12; Richard B. Morris, ed., *Select Cases from the Mayor's Court of New York City, 1674–1784* (New York: American Historical Association, 1935), 741.

13. Samuel McKee Jr., *Labor in Colonial New York, 1664–1776* (New York: Columbia University Press, 1935), 99–100; Van Laer, *Minutes of the Court of Albany, Rensselaerswyck and Schenectady*, 2: 401, 405, 414–418.

14. Van Laer, *Minutes of the Court of Rensselaerswyck 1648–1652*, 52; Van Laer, *Minutes of the Court of Albany, Rensselaerswyck and Schenectady*, 2: 322–323.

15. Van Laer, *Minutes of the Court of Rensselaerswyck 1648–1652*, 33, 107; Van Laer, *Minutes of the Court of Albany, Rensselaerswyck and Schenectady*, 1: 28, 99.

16. A. J. F. Van Laer, ed., *Correspondence of Jeremias Van Rensselaer 1651–1674* (Albany: The University of the State of New York, 1932), 170, 263; Van Laer, *Minutes of the Court of Albany, Rensselaerswyck and Schenectady*, 1: 34, 56, 72, 104, 111, 130; 2: 259–260.

17. Morris, *Government and Labor*, 359; Van Laer, *Minutes of the Court of Fort Orange and Beverwyck*, 2: 64–65.

18. Van Laer, *Minutes of the Court of Albany, Rensselaerswyck and Schenectady*, 1: 20–21, 168–169.

19. Van Laer, *Minutes of the Court of Fort Orange and Beverwyck*, 2: 25–26, 170–171, 282.

20. Ibid., 279–282.

21. Van Laer, *Minutes of the Court of Albany, Rensselaerswyck and Schenectady*, 1: 94, 102.

22. Ibid., 1: 21; 3: 367.

CHAPTER SIX

Daniel Defoe's London

Jack was a boy living in the city of London at the beginning of the 18th century. Like so many thousands at the time, he was a homeless waif living on the streets. Jack's parents were well to do, but he was a bastard and forsaken by his mother and father for a nurse, who brought him up with funds provided by the father. Jack knew nothing of his parents and did not even know his surname. When Jack was 10 years old, his nurse died, and he was abandoned to the streets to live with whatever companions he could contrive to associate with. He lived in a neighborhood of east London near the Tower on Rosemary Lane. The parish authorities of St. Botolph Aldgate were satisfied that if a child could take care of him- or herself then they had no need to take the trouble. Jack and his compatriots were able beggars and thieves who could beg and steal what they needed to survive. Rosemary Lane hosted the shops, smells, colors, and noise of Rag Fair, where any sorts of clothes or cloth could be bought or pawned. It was a crowded, gaudy, noisy thoroughfare, the kind that a young boy could lose himself in—and this Jack did. Even though he was homeless and poor, he was as jolly as the rest of the people, at least according to a contemporary account by Ned Ward: "Amongst all that I beheld as I pass'd thro' 'em, I saw not one Melancholy or Dejected Countenance amongst 'em; but all showing in their Looks more Content and Chearfulness than you shall find in an Assembly of Great and Rich men on a Publick Festival: From whence we may Conjecture, that Poverty is commonly attended with such a Careless Indifference, that frees the Mind from reflecting on its Miseries."[1] Jack made this his young-life work. He found sufficient food by begging at the doorsteps of merciful townspeople. He slept at the parish watch house with other beggars and ne'er-do-wells in warm weather or in the warm ashes of the lower brick foundations of glass houses when it was cold. One of his chief activities was avoiding people called "spirits," who found the number of homeless children on the streets of London ripe pickings for supplying ship's captains with servants bound for America. Ned Ward, again, described spirits and their pawns on one occasion in London: "We peep'd in at a Gateway, where we saw Three or Four Blades well drest, with Hawkes Countenances, attended with half a Dozen Ragamuffinly Fellows, showing Poverty in their Rags, and Despair in their Faces, mixt with a parcel of young Wild Striplings like Run-away Prentices." Upon inquiry, Ward discovered "that House, says my Friend, which they are entering, is an Office where Servants for the Plantations, bind themselves to be miserable as long as they Live, without an especial Providence prevents."[2]

One of Jack's friends became associated with spirits who kidnapped children, so Jack knew the dangers involved and had to keep his wits about him to ensure his own safety. This friend was of a wicked turn of mind; he would kidnap the youngsters (although he was himself only 13 years) and hold their mouth or bind their throat to ensure that they would not call out, in the process most horribly injuring the child. The authorities finally caught up with him and committed him to Newgate.

Newgate was the most notorious of the London prisons in the 16th, 17th, and 18th centuries. Here the most desperate felons were kept, particularly those who had been condemned to be hanged by the neck at Tyburn. All London prisons, whether they went by the name of Bridewell, Old Bailey, or Newgate, were filthy places, the same as dungeons, with every conceivable pestilence, the miserable and dying, and the condemned and those awaiting to be transported, languishing in despair. Such gaols were often private, profit-making concerns for jailers and their owners. Newgate had a reputation for harboring typhus, so it was a brave magistrate indeed who was willing to venture within its walls to inspect the prison. Here the basic necessities, such as food and water, were bought at a price. Without money, the poor suffered from malnutrition, cold, and want of clothing. People had to live in their own filth, sometimes chained to a spot. Here girls and women were forced to prostitute themselves; many babies (such as Daniel Defoe's fictional character, Moll Flanders) were born in Newgate. Jailers inflicted corporeal punishment on malefactors of any age, boys and girls. Jack's friend, when committed to Newgate, was flogged on several occasions, bloodying and scarring his back.[3]

As Jack went through adolescence, he became associated with bands of thieves who stole, pickpocketed, and pawned their way to a precarious living. Henry Fielding would in time comment on the "great Gang of Rogues" who have made "Theft and Robbery into a regular System." These gangs were adept at "evading the law" and springing their caught comrades from gaol.[4] Jack readily picked up the art of picking a person's pocket especially among the bumpkins and fools who came to London without a care in the world for their property or person. London inhabitants themselves, according to Defoe's portrayal in *Life and Adventures of Duncan Campbell*, were superstitious and superficial, believing in talismans, predictions of fortune-tellers, star charts of astrologers, and Gypsy palm readers. Such people were easy marks for an intelligent thief. As Jack grew to manhood he grew in his profession, though he had qualms about stealing from the very poor and decrepit, and refused to go to the extreme of most of his companions in whoring, cursing, and drinking. There was definite opportunity for the latter activity, as just about everywhere a person turned in London there was a public house offering gin at a cheap price. In some parts of London, such as St. Giles, the ratio of public houses to other establishments was one in four. Judge Henry Fielding once wrote that "wretches are often brought before me, charged with theft and robbery, whom I am forced to confine them before they are in a condition to be examined; and when they have afterwards become sober, I have plainly perceived, from the state of the case, that the Gin alone was the cause of the transgression, and have been sometimes sorry that I was obliged to commit them to prison."[5] Partly because he remained sober, Jack was never arrested and brought before a justice, but many of his friends were; Jack had the unhappy experience of watching his friend and mentor, who was just a few years older, be arrested, held fast in irons in Newgate, and eventually hung by the neck at Tyburn.

England in the 18th century had scores of capital crimes that applied to anyone over the age of seven, caught and convicted. Crimes ranged from the very violent, such as rape, to the innocuous, such as associating with Gypsies. From the Glorious Revolution, when there were 50 such crimes deserving death, to the end of the 18th century, when there were two times as many, the constancy was that the condemned, reprieved, and executed fit no prescribed mold, but were as haphazard as London life itself. If initially English magistrates and lawgivers considered transportation a means by which idleness could be made productive, and evil turned to good, in the 1700s it became more a desire to be rid of the rogues and their kind.[6]

Jack, Daniel Defoe's creation in his novel, *Colonel Jack*,[7] was representative of so many young English boys and girls, men and women, who roamed the streets of London stealing because they knew nothing else. Londoners had not developed the necessary community infrastructures and institutions to match the city's burgeoning population of two-thirds of a million people at the time that Defoe wrote. Trade and manufacturing (and wars) flourished but not enough to employ the thousands thronging the streets. Lacking a system of public education, lacking sufficient orphanages and such charitable organizations to care for children, the "street Arabs" of London had the run of the thoroughfares. Defoe's creations of Colonel Jack and Moll Flanders perfectly capture the experience of these young ne'er-do-wells.

A contemporary figure to Defoe's Jack was James Revel, who was as real or as fictional as Colonel Jack. In the early 18th century, a poem appeared by one James Revel titled *The Poor Unhappy Felon's Sorrowful Account of the*

Fourteen Years Transportation at Virginia, in America. The verse describes a young man brought up in west London by hard-working good people. The boy was apprenticed to a tin man near Moorfields, a rough place akin to Rag Fair, though on the more western side of the city. Here the young apprentice fell into "wicked company," a "gang of thieves" that "rov'd about the streets both night and day." In spite of the earnest entreaties of his parents and master, the lad continued his thieving ways, allowing "strong liquor" to banish "the thoughts of fear" that justice would one day catch up to him. This day came: several of his companions were executed, but James was transported to Virginia. The voyage lasted seven weeks, during which some of the transported felons died, but not James. Once they reached America, their lousy clothes were exchanged for clean apparel; they were put on exhibition for potential buyers. James unfortunately had his contract purchased by "a grim old man" who owned land up the Rappahannock River. Here James exchanged his good clothes for "a canvas shirt and trowsers" as well as "a hop-sack frock." He was barefooted no matter the season. He worked in the tobacco fields next to African slaves; they worked six days for the master and one day on their own small plot of ground growing the food they ate. They harvested their own maize and hauled it to the mill to grind it into flour. Escape was fruitless; when caught, extra time was added to the sentence. To steal or murder was to sign your death sentence. When he fell ill, he received no respite from work and gained more empathy from his fellow slaves than his master. Eventually his master died and James was purchased by another, a cooper, who lived at Jamestown, and who treated his servant fairly. After 14 years, James was released and returned to London, where he refused to take up his old ways and lived a good and sober life.[8]

Precisely when James Revel served in Virginia is unclear, though throughout the colonial period English magistrates transported felons to that colony. In 1661, after the restoration of Charles II to the English throne, the Council for Foreign Plantations met "to consider of the best ways of encouraging and furnishing people for the Plantations, and how felons condemned to death for small offences, and . . . sturdy beggars, may be disposed of for that use, and to consider an office of registry for the same." A few years later, there was a proposal "to the King and Council to constitute an office for transporting to the Plantations" felons of England. There were sufficient numbers of felons transported during the Commonwealth and after the Restoration (in 1660) that the House of Burgesses in 1670 passed legislation to prevent "the great numbers of Felons and other desperate villaines sent hither from the several prisons of England." By this time, numbers of transported felons were dropping, although the diarist Narcissus Luttrell in 1692 noted that London magistrates ordered the transportation of 50 lewd women and 30 prostitutes to Virginia.[9]

Such a life continued to elude Defoe's Jack, who escaped to Scotland to avoid a similar fate of his executed friend; he enlisted in the army but soon deserted, and eventually returned to England crossing the Tweed to New-castle, where he found himself in a tavern with little money, and less hope. A friendly woman kept the tavern; she lamented Jack's misfortune, and told him of a way to get to London by sea cheaply and offered to provide some refreshment while he waited. Jack was soon too intoxicated to resist when the spirits escorted him aboard the ship that, it turned out, was heading to America. The captain excused himself from knowing the source of his human cargo, only that his job was to transport them to America and there sell them to the highest bidder. The ship sailed north around Scotland then pursued a southwesterly course, arriving at the Chesapeake Bay and sailing north to the Potomac River. There, Jack realized that he deserved his fate: "I was bred a vagabond, had been a pickpocket and a soldier, and was run from my colours, and . . . I had no settled abode in the world, nor any employ to get any thing by, except that wicked one I was bred to, which had the gallows at the heels of it." At first, Jack found that his situation did not seem so bad: at the end of his term of service, "I should have the courtesy of the country, (as they called it) that is, a certain quantity of land to cultivate and plant for myself. So that now I was like to be brought up to something, by which I might live, without that wretched thing called stealing; which my very soul abhorred, and which I had given over, as I have said, ever since that wicked time that I robbed the poor widow of Kentish-Town."[10]

Meanwhile, Jack worked hard, along with other servants and slaves. Periodically his master received new servants from England, reprieved felons who had been transported to America. When they arrived at the plantation, his master addressed them, saying that many in Virginia had begun in such circumstances, but if they worked hard, and acted correctly, they might someday own land. Such speeches affected Jack, who was befriended by his master, who eventually raised Jack up to be an overseer on his plantation. Jack learned that the only way to treat servants and slaves was through mercy rather than threats; his plantation workers willingly worked for such a kind master.

Daniel Defoe, in his fiction and essays, concerned himself with the impoverished of England. He believed that one answer to the large numbers of sturdy poor and indigent criminals was transportation to America. Defoe realized that for some people, as his imaginary creation Colonel Jack lamented to himself, it was "a sad thing to be under a necessity of doing evil, to procure that subsistence, which I could not support the want of, to be obliged to run the venture of the gallows, rather than the venture of starving, and to be always wicked for fear of want." As Defoe preached in *Colonel Jack*: "Every Newgate wretch, every desperate forlorn creature, the most despicable ruined man in the world, has here," in America, "a fair opportunity put into his hands to begin the world again, and that upon a foot of certain gain, and in a method exactly honest; with a reputation that nothing past will have any effect upon: and innumerable people have raised themselves from the worst

circumstance in the world, namely, from the cells in Newgate." Defoe imagined an educated, "clever fellow," transported to America and purchased by
plantation owner Colonel Jack. The felon "acknowledged . . . being driven to
extremities"; he "took to the highway, for which, had he been taken, he would
have been hanged; but falling into some low-prized rogueries afterwards, for
want of opportunity to worse, was catched, condemned, and transported,
and, as he said, was glad he came off so." He said further: "How much is the
life of a slave in Virginia to be preferred to that of the most prosperous thief
in the world! Here I live miserable, but honest; suffer wrong, but do no wrong;
my body is punished, but my conscience is not loaded; and, as I used to say,
that I had no leisure to look in, but I would begin when I had some recess,
some time to spare; now God has found me leisure to repent." Defoe, a deeply
religious man, believed that fate is but God's will, and that such people, as
Colonel Jack or Moll Flanders, suffered deeply so they would repent and
change and, being forgiven, would thrive again. "Virginia, and a state of
transportation, may be the happiest place and condition they were ever in for
this life, as, by a sincere repentance, and a diligent application to the business
they are put to, they are effectually delivered from a life of flagrant wicked-
ness, and put in a perfect new condition, in which they have no temptation to
the crimes they formerly committed, and have a prospect of advantage for the
future." Others agreed with Defoe. Author and reformer Patrick Colquhoun,
who lived in America before the War of Independence, in 1806 wrote, apparently from experience, that from 1718 to 1775 "great numbers of felons were
sent chiefly to the Province of Maryland" where they experienced "rigid discipline which the colonial Laws authorized the masters to exercise over servants." These felons, "after the expiration of their Servitude, . . . mingled in
the Society of the Country, under circumstances highly beneficial to themselves and even to the colony. Possessed in general . . . of good natural abilities, they availed themselves of the habits of industry they acquired in the
years of their Servitude—became farmers and planters on their own account;
and many of them . . . also in their turn became masters, and purchased the
Servitude of future Transports sent out for sale." English writers had long
written in such vein. Joshua Gee, in his 1730 treatise *The Trade and Navigation
of Great-Britain Considered*, argued that the idle poor of England would find a
useful life in America: "Now as there cannot be an Act of greater Charity or
Humanity, than to put those People into a Way of getting Bread for themselves; if they were sent into the Colonies, and put upon raising and dressing
Hemp and Flax, I am of Opinion, they might not only find a most profitable
Employment, but also those that are condemned for petty Larceny, or any
other Crime less than the Penalty of Death, being sent thither might be rendered useful." William Eddis, who lived in Maryland for several years before
the American War of Independence, had a slightly different view. Most felons, either those who were banished to America and could pay their own

way, or those who had to be bound to service, "seldom establish their residence in this country: the stamp of infamy is too strong upon them to be easily erased: they either return to Europe, and renew their former practices; or, if they have fortunately imbibed habits of honesty and industry, they remove to a distant situation, where they may hope to remain unknown, and be enabled to pursue with credit every possible method of becoming useful members of society."[11]

Colquhoun believed that transported felons became very valuable in Maryland and usually "had better abilities than those who voluntarily engaged themselves to go to America." In this he was referring to indentured servants, whom Defoe thought nevertheless could benefit from their experience of voluntary transportation to America: those "that go voluntarily over to those countries; and, in order to get themselves carried over, and placed there, freely bind themselves there; especially if the person into whose hands they fall, do any thing honestly by them; for, as it is to be supposed, that those poor people knew not what course to take before, or had miscarried in their conduct before, here they are sure to be immediately provided for, and, after the expiration of their time, to be put in a condition to provide for themselves."[12]

In Defoe's nonfiction writing, such as *Giving Alms No Charity*, he joined a chorus of other writers, jurists, and analysts who were trying to discover the causes of idleness, poverty, and crime, which plagued England, and particularly London, for centuries. Henry Fielding, a justice of the peace, essayist, and novelist of the mid-18th century, wrote in 1751 *An Enquiry into the Causes of the Late Increase of Robbers, &c.* Fielding argued that crime was increasing because of idleness and indulgence, which were consequences of changes in the economy and class structure of England. He longed for the good old days when a peasant knew his or her place next to the lord of the manor. So many villeins had been driven from the farm to the city in England, where they had to take up a different kind of work: mechanical labor, craft labor, trade, and shopkeeping. Rather than the old pleasures of the land, hard work from sunup to sundown followed by a bowl of porridge by the scant fire of the one-roomed dwelling, the urban worker looked at the ways of his betters, and their luxurious habits, and thought that he, too, deserved such luxury. Although God ordained that the mass of humankind must labor for their paltry pleasures, these English upstarts actually believed they deserved to live in luxury, idleness, and sin. The solution, thought Fielding, to this problem was to limit the gin houses and gaming establishments and counter the idleness of those who wish to enjoy life without work.[13]

A half-century later Patrick Colquhoun, a like-minded reformer, argued that as long as England refused to provide for the education of youths, immorality and crime would continue. Youngsters such as Defoe's Jack have "the worst possible examples daily before them and . . . as they advance to maturity, become victims of those vices, which . . . render them bad and noxious members of society instead of becoming good servants." Indeed, "the prosperity of every state depends on the good habits, and the religious and moral instruction of the labouring people. By shielding the minds of youth against vices . . . much is gained to society in prevention of crimes, and in lessening the demand for punishments." Of course, too much education might give these people unfortunate ideas about elevating themselves above their station in life. Nevertheless, Colquhoun wrote, "if we suffer them to be ill educated, and then punish them for those very crimes to which their bad education and miserable condition exposed them, the result is, that by such an oversight we make delinquents, and then punish them." What Defoe had described in his novels a century before still existed in London in Colquhoun's time: "Many useful subjects are lost to the state by premature death on the scaffold, by transportation, at an enormous expense to the country, and by being rendered idle, useless, hardened and depraved, from the evil habits they contract in gaols."[14]

Fielding believed that one of the greatest problems facing England was the inadequacy of the poor relief system, which tended to impoverish rather than to relieve. "It must be a matter of astonishment," he wrote, "to any man to reflect, that in a country where the poor are, beyond all comparison, more liberally provided for than in any other part of the habitable globe, there should be found more beggars, more distressed and miserable objects than are to be seen throughout all the states of Europe."[15] English laws addressing the needs of the poor began during Elizabeth's reign, almost 200 years before Fielding wrote, and had led to a variety of almshouses, workhouses, houses of correction, hospitals, acts of settlement, encouragements to emigrate, transportations of felons, and laws against vagrancy. But still, there were more and more impoverished people. Why?

Daniel Defoe believed that he had the answer, as presented in his essay, *Giving Alms, No Charity*. Published in London in 1704, the subtitle explains, "Being an Essay upon this Great Question, whether Workhouses, Corporations, and Houses of Correction for Employing the Poor, as now Practised in England . . . are not mischievous to the Nation, tending to the Destruction of our Trade, and to Increase the Number and Misery of the Poor." Defoe wrote that Elizabeth I was wise in taking advantage of the fall of Flemish cloth industry under the Spanish occupation in the 16th century, such that, whereas before English goods went to Flanders to be manufactured, instead Flemish workers came to England where the raw materials (wool) were being produced. This shows that the key to relieving poverty in England is to provide work for workers, which Defoe argued had been done: English manufacturing was in his time providing enough work, so the problem with poverty and begging in England was simply that the English poor lacked the will to work. Defoe once discovered, as recorded by Frederic Eden, that "when I wanted a man for work, and offered 8 s per week to strolling fellows at my doore, they have frequently told me to my face, that they could get more a begging." Begging had become an employment by which to earn a living; as a result, there was more work in England than workers. Therefore, he argued, it was nonsensical to require parishes to construct workhouses to employ the poor, when there were already sufficient manufacturing places and the like to employ the poor laborer. The problem was not that there was insufficient work for the poor; rather, that the poor were indolent and chose not to work. To force people into the workhouse was to take away the living of an honest poor person somewhere who wished to work. Defoe had made a study of the domestic economy, which he argued was stable because products were developed in various parishes and shipped to London, the center for manufacturing, whereupon manufactured items were then shipped back to parishes for consumption. If, however, every parish was a manufacturing center by means of its workhouses and houses of correction, then manufacturing would become decentralized and healthy trade disrupted—all for the sake of forcing the sturdy poor to work. It was similarly absurd that the English army and navy had to recruit in gaols when there were able-bodied men who could take the job.[16]

In the wake of war, such as after the treaty ending the War of the Spanish Succession in 1713, the number of soldiers returning home, as well as the reduced demand for troops, resulted in crushing numbers of poor and criminals appearing before justices and being sent to Newgate and Bridewell. The House of Commons responded with legislation to allow judges to transport criminals. Patrick Colquhoun wrote in 1806 that "transportation is commonly understood to have been first introduced, anno 1718, by the act of the 4th George I. Cap. 11; and afterwards enlarged by the act 6th of George I. c. 23 which allowed the court a discretionary power to order felons who were by law entitled to their clergy, to be transported to the American plantations for seven or fourteen years, according to circumstances." True, the system of convict transportation blossomed under the Hanovers, beginning with George I, but there had been instances previously, where rogues and convicts were banished, transported, to other parts of the realm, or elsewhere. According to a law under Elizabeth I, desperados "who had taken sanctuary might abjure the realm." Under the Commonwealth political prisoners could be sent to the colonies. One 17th-century law condemned people who destroyed crops to be transported to America for seven years. Before Parliament took control of convict transportation during the beginning years of the reign of George I, often individuals who had their capital sentences reprieved by royal decree were transported for a term of years up to life at the discretion of the king. Sir John Towers, for example, had "long lain in a loathsome prison" when he petitioned Charles II to intervene to carry out the transportation to the colonies. There was some movement during the early years of Charles II's reign to systematize the transportation of "vagrants, rogues, and idle persons that can give no account of themselves, felons who have the benefit of clergy, such as are convicted of petty larceny, vagabonds, gypsies, and loose persons, making resort to unlicensed brothels, such persons to be transported from the nearest seaport, and to serve four years according to the laws and customs of those islands, if over 20 years of age, and seven years if under 20." Such a system, however, did not develop for another 50 years. By the end of the reign of Queen Anne, in 1714, England was moving toward adopting a clear system of transportation. An act in 1714 allowed justices of the peace to apprehend vagabonds and beggars who were deemed incorrigible and bind them in service or labor for seven years in England or in the American plantations.[17]

The system of convict transportation began in earnest under George I in the fourth year of his reign, 1717. According to a law passed by Parliament during this year, paupers or criminals who would normally be sentenced to the bridewell or house of correction for such corporeal punishment as whipping and branding could be, at the discretion of the justice, sent to America to serve for seven years, bound to a master in service. Criminals subject to execution could be sentenced for fourteen years. Any such felon so transported who returned to England before the conclusion of their term of servitude was subject to summary execution. This act further systematized the binding of youths into service in the colonies. Any person between the ages of 15 and 21 who sought to be transported to America could be bound to a ship captain for such purpose, as long as justices of the peace and the Lord Mayor of London agreed. The youth would be bound for eight years.[18]

Defoe's London was such that the poor were increasing notwithstanding the poor laws; the numbers of criminals were increasing notwithstanding the capital crimes committed in the shadow of Tyburn; and Newgate, Old Bailey, Bridewell, and all of the other gaols of England were overflowing with indebted paupers, hardened criminals, prostitutes and their babies, and those caught for committing minor transgressions. These prisons were insufficient for long-term imprisonment, save for debtors awaiting a change of heart of their creditors. Transportation appeared to be the one way to deal with social problems that seemed unsolvable. Gaols could be spared numbers, people could be redeemed from execution, and commerce served. Even if the poor and transported did not benefit, labor, production, trade, and hence the wealth and power of the realm, would benefit. The system of transportation would also allow legislators and jurists to push back the problem of reforming criminal law and gaols until another day.

Of course, if a person were convicted of a capital crime but not executed this could lessen the implied threat of the hangman's rope. Judges figured out a way to keep the pretenses of capital crimes and the ultimate threat of hanging at the same time that they could spare those who seemed not so hardened in crime, or those who were caught in the wrong situation at the wrong time, or those who were able-bodied and could do a full day's work on the tobacco plantation. People could be spared hanging for transportation by pleading the "benefit of the clergy." The legal basis for pleading the benefit of the clergy harked back to medieval England, when Roman Catholic clerics sought trial in ecclesiastical rather than secular courts. During the Tudor period, with the creation of the Church of England, pleading the benefit of the clergy was allowed for clerics and lay people if the person under trial, or person condemned, were literate and could read from Psalm 51, asking God and the court for mercy. Benefit of the clergy continued with little change under the Stuarts, but in the 18th century the literacy requirement was dropped. Generally, the benefit of the clergy allowed a person to exchange execution for branding and hard labor for a year or more; after 1717, the alternative was transportation to the colonies for seven years. If a person could not claim benefit of the clergy but obtained a royal pardon, also occurring with more frequency, then the term of service was fourteen years. Increasingly during the 18th century, benefit of the clergy became but a formality for allowing a person to escape execution for a life in the colonies.[19]

Notwithstanding Defoe's portrayal in *Colonel Jack* and *Moll Flanders* that transportation of prisoners to the colonies was beneficial for both felon and master, hence for the colonies and the mother country alike, colonials often felt dubiously toward the system. Estimates vary on the number of felons transported to the colonies—perhaps as many as 30,000. Of these, 10,000 came from Old Bailey prison in Middlesex County, London, before the outbreak of the American War of Independence. Numbers were of course greater after 1717, and most felons during the Hanoverian period ended up in Maryland, where there continued to be a great demand of white servants. Virginia during the early to mid-18th century was moving toward slavery rather than servitude, and throughout the colonies there was increasing resistance at midcentury to the colonies being a dumping ground for English felons.[20]

One of the more vocal American opponents to English convict transportation was the polymath Benjamin Franklin of Philadelphia. Franklin was much traveled, having spent many years in England. He knew the English mentality regarding labor and people. He was a student of demography and human affairs. He was an almanac writer and publisher and a printer of note and fame. Franklin made it his business to know what was happening throughout the colonies. He kept track of ideas, customs, commerce, habits, and opinions and was not one to silence his own opinionated voice. In May 1751, for example, Franklin sent an opinion piece to the *Pennsylvania Gazette*, signed "Americanus." It disturbed Franklin that Parliament's response to colonial laws to prevent the importation of transported felons was "that such Laws are against the Publick Utility, as they tend to prevent the Improvement and Well Peopling of the Colonies." Franklin, who loved to use his wit to full effect, responded that "such a tender *parental* Concern in our *Mother Country*

for the *Welfare* of her Children, calls aloud for the highest *Returns* of Grati-
tude and Duty." Franklin jokingly asserted, therefore, his "Endeavour" to
show America's "grateful Disposition" by shipping, in return, some of the
products of its soil, to improve England according to the same logic that justified transporting felons to America. "In some of the uninhabited Parts of
these Provinces, there are Numbers of these venomous Reptiles we call
Rattle-Snakes; Felons-convict from the Beginning of the World." Although
Americans tended to kill them when they found such snakes, Franklin
thought that "they may possibly change their Natures, if they were to change
the Climate," to England. He proposed "that this general Sentence of *Death*,"
so deserved by the felons in England as well as the rattlesnakes of America,
"be changed for *Transportation*." Some might argue against the inconvenience
of such an action. Likewise, Americans had argued that to empty "the New-
gates and Dungeons in Britain . . . into the Colonies" was highly inconve-
nient, since "Thieves and Villains [are] introduc'd among us," which "spoil
the Morals of Youth in the Neighbourhoods that entertain them, and perpe-
trate many horrid Crimes." After all, "What is a little *Housebreaking, Shoplift-
ing*, or *Highway Robbing*; what is a *Son* now and then *corrupted* and hang'd, a
Daughter *debauch'd* and pox'd, a Wife *stabb'd*, a Husband's *Throat cut*, or a
Child's *Brains beat out* with an Axe, compar'd" to the overall "*publick Utility*"
of the Parliamentary decision, which would help with the "improvement and
WELL PEOPLING of the Colonies!" "*Rattle-snakes*," Franklin concluded,
"seem the most *suitable Returns* for the *Human Serpents* sent us by our *Mother*
Country." But even here the colonies would have the worst of the trade, "for
the *Rattle-Snake* gives Warning before he attempts his Mischief; which the
Convict does not."[21]

Franklin was one of many voices. During the same month and year, a
writer in the *Virginia Gazette* opined, similarly: "When we see our Papers
fill'd continually with accounts of the most audacious Robberies, the most
Cruel Murders, and infinite other Villanies perpetrated by Convicts transported from Europe, what melancholy, what terrible Reflections must it occasion! What will become of our Posterity? These are some of thy Favours
Britain. Thou art called our Mother Country; but what good Mother ever sent
Thieves and Villains to accompany her children; to corrupt some with their
infectious Vices and murder the rest? What Father ever endeavour'd to spread
the Plague in his Family?"[22]

Yet one Virginia planter, renowned for his common sense and good
judgment—George Washington—purchased convict labor for Mount Vernon
around this time—1766. Eight years later, Washington sent an agent to Baltimore to purchase "four men convicts, four indented servants for three years,
and a man and his wife for four years." The man who sold the servants wrote
Washington that "the price is, I think, rather high; but as they are country,
likely people, and you at present wanted them, you [will] be satisfied with

[the] bargain." During the same year, 1774, Washington, wishing to obtain a labor force to develop some lands he owned in the Ohio Valley, wrote to a merchant for information about importing Palatines, or *Redemptioners*, from Continental Europe. Washington knew of the reputation of German immigrants for industriousness and wished "to make matters as easy and agreeable as possible to these emigrants." He proposed to pay for their passage to America and passage to the Ohio, for which he expected reimbursement through labor, and secure himself from economic loss, to indenture these people until the terms were satisfied, whereupon they shall be "freemen and tenants." Washington also wished to assure these people that he would in no way restrain them "in their civil or religious principles," which all "mankind are solicitous to enjoy."[23] Washington hoped, therefore, to encourage people by their own free will to come to America to labor for him.

Notes

1. Ned Ward, *The London Spy Compleat*, 1703. http://grubstreetproject.net/works/T119938?image=338

2. Ibid. http://grubstreetproject.net/works/T119938?image=62

3. Albert Crew, *London Prisons of Today and Yesterday* (London: Ivor Nicholson and Watson, 1933), 30–32, 43; Sidney Webb and Beatrice Webb, *English Prisons under Local Government* (London: Longmans Green, 1922), 4–7, 16, 18–20.

4. Henry Fielding, *An Enquiry into the Causes of the Late Increase of Robbers, &c*, 2nd ed. (London: Millar, 1751), 3–4.

5. Leon Radzinowicz, *A History of English Criminal Law: And Its Administration to 1750* (London: Stevens, 1948), 400, 406.

6. Ibid., 3, 11, 12; A. G. L. Shaw, *Convicts and the Colonies: A Study of Penal Transportation from Great Britain and Ireland to Australia and Other Parts of the British Empire* (London: Faber, 1966), 22, 25, 31.

7. Daniel Defoe, *Life of Colonel Jack, in Two Volumes* (Edinburgh: James Ballantyne, 1810).

8. James Revel, *The Poor Unhappy Felon's Sorrowful Account of the Fourteen Years Transportation at Virginia, in America* (York: Croshaw, n.d.).

9. Marcus W. Jernegan, *Laboring and Dependent Classes in Colonial America, 1607–1783* (New York: Frederick Ungar, 1965), 48; Abbot E. Smith, "Indentured Servants: New Light on Some of America's First Families," *Journal of Economic History* 2 (1942): 50; Eugene I. McCormac, *White Servitude in Maryland, 1634–1820* (Baltimore: Johns Hopkins Press, 1904), 94; W. Noel Sainsbury, ed., *Calendar of State Papers, Colonial Series, America and West Indies, 1661–1668* (London: Longman, 1880), 221.

10. Defoe, *Colonel Jack*, 1: 191.

11. Patrick Colquhoun, *A Treatise on the Police of the Metropolis*, 7th ed. (London: Bye and Law, 1806), 436, 454–455; Defoe, *Colonel Jack*, 2: 25–26; Joshua Gee, *The*

Trade and Navigation of Great-Britain Considered (London: Buckley, 1730), 59; William Eddis, *Letters from America, Historical and Descriptive* (London: privately printed, 1792), 66.

12. Colquhoun, *Treatise on the Police*, 455; Defoe, *Colonel Jack*, 2: 25–26.

13. Fielding, *Enquiry*, 6–11.

14. Patrick Colquhoun, *A New and Appropriate System of Education for the Labouring People* (London: Savage and Easingwood, 1806), 10, 12, 69, 77.

15. Ibid., 38.

16. Daniel Defoe, "Giving Alms No Charity," in *The Works of Daniel Defoe*, ed. John S. Keltie (Edinburgh: William Nimmo, 1870); Frederic Eden, *The State of the Poor*, 3 vols. (London: Davis, 1797), 263.

17. Colquhoun, *Treatise on the Police*, 436; Shaw, *Convicts*, 21, 23; George Nicholls, *A History of the English Poor Law*, 2 vols. (London: Murray, 1854), 1: 304, 380; McCormac, *White Servitude in Maryland*, 94–95.

18. Nicholls, *History of English Poor Law*, 2: 4.

19. A. L. Cross, "English Criminal Law and the Benefit of the Clergy during the Eighteenth and Early Nineteenth Centuries," *American Historical Review* 22 (1917); Abbot E. Smith, *Colonists in Bondage: White Servitude and Convict Labor in America, 1607–1776* (New York: W. W. Norton, 1947), 111.

20. Smith, *Colonists in Bondage*, 117; Jernegan, *Laboring and Dependent Classes*, 48; McCormac, *White Servitude in Maryland*, 104, 107.

21. "Felons and Rattlesnakes, 9 May 1751," *Founders Online*, National Archives, last modified October 5, 2016. http://founders.archives.gov/documents/Franklin /01-04-02-0040

22. Smith, *Colonists in Bondage*, 130.

23. Worthington C. Ford, *Washington as Employer and Importer of Labor* (Brooklyn: privately printed, 1889), 16–17; Jared Sparks, ed., *The Writings of George Washington*, vol. 2 (Boston: Little, Brown, 1847), 383–386.

CHAPTER SEVEN

The Voyage of the Free-Willers

In the history of the human propensity for war, few places have endured more conflict and devastation than the Rhine River valley. The Rhine was for centuries the bloody historical barrier between the Roman Empire and the Germanic tribes. Frankish conquests and rule, followed by the region's incorporation in the Holy Roman Empire and subsequent struggles between rival despots for the control of the east and west banks of the Rhine, exhausted the farmers and burghers of the Rhineland. War continued, however, during the Thirty Years War and War of the League of Augsburg during the 17th century and the War of the Spanish Succession of the early 18th century, forcing many of the noncombatants of the Rhineland to consider emigrating to safer and more prosperous regions.

Among the many thousands of emigrants fleeing the Rhineland, especially the region known as the Palatinate, was a schoolmaster, Gottlieb Mittelberger. A native of Enzweihingen, a small town in the Duchy of Württemberg in the Holy Roman Empire, Mittelberger emigrated in response to an offer to teach and serve as organ master at a German church in the town of New Providence in Pennsylvania. He kept a journal of his travels from Germany to America. Departing in May 1750, he traveled to Heilbronn on the Neckar River, where he directed the careful loading of an organ bound for America; prospective organ master and organ descended the Neckar by boat to its confluence with the Rhine River near Mannheim. The voyage down the Rhine took many more weeks, so that it was not until July that Mittelberger found himself at the mouth of the Rhine. Accompanying Mittelberger during his seven-week voyage from the Palatinate to Rotterdam were many families from Palatine and Württemberg, others whom Mittelberger called Durlackers who joined at the confluence of the Neckar and Rhine, as well as some Swiss travelers—hundreds of people who journeyed down the Rhine to the Atlantic, hoping for a new life in America. But it would take them just short of half a year to get to Pennsylvania, by which time most of the people aboard, if they were not impoverished when they departed Germany, were so upon arriving at the Delaware River.[1]

The voyage down the Rhine took so long because ships stopped at "36 custom-houses, at all of which the ships are examined, which is done when it suits the convenience of the custom-house officials. In the meantime, the ships with the people are detained long, so that the passengers have to spend much money." After a voyage of four to six weeks, the ships arrive at Rotterdam, where "they are detained . . . likewise 5 or 6 weeks." The prices for food and other such items "are very dear there" so that "the poor people have to spend nearly all they have during that time." The conditions that the emigrants endured at the mouth of the Rhine astonished Mittelberger. "Both in Rotterdam and in Amsterdam the people are packed densely, like herrings so to say, in the large sea-vessels. One person receives a place of scarcely 2 feet width and 6 feet length in the bedstead, while many a ship carries four to six hundred souls." From Rotterdam, the ships sailed across the Channel to Cowes, a port on the Isle of Wight, south of Portsmouth. The winds of the Channel were often so contrary that it could take weeks to make the short voyage from Rotterdam to Cowes, and once there, the ship might lie to for several weeks taking on cargo. "During that time every one is compelled to spend his last remaining money and to consume his little stock of provisions which had been reserved for the sea; so that most passengers, finding themselves on the ocean where they would be in greater need of them, must greatly suffer from hunger and want."[2]

Ultimately, having been on board a ship up to three months, the exhausted, impoverished people finally set forth toward America, a voyage that could last another three months, depending on the wind. "But during the voyage there is on board these ships terrible misery, stench, fumes, horror, vomiting, many kinds of sea-sickness, fever, dysentery, headache, heat, constipation, boils, scurvy, cancer, mouth-rot, and the like, all of which come from old and sharply salted food and meat, also from very bad and foul water, so that many die miserably." Lice took over the ship; Mittelberger saw people scraping the vermin from their bodies. Storms lasting several days kept everyone below decks, where the misery increased. Constant lamentations broke from the people that they were to die of shipwreck, that they would never see their homeland again, that they were forsaken. Waves lashed the vessel making the ill of body and mind suffer even more. In the crowded conditions below deck, as the ship rolled from side to side so did the people, one on top of another, the sick upon the well and vice versa. Mittelberger experienced it all, even sickness.[3]

Mittelberger, apparently the only willing lay pastor on board the ship, consoled the distraught passengers "with singing, prayer and exhorting; and whenever it was possible and the winds and waves permitted it, I kept daily prayer-meetings with them on deck. Besides, I baptized five children in distress, because we had no ordained minister on board. I also held divine service every Sunday by reading sermons to the people; and when the dead were sunk in the water, I commended them and our souls to the mercy of God." Mittelberger took a heavy task upon himself: to be a counselor for the mourning, a referee between the dozens of fights that broke out over food, water, those who blamed others for their misfortunes, husbands and wives who could not reconcile their losses with each other. The laments and cries were unceasing. So many people were buried at sea, "which drives their relatives, or those who persuaded them to undertake the journey, to such despair that it is almost impossible to pacify and console them." Pregnant women who gave birth inevitably were committed to the waves with their dead newborns. A singular instance involved a woman who could not give birth, and she died with the child within her; the sea was so rough that they had to push the body through a port hole into the sea. "Children from 1 to 7 years rarely survive the voyage; and many a time parents are compelled to see their children miserably suffer and die from hunger, thirst and sickness, and then to see them cast into the water." Worms and spiders spoiled the biscuit; the water was black and worm filled. It is no wonder that 32 children died on this voyage. "The parents grieve all the more since their children find no resting-place in the earth, but are devoured by the monsters of the sea." Often whole families died of disease, and sometimes in such rapidity that the "dead persons lie in the berths beside the living ones." Too often, ships arrived in America with their human cargo starving to death. Even as late as 1805, a ship arrived with starving free-willers: "The hunger was so great on board that all the bones about the ship were hunted up by them, pounded with a hammer and eaten; and what is more lamentable, some of the deceased persons, not many hours before their death, crawled on their hands and feet to the captain, and begged him, for God's sake, to give them a mouthful of bread or a drop of water to keep them from perishing, but their supplications were in vain; he most obstinately refused, and thus did they perish."[4]

Upon reaching land, many people experienced a false joy, thinking that their suffering was at an end. The majority of passengers, however, had long run out of money and were in arrears for their passage to the captain, who would not allow them to depart until they could satisfy payment one way or another. Those who could not raise the funds, or had no relatives or friends to advance them monies, were sold as servants; the healthy ones went first; the sick and dying often stayed aboard ship to die. Meanwhile, English, Dutch, and German planters and merchants boarded the ship to negotiate with passengers how long they would work to pay for the passage. Adults signed a contract with the master for "3, 4, 5 or 6 years for the amount due by them, according to their age and strength." Youngsters had to serve until age

21. Parents of children suffered accordingly. Parents of children under age five had their children taken away to serve a master until they reached adulthood. Children over the age of five could be sold into servitude to pay for their parent's debt. "But as the parents often do not know where and to what people their children are going, it often happens that such parents and children, after leaving the ship, do not see each other again for many years, perhaps no more in all their lives." Husbands and wives had to take on the service of sick or deceased spouses; orphans had to serve for themselves and their parents; the sick, if they were not sold, were taken to a hospital, either to die or recover, when they must serve time for their passage.[5]

Work, for most of these people who had come to America on their own free will, consisted of clearing land for planting: cutting down trees, uprooting oaks, and building fences. "Work and labor in this new and wild land are very hard and manifold, and many a one who came there in his old age must work very hard to his end for his bread." But, the pious Mittelberger added, is this not what God ordained as the consequences for human sin? Runaways were common, though such people "cannot get far. Good provision has been made for such cases, so that a runaway is soon recovered." For the amount of time absent from their master, the recovered servant had to pay in labor: one week of work for one day absent; one month work for one week absent; one-half year work for one month absent. The standard freedom dues for servitude existed in Pennsylvania, according to Mittelberger: "When one has served his or her term, he or she is entitled to a new suit of clothes at parting; and if it has been so stipulated, a man gets in addition a horse, [and] a woman, a cow." These freedom dues in Pennsylvania were established by law; they were often referred to as the "custom of the country." In the 1690s, these included 50 acres and a "years provision of corn." In 1700, the "servant that shall faithfully serve, four years or more, shall at the expiration of their servitude, have a discharge, and shall be duly clothed with two Compleat Suits of Apparel, whereof one shall be new, and shall also be furnished with one Axe, one Grubbing hoe, and one Weeding-hoe, at the charge of their master or mistress." The courts protected the servants in their rights. One man released from servitude in 1693 sued for his freedom dues and received by order of the court "a hat, coat, waistcoat, breeches, drawers, stockings, and shoes, all new, and also ten bushels of wheat or fourteen bushels of corn, two hoes and One Axe."[6]

At the same time, the people of Pennsylvania expected the newcomer to act honorably during the term of servitude. Males, upon arriving, had to sign the following declaration:

> We subscribers, natives and late inhabitants of the Palatine upon the Rhine and places adjacent, having transported ourselves and families into this Province of Pennsylvania, a colony subject to the crown of Great Britain, in hopes and expectation of finding a retreat therein, Do solemnly promise

and engage that we will be faithful and bear true allegiance to His present *Majesty, King George the Second*, and His successors, Kings of Great Britain, and will be faithful to the proprietor of this Province; and that we will demean ourselves peacefully to all His said Majesty's Subjects, and strictly observe and conform to the Laws of England and of this Province, to the utmost of our power and the best of our understanding.[7]

Mittelberger's own experience (which was satisfactory) notwithstanding, he believed that the people of Germany were better off staying home to suffer rather than suffer two- or threefold in America. "Who therefore wishes to earn his bread in a Christian and honest way, and cannot earn it in his fatherland otherwise than by the work of his hands, let him do so in his own country and not in America: for he will not fare better in America. However hard he may be compelled to work in his fatherland, he will surely find it quite as hard, if not harder, in the new country." There were so many other undesirable conditions to discourage Germans from voluntarily journeying to America: the cost, which bankrupted almost all passengers, and those not bankrupted inevitably had the remainder of their resources stolen. The chance of death at sea was great, either because of malnutrition and disease or shipwreck. Further, there was a downside to the freedom of religion offered in Pennsylvania. William Penn had purposely established liberal standards for settlement, citizenship, and religion in the colony of Pennsylvania. Such freedom included as well the freedom to disbelieve, to live lives as freethinkers and infidels. Many children sold into servitude ended up with such people, so that they were not raised as proper Christians, with eternal consequences.[8]

More ominous were what Mittelberger called the "man-thieves," usually referred to as Neulanders. These people were like the spirits, or crimps, of England who tried to "sell" America to the unwitting and desperate. William Eddis, in *Letters from America*, described the arts by which such sellers of America presented "colours so alluring, that it is almost impossible to resist their artifices. Unwary persons are accordingly induced to enter into articles, by which they engage to become servants." Spirits convinced the unwary that they will find "tenderness and humanity during the period of servitude" and "a competent provision for the remainder of their days." Agents in England like Neulanders in Europe used "fallacious pretences, by which numbers are continually induced to embark for this continent" of America.[9] Neulanders used lies to convince families in Germany that their relatives in America sent them to help them emigrate. They used their wiles on poor as well as wealthy. Mittelberger heard of "persons of rank, such as nobles, learned or skilled people, who cannot pay their passage and cannot give security, . . . treated just like ordinary poor people, and must remain on board the ship till some one comes and buys them from the captain." Rank and importance mattered little in America, where labor was most important. "Such people, who are not accustomed to work, are treated to blows and cuffs, like cattle, till they have learned the hard work." These "dealers in human flesh" often worked with merchants and captains to bring the emigrants to places other than Philadelphia to fetch the highest price. "Thus emigrants are compelled in Holland to submit to the wind and to the captain's will, because they cannot know at sea where the ship is steered to." The Neulanders were so convincing in their craft, that often people trusted them with all of their funds, only to find that the thieves absconded with the lot, leaving them destitute, with no other course than to bind themselves into service. The Neulanders also knew expert forgers who could forge handwriting and names to convince the unwitting in Germany that they had received a message from home asking them to come. Mittelberger's own family was almost deceived in this way. Monopolies dealing with the transportation of humans operated in Europe among Neulanders and merchants, who sought as many people as possible to put on board their ships; even if many died, their relatives would be responsible for paying for the deceased person's passage either in funds or service.[10]

Such was the evil practiced upon the German people by these Neulanders that compelled Mittelberger to write his book. "Würtembergers, Durlachers and Palatines . . . implored me with tears and uplifted hands, and even in the name of God, to make this misery and sorrow known in Germany, so that not only the common people, but even princes and lords, might learn how they had fared, to prevent other innocent souls from leaving their fatherland."[11]

Notwithstanding the Neulanders, in the end these people were free-willers who came on their own accord. They arrived at a colony, Pennsylvania, with a long history of servitude. The original proprietor, William Penn, to settle his land, a grant from Charles II, had himself engaged in promotional literature, having his work translated into Dutch and German to encourage the desperate of the Rhineland to emigrate to this new land. Penn was agreeable to an institution by which immigrants to his colony could work off the cost of their transport by a set number of years of labor. More substantial colonists and immigrants who imported or brought with them people to settle the land received a headright of 50 acres. Penn, in a letter to James Harrison in August 1681, wrote that he offered "fifty acres a servant to the master, and fifty to the servant. This is done for their sakes that can't buy; for I must either be paid by purchase or rent, that is, those that can't buy may take up, if a master of a family, 200 acres at a penny an acre. . . . [To] encourage poor servants to go and be laborious," he reduced the rent to a half-penny per acre. "For those that can't pay their passage, let me know their names, number and ages; they must pay double rent to them that help them over. But this know, that this rent is never to be raised, and they are to enjoy it for ever." Once the debt for transportation was paid, the servant, now a freedman, retained the land as a freedom due. In this spirit, Penn and his agents were able to attract immigrants to the colony for scores of years. These immigrants included large numbers of servants from Wales, England, the Netherlands, Scotland, Ireland, and Germany. Of the latter country, many fled the wars of Europe for England, and there sought transportation to America. As in other colonies, not all of the servants in Pennsylvania were paying off the debt of transportation; many were poor, especially children, bound to a master; local courts imposed servitude on malefactors or debtors. Many servants, upon conclusion of their original indenture, bound themselves again in servitude for the security that it offered. In this way, the system of servitude slowly, over the course of the colonial period, became, for some people, little more than a contract of employment.[12]

Many German Palatines who made the voyage to America in the early 18th century arrived first in New York per an agreement made by the English Board of Trade with the colony to receive thousands of these servants to "employ them in the manufacture of naval stores, tar, pitch, and turpentine, in the pine forests" in return for transport; "each man was to receive five pounds, and forty acres of land, at the time of settlement, and was not to leave the place designated by the Governor to be settled, without his consent." Many, however, died on the voyage, and others found the attitude of the New Yorkers intolerable, so that, after about 10 years, they relocated to Pennsylvania under more favorable terms. Henceforth, word got out in Europe that Pennsylvania rather than New York was the desirable destination.[13]

All noteworthy and laudable plans eventually succumb, at least in part, to avarice and corruption. By the mid-18th century, Pennsylvania was like all of the colonies—subject to abuses in the transportation of laborers to America. Peter Williamson, for example, a Scottish lad who lived in Aberdeen, was at some indeterminable point in the 18th century kidnapped by an unscrupulous captain and crew and taken, along with many other youths, to America. Upon arriving, the ship ran aground, and the crew abandoned ship, though when the boat did not sink, they returned the next morning to gather their human cargo. Williamson was sold in Philadelphia to a master who had himself many years before been kidnapped and brought to America. The man treated young Williamson well, taught him to read and write, and even left him a substantial inheritance when he died. Chance and luck were apparently with Williamson, though others of his kind were not so fortunate.[14]

Not only Scots but Irish experienced such tribulation. An Irish lad named John King, during the Commonwealth period, "with divers others were stolen in Ireland, by some of the English soldiers, in the night out of theyr beds & brought to" a ship "ready to receave them, & in the way as they went, some others they tooke with them against their Consents, & brought them aboard the said ship, where there were divers of their Country men, weeping and Crying, because they were stolen from theyr fr[i]ends." The Irish version of spirits cajoled and tempted the innocent into their power. Cromwell during the Commonwealth decimated Ireland, and many hapless men, women, and children were sent to America. In 1653, from Ireland, 400 children, 250 women, and 300 men were sent to Boston.[15]

Like slavery, the individual servant's experience of the system of servitude depended largely on the character of the master. Those unfortunates whom chance or destiny stuck to a violent or criminal master often ran away in despair. Pennsylvania, like all of the colonies, had laws in place to prevent runaways and to enable their speedy recapture. Some local and provincial laws required local magistrates and tavern keepers to check on the status of travelers who appeared to be ne'er-do-wells. Such was the experience of young Ben Franklin, running away from Boston to Philadelphia; stopping at an inn, "I was suspected to be some runaway servant, and in danger of being taken up on that suspicion." Again, after arriving in Philadelphia, while having dinner at a tavern, "several sly questions were asked me, as it seemed to be suspected from my youth and appearance, that I might be some runaway." An actual 18th-century Pennsylvania runaway was "an Irish servant lad named William Dobbin, about 18 years of age, speaks good English, fresh colour'd, thick and well set in his body, has light colored curled hair, some what resembling a wig; Had on when he went away, an old felt hat, ozenbrigs shirt, an old dark brown colour'd coat, too big for him, and breeches of the same, grey worsted stockings, and a pair of old shoes, with brass buckles, one of the buckles broke." This meticulous description betrayed a master who knew his servant well and wanted him back. Thomas James offered a 20-shilling reward for his return.[16]

Compensation for criminal acts by servants in Pennsylvania, such as running away, theft, gambling, and loitering, included added time of service but as often the colony imposed corporeal punishments. Servants rarely had the funds to pay fines; unless the master paid fines, the servants suffered physically. White servants typically suffered the same treatment doled out to slaves for various infractions; masters and magistrates made frequent use of the whip to the bare back. One law of 1751 subjected servants and slaves to an initial punishment of whipping, 21 lashes at the public post, followed by three days on bread and water doing hard labor at the workhouse; for the second infraction the servant received 31 lashes with the whip and six days of hard labor at the workhouse.[17]

Colonial America could be a violent time for men, women, children, whites, blacks, and Indians. Whipping and such corporeal punishments were common for a variety of people, not just those in service or enslaved. But the person bound to service for life, or a person bound to another for a set number of years, had fewer rights than the freeholders and citizens of Pennsylvania and other British American colonies and, therefore, suffered more. William Eddis, in *Letters from America*, argued that English and

European servants had a tougher time in America even than slaves. A slave was a possession, and severe injury or death was "a material loss to the proprietor." But servants were temporary workers whom the master would have for a limited time; hence, the master "exercised an inflexible severity" over the servant, especially the transported felon. "They are strained to the utmost to perform their allotted labour; and, from a prepossession in many cases too justly founded, they are supposed to be receiving only the just reward which is due to repeated offences." Servants, Eddis claimed, "groan beneath a worse than Egyptian bondage," from which many try to escape, "but very few are successful; the country being intersected with rivers, and the utmost vigilance observed in detecting persons under suspicious circumstances." Captured, "the unhappy culprit is doomed to a severe chastisement; and a prolongation of servitude is decreed in full proportion to expences incurred, and supposed inconveniences resulting from a desertion of duty."[18]

The experience of the free-willers was, according to Eddis, even worse. The colony of Maryland, which after the mid-18th century was the great repository of transported felons, also received a large share of Redemptioners from Europe. "The situation of the free-willer" Eddis wrote, "is, in almost every instance, more to be lamented than either that of the convict or the indented servant; the deception which is practiced on those of this description being attended with circumstances of greater duplicity and cruelty. Persons under this denomination are received under express conditions that, on their arrival in America, they are to be allowed a stipulated number of days to dispose of themselves to the greatest advantage. They are told that their services will be eagerly solicited, in proportion to their abilities; that their reward will be adequate to the hazard they encounter by courting fortune in a distant region; and that the parties with whom they engage will readily advance the sum agreed on for their passage; which, . . . they will speedily be enabled to repay, and to enjoy, in a state of liberty, a comparative situation of ease and affluence."[19]

Clearly, what Mittelberger portrayed in his journal occurring in 1750 continued 25 years later in the same region of America. The free-willers that Eddis described were good people, not the felons of England; they were people "whose characters are unblemished, whose views are founded on honest and industrious principles"; people seeking a new start, with "fond hopes," which upon arriving in America "are cruelly blasted, and they find themselves involved in all the complicated miseries of a tedious, laborious, and unprofitable servitude" due to "avarice and delusion" brought upon them by others, the Neulanders; and the free-willers find themselves among "the most profligate and abandoned of mankind." Many of the free-willers who arrived in America, Eddis discovered, were treated not according to their status or previous position in life but rather as chattel labor. "Character is of little importance" to masters who sought strong, healthy people to do hard work.

Masters had quite a number from which to choose: over 3,000 servants worked in Philadelphia during the three decades prior to the American War of Independence.[20]

William Eddis proclaimed himself astonished that such a system of labor—of abusing and exploiting people—was so well known and yet little was done to curb it, to help these poor people. But such was the America of his time, when people began to rebel for their liberties while being all too willing to ignore the liberties and sufferings, of so many people—white, black, Indian—who labored on farms and plantations and were cruelly used and abused, all for the sake of profit, by a class of people who otherwise worried about their own freedoms and felt themselves ill-used when a king and Parliament so many thousands of miles away should deign to impose themselves on the American people with taxes, trade regulations, and the imposition of order.

Notes

1. Carl Eben, trans., *Gottlieb Mittelberger's Journey to Pennsylvania in the Year 1750* (Philadelphia: McVey, 1898), 13–14.

2. Ibid., 18–19.

3. Ibid., 20–21.

4. Ibid., 21–24; Karl F. Geiser, *Redemptioners and Indentured Servants in the Colony and Commonwealth of Pennsylvania* (New Haven: Yale Publishing, 1901), 48–49.

5. Eben, *Gottlieb Mittelberger's Journey to Pennsylvania*, 25–28.

6. Ibid., 28–30; Geiser, *Redemptioners*, 72.

7. Quoted in Geiser, *Redemptioners*, 34,

8. Ibid., 30–32.

9. William Eddis, *Letters from America, Historical and Descriptive* (London: privately printed, 1792), 68–69.

10. Ibid., 38–41; Geiser, *Redemptioners*, 47. Likewise, Abbe Raynal: "The greatest part of the strangers who go over to America under these conditions, would never go on board a ship, if they were not inveigled away. Simple men seduced by these magnificent promises blindly follow these infamous brokers engaged in this scandalous commerce, who deliver them over to factors at Amsterdam, or Rotterdam." Quoted in Geiser, *Redemptioners*, 19.

11. Eben, *Gottlieb Mittelberger's Journey to Pennsylvania*, 16.

12. Geiser, *Redemptioners*, 10–12, 26–28, 69–70; Samuel M. Janney, *The Life of William Penn: With Selections from His Correspondence and Autobiography*, 2nd ed. (Philadelphia: Lippincott, 1852), 175.

13. Geiser, *Redemptioners*, 30–31.

14. *The Life and Curious Adventures of Peter Williamson* (Abderdeen: privately printed, 1826), 9–11, 13.

15. Abbot E. Smith, *Colonists in Bondage: White Servitude and Convict Labor in America, 1607–1776* (New York: W. W. Norton, 1947), 166, 168.

16. John Bigelow, ed., *Autobiography of Benjamin Franklin* (Philadelphia: Lippincott, 1868), 109, 113; Geiser, *Redemptioners*, 80.

17. Geiser, *Redemptioners*, 88–89.

18. Eddis, *Letters from America*, 70–71.

19. Ibid., 71–72.

20. Ibid., 73, 75, 76; Christopher L. Tomlins, *Freedom Bound: Law, Labor, and Civic Identity in Colonizing English America, 1580–1865* (New York: Cambridge University Press, 2010), 46.

CHAPTER EIGHT

Infortunate Servants

When Benjamin Franklin arrived in Philadelphia in 1723, the small city on the Delaware River had a population of over 5,000 people and was a busy seaport handling extensive trade in goods and people. Franklin was a 17-year-old runaway, having left Boston, and his family, to seek his fortune in another city. He had served his brother, publisher of the *New England Courant*, as a printer's apprentice, for five years; the indenture, which called for him to serve until he was 21, was altered when he was 17. His brother Josiah Franklin having been too critical of the provincial government, the General Court demanded that he cease publication; but in a clever ruse, he discharged Benjamin from his indenture and made him the figurehead owner of the paper. These shenanigans, as well as his brother's violent ways, impelled Benjamin to leave his brother's service. Neither his brother nor his father agreed with this decision, which convinced young Franklin to run away. He took ship to New York, and there learned that a printer in Philadelphia might be in need of a skilled worker, so he took ship to Philadelphia, suffered through a horrible voyage, had to walk part of the way, and arrived in the city looking something like a beggar. Franklin's adventures were akin to those of fictional characters such as Moll Flanders and Robinson Crusoe, penned by Daniel Defoe, whose writing Franklin knew well.[1]

A skilled printer, Franklin quickly went to work in Philadelphia and thrived. He met influential men, such as the governor of the province, who encouraged Franklin to travel to London to buy supplies to set himself up as owner of his own Philadelphia printing house. After spending about a year and a half in London, where he learned more about business and made useful connections, Franklin returned to Philadelphia; his old employer Samuel Keimer hired him to run his printing operation. Franklin had under him five workers, two free laborers and three servants. One servant had come from Ireland; Keimer had purchased his indenture, in which the servant, named

John, would serve for four years—or at least he would have served this term had he not run away. Another servant was an apprentice named David Harry. The third was George Webb, an Englishman, whose four-year service Keimer had purchased from a captain trading in human cargo.[2]

George Webb was well educated, growing up in Gloucester, England. He was a gifted student, had matriculated at Oxford, but being a person with little common sense and much frivolity, he ran away to London, where he found himself penniless. Soon a spirit, or crimp, selling America accosted him, and used such sales techniques to get the young man, but 18 years of age, to sign an indenture, bound for America.[3]

There were many other educated British inhabitants besides Webb whom chance or destiny had brought to America. At about this time, December 1729, William Moraley arrived in Philadelphia aboard the ship *Bonita* from London. Moraley, an Englishman living in Newcastle who had been disinherited by his mother after his father's untimely death, met with a spirit in London after Moraley had seen an advertisement describing the wonders of America. The man bought Moraley a pint of beer and described how Moraley could make himself new if he signed up for the voyage. The spirit told Moraley that if he had husbandry or mechanical skills he could sign up for a four-year stint in America; Moraley, trained as a clockmaker, which was not as much in demand, had to settle for five years. Accordingly, Moraley and the spirit went to the Lord Mayor of London, where Moraley attested to his unmarried, unbound state. Being single and free to go, without restrictions, Moraley signed the indenture to sail to Pennsylvania to serve for five years. The spirit took Moraley to Billingsgate, then Limehouse, where the 200-tun ship was moored. He was taken aboard, and found himself with 20 others who had likewise signed indentures. These men and boys mostly looked dejected, but when Moraley saw raisins, and beer, and mutton, he felt himself well treated and happily resigned himself to the voyage. Moraley kept a journal either on paper or in his mind, from which he re-created his experiences, many years later, in a book that he titled *The Infortunate*.[4]

Arriving at Philadelphia after a three-month voyage, Moraley was one of "a Parcel of very likely Servant Men and Boys, of sundry Trades, as well as Husbandmen." He and the others were not as optimistic as when they had set out in September 1729, as the food was rationed severely and was of poor quality, during the voyage. They lived on ship's biscuit, a thimble of brandy every day, salt beef and dried fish, and whatever other food they could catch: dolphins and flying fish. By the time they reached the Delaware River in early December, Moraley and many of his companions were ill. Moraley drank from the Delaware, which had a purgative effect, which he claimed would only be relieved by drinking rum—repeatedly for several months! Indeed, the captain uncharacteristically gave Moraley the run of Philadelphia before the auction, during which Moraley sold his coat for a "Quart of Rum."

Eventually he was sold to a clockmaker and goldsmith of Burlington, New Jersey, one Isaac Pearson, who, according to Moraley, "was a Quaker, but a Wet one," meaning not devout.[5]

For three weeks, Moraley enjoyed the friendly city, the markets and houses of entertainment in particular. He enjoyed observing the architecture of the city, such as what came to be called Independence Hall, then under construction, the Quaker meetinghouse, and the Anglican house of worship, Christ Church, also under construction. The city allowed religious freedom to a degree, as long as one was a Christian; Moraley did not profess his belief, but his birth was registered at Christ Church, Newgate, in London, where he was undoubtedly baptized. Moraley was a lover of wealth and ostentation, so he made special notice of the wealthiest Philadelphians and their abodes. He strolled about market square and down by the wharves to see the goods coming and going. He made note of the three watchmakers of the city, perhaps examining their goods for sale. The variety of people impressed the newcomer; Moraley saw many Germans, especially Palatines, arriving by ship, some of whom would find their way to Germantown, a German hamlet a few miles away. There were plenty of slaves and servants on the streets of Philadelphia. They were easy to spot by their clothing, a very coarse apparel that Moraley termed "Osnabrigs," originating from Germany.[6]

Moraley after several weeks made his way by boat 20 miles up the Delaware to Burlington, situated on the New Jersey shore of the river. Isaac Pearson did not appear to be a demanding master, feeding Moraley well upon arrival and allowing him a day to acclimate himself to the small town. Burlington had, Moraley wrote, 300 houses that were well made and pretty, with delightful gardens. The city enjoyed some trade, as the town harbor could host large oceangoing vessels. Burlington had three churches, one of which, the Anglican, Moraley must have occasionally attended, as he became acquainted with the rector, Robert Wayman, whom Moraley described as "a Gentleman of Parts, and the most extensive Goodness." Moraley found that the Quakers of the town were similarly benevolent and charitable.[7]

Although Moraley's master seemed, compared to others, tolerant and easy, the servant disliked Burlington, wishing instead to live in Philadelphia. Moraley had signed an indenture but nevertheless demanded that Pierce sell him to another master, one in Philadelphia, upon the same terms of the indenture. Pierce understandably refused. His inconstant servant decided to take matters into his own hands and escape. He was recaptured, apparently in Philadelphia, and temporarily jailed. Master and servant agreed to appear before the mayor of Philadelphia, Thomas Griffitts, who reconciled them, the terms being that Moraley would return to Burlington but his time of service would be lessened by two years. This was a singular and fortunate agreement for an escaped servant! After which, Moraley wrote, "I was ever after perfectly pleased with my Master's Behaviour to me, which was generous."[8]

Moraley served alongside another indentured servant, Aaron Middleton, and an unnamed black slave. Middleton was a clockmaker as Moraley was, and he was similarly distraught with Isaac Pearson on some occasion or another, for he escaped, at least once. In Moraley's *The Infortunate*, he lamented the lack of rights of "bought servants," to whose testimony justices of the peace generally did not give the same weight as to the master's. Moreover, anyone traveling throughout the colonies—at least according to Moraley's experience—had to have a "pass," issued by the master. Servants who ran away without a pass were usually captured, with the consequence that they had extra service added to their terms—although this was not the case when authorities returned Moraley to his master. Moraley witnessed the experience of slaves and their treatment at the hands of the colonial establishment. Corporeal punishment was an acceptable means of correction; sometimes it was so severe as to kill the unfortunate slave. Moraley believed that slaves tolerated their condition because the colony (in this case, New Jersey) allowed the observance of the Sabbath to extend to slaves. On Sundays, therefore, slaves were free to work for themselves and their families and enjoy family and community life. They forgot their enslavement, Moraley thought, until they were back at it on Monday morning.[9]

One way that Moraley tolerated his experience of servitude was his ability to travel throughout the countryside on errands for his master. Pearson would use Moraley as a traveling clock and watch cleaner/repairer. Moraley was intelligent and observant and used these excursions to make notes on the countryside and the people of New Jersey and Pennsylvania. He appears to have been an engaging, loquacious man, who made friends easily, sometimes with the free property owners of the region. With such companions, he explored the Delaware River and tributaries, learning about their supposed source in Canada, the wildlife that inhabited its banks, and other natural phenomena, such as fossils.[10]

Like other 18th-century observers of natural history, Moraley found the natural environment of America evidence of the works and benevolence of God. The plenty of fish, forest fauna, and flora was astonishing. He was impressed by the huge sturgeon found in Delaware River. He compared the wildlife of America to Europe, commenting on unique species such as the skunk and the opossum. The rattlesnake inspired terror and fascination. Moraley enjoyed observing and describing hummingbirds, eagles, mockingbirds, pigeons, and whip-poor-wills. He observed and described in detail the local entomology, such as wasps, beetles, bees, and butterflies.[11]

A recent immigrant from England, Moraley compared his experiences in America with those of his home country. He denoted the region of the Delaware River "the best Poor Man's Country in the World." Himself a servant, he fully believed the rhetoric of English promoters that here, in America, was the promise of the English poor. Unlike England, where farmers were

beholden to landowners, paying exorbitant rent, in America land was sufficiently available that just about everyone who wished to have it could: "so
that instead of finding the Planter Rack-rented, as the *English* farmer, you will
taste of their Liberality, their living in Affluence and Plenty." Freeholders
could make a profitable living with the plentiful availability of labor, whether
servants, apprentices, or slaves. The land was fertile, and in the Delaware
valley maize grew well with a little work, providing food for humans and
their livestock.[12]

Moraley the indentured servant was interested in the aboriginal inhabitants, having frequent interaction with them on his varied travels. He
attempted to discover their history, but learned that they had no written
records, so relied on hearsay. As a result, much of his information about the
American Indians provided in *The Infortunate* is inaccurate or superficial.
Moraley, himself given to drink, paid attention to the drinking practices of
the Indians, and observed them on occasions in a complete stupor from
intoxication.[13]

Moraley found himself in such a state quite often, which is the implication
of *The Infortunate*. As throughout the colonies, alcoholic beverages were plentiful and widespread among all ages, sexes, races, and social and economic
conditions. There were fermented beverages from grain and fruits, especially
cider from apples, as well as Madeira wine, and rum and various drinks
made from rum, such as Bombo, made from rum and beer, and Sampson,
made from rum and cider. The climate of Pennsylvania was good for fruit
trees, guaranteeing plentiful amounts of cider, perry, and wines, which com-
plemented meals of boiled and buttered maize and potatoes, and fish.
Moraley was a fisher, availing himself of the Delaware and tributaries and
ponds for that purpose, catching perch, roach, and trout. On at least one
occasion Moraley caught so many roach that he had enough to feed a large
family besides selling dozens, which allowed him to purchase rum and sugar
"to wash them down." If the fisher was unsuccessful, the local markets always
had a profusion of fish, of good quality and cheaper, Moraley discovered,
than Newcastle upon Tyne back home in England.[14]

Moraley was sufficiently well read to be able to imitate in *The Infortunate* a
variety of styles of writing: pathos of life, rhymes about the human condition,
social commentary, traveler's descriptions, and natural science. He was a fair
observer of humans and nature and provided brief if laudatory assessments
about the colony of Pennsylvania and its environs. He was amazed by the
land's productivity, and thought it as fine as any other place save for the
swings in temperature during the change of seasons. In winter, it was cold
enough to freeze the Delaware, so that people would cross it on horseback
and foot and in carriages, sleighs, and sleds. Moraley and a friend hit a thin
patch on one winter's day, and the friend fell through the ice and drowned.
Moraley complained that his outdoor chores sometimes led to intense cold so

that he yearned to return to England as a prodigal son. In summer, the heat was often severe enough to cause death. Moraley claimed that on very hot days it was wrong to drink water, rather hot liquor was preferable and more easily tolerated! In some stretches of his prose he brandished an artist's brush in words to paint a portrait of God's wonderful creation along the Delaware River.[15]

In 1730, Isaac Pearson purchased land near Burlington upon which he and some partners erected an ironworks; Moraley was sent there to work. He appears to have enjoyed the solitude of the place. He claimed that he was a blacksmith, fisher, shepherd, and drunk during his time there. Finally, his time of servitude of three years concluded; Pearson gave him freedom dues of "indifferent" clothes. Moraley traveled south to Philadelphia and worked in short order for several clockmakers then set forth as something of an itin-erant clock cleaner, which ultimately did not serve him well, and he often was desperate for lodging, food, and drink. On one occasion he was taken for a runaway servant and brought to Burlington, where he appealed to his for-mer master Pearson for copies of the indenture proving his freedom. He con-tinued his itinerant lifestyle, working here and there, for a time working for a Burlington blacksmith. He borrowed more than he earned, was pursued by creditors from Philadelphia, so he fled to New York, where those same credi-tors found him, which caused Moraley to serve briefly as a soldier, then as a servant, or butler, to a Spanish gentleman.[16]

Freedom was a challenge for Moraley, perhaps because he resorted to hab-its of life that in England had compelled him to servitude in the first place. He decided to return to Burlington, where Pearson hired him to work at the ironworks, as before. This was not satisfactory, so Moraley went to work for the Burlington blacksmith again but, soon after, determined to take ship back to England; he joined a vessel as a cook. The vessel was at moorings, awaiting freight and passengers, so Moraley went on another excursion throughout the region before making it back in time for the ship to weigh anchor and descend the Delaware River.[17]

Moraley's fondness for drink and indifference toward stable employment inclined him to leave America for England, where he traveled about from ale shop to ale shop until he reached Newcastle. There he lived with his mother until her death, after which he was thrust out into the world on his own, with predictable consequences.

Having departed from the Delaware valley and Philadelphia, Moraley's place was taken by many immigrants arriving daily, yearly, people under indenture, seeking to make their way in a new world. The records of Phila-delphia for 1745 illustrate the many people who arrived aboard ship to become indentured servants. Terse records only hint at lives lived and time spent working for a master assigned by chance. William Adair, for example, a servant to William Campbell, had his indenture transferred to mariner

William Clymer of Philadelphia, to serve two years at the end of which the
"customary [freedom] dues" were to be paid. Other mariners, or ship captains, manned their ships with servants. For example, Edward Dowers, who
captained the ship *Bolton*, having transported Irishman James Simple to
Pennsylvania, assigned Simple to serve him as mariner for nine years in
return for freedom dues of "two suits of apparel." One Anthony Adams
arrived to Philadelphia on October 4, 1745, aboard the galley *Anne*. Adams,
according to the record, was "an East Indian from Scotland." He was bound
for six years to Thomas Mullan. Another arrival the same day on board the
snow *George* was Patrick Kirk, from Dublin, who was bound to Edward Ash,
a Philadelphia butcher, for five years in return for "customary dues" as well as
training as a butcher. Some immigrants arrived without indenture, and once
a prospective master paid the ship captain for passage received the debtor as
servant for a set number of years. These included Irishman John Gardner,
who arrived in October, 1745, aboard the brig *Cleveland*; a cordwainer, John
Faires of Philadelphia, paid the £8 transport fee, in return for which Gardner
was to serve Faires for 18 months. When James Mahan arrived from Ireland
aboard the ship *Bolton*, he agreed to pay the £16 transport fee by serving
"three years eleven months & twenty days"; his freedom dues consisted of
clothing as well as "forty shillings." James Gardner of Lancaster County did
not bind himself into service to pay for passage, rather to pay for a debt of
£22 that he owed to John Howell of Philadelphia; he agreed to serve Howell
for three years to pay the debt. Likewise, John Collins, a farm laborer in debt
to Daniel Boyle, yeoman farmer, bound himself to Boyle to serve 18 months
to pay the debt.[18]

Others bound themselves into service for the sake of learning a trade or
for maintenance. These apprentices usually served until age 21 or 5 years. An
example was James Thomson of New Brunswick, New Jersey, who bound
himself to a potter, Jonathan Durell of Philadelphia, in order "to learn the art
and mystery of a Potter for five years" including "to have two quarters of year
night schooling and at expiration of the said term to have two suits of apparel,
one whereof to be new." Elizabeth Downey, at the same time, was a child of
10, very poor, under the charge of the overseers of the poor of a township
next to Philadelphia known as Northern Liberties. Downey was bound to
Charles Juisian of Philadelphia as an apprentice, trade unknown; she was "to
be taught to read & write, and at expiration of the said time to have two suits
of apparel, one of which is to be new." Deborah Dodson, who was not yet
three years old, was bound by the overseers of Northern Liberties to Frederick Gyer for 15 years; he was to teach her "to read and write the English language, and to knit, sew and spin." Another "infant," Robert Black, "seven
years old or thereabouts," was bound to Andrew Hodge of Philadelphia, a
baker, "for thirteen years and five months" to learn the art of baking as well
as to be "taught to read and write." Jane Jones in 1745 decided to bind her

one-year-old daughter for 17 years to John and Mary Warmes; they were to teach the infant, named Mary, to read and to have "the customary dues." John Freeman apparently wished not only to learn the cobbler trade but also the German language; his mother bound her son as apprentice to John Moses Conty for eight years. For his freedom dues, Freeman wanted £5. Another apprentice, Thomas Williamson, in return for his passage to Philadelphia from Ireland, agreed to serve Robert Fleming for four years in return for Fleming teaching him the crafts of barbering and wig making. A more detailed apprenticeship arrangement was signed on October 22, 1745, when Abram Mason of Kent County agreed to serve as apprentice to Joseph Jones of Philadelphia "for six years, three months and twenty-one days" in return for "two winters schooling at a boarding school to learn to write and cypher, one of the said winter to be paid for by Joseph Jones, the other by Joseph Mason, brother to Abram." In addition, Mason was to teach Abram "the art of mystery of a joiner or cabinet maker."[19]

The many 18th-century immigrants who disembarked from ships after crossing the Atlantic from Ireland, Scotland, and England were, like those who arrived in Philadelphia in 1745, people of varying sorts: skilled and unskilled; educated and ignorant; old and experienced and young, willing to learn a skill; women and men seeking money to pay their passage; some fleeing famine, others war, others debt, others mistakes and errors of the past. They all believed that America represented a chance: an opportunity for shelter and food; for honest labor; to become solvent; to learn a skill; to escape the past; to forge a different future. Like all humans, past and present, some of these people fulfilled their ambitions, aspirations, and expectations, while others failed—became ill, died prematurely, gave up hope, or like William Moraley, served their time, refused to change their ways, and returned to England for much of the same.

Notes

1. John Bigelow, ed., *Autobiography of Benjamin Franklin* (Philadelphia: Lippincott, 1868), 92, 104, 105, 112.

2. Ibid., 157–158.

3. Ibid., 158–159.

4. Susan E. Klepp and Billy G. Smith, eds., *The Infortunate: The Voyage and Adventures of William Moraley, an Indentured Servant*, 2nd ed. (University Park: The Pennsylvania State University Press, 2005), 12, 14, 16, 17, 27.

5. Ibid., 23–24, 26.

6. Ibid., 6, 32–35.

7. Ibid., 41, 44, 45.

8. Ibid., 46.

9. Ibid., 46, 58–61.

10. Ibid., 48–51.

11. Ibid., 52–57.

12. Ibid., 51–53, 57.

13. Ibid., 49–50, 64.

14. Ibid., 69–70.

15. Ibid., 70–72.

16. Ibid., 73–79.

17. Ibid., 87–88, 91.

18. "Servants and Apprentices Bound and Assigned before James Hamilton Mayor of Philadelphia, 1745," *Pennsylvania Magazine of History and Biography* 30 (1906): 348, 350, 352, 427–428, 431, 433, 436.

19. Ibid., 351, 429, 434–436.

CHAPTER NINE

Oglethorpe's Dream

In Defoe's London during the first several decades of the 18th century, as the poor continued to seek relief and the criminally minded committed their various transgressions against the people of England, so that the prisons were filled and convicts were being transported to America, a member of Parliament devised a plan to solve these age-old problems. When James Oglethorpe learned that one of his friends, Robert Castell, incarcerated in Fleet Prison, had died, he urged the House of Commons to form a committee to investigate the condition of these prisons. In 1729, he headed a committee that visited Fleet, and found the conditions were horrendous. Oglethorpe pushed through measures in the House of Commons to reform Fleet, but he realized that there was a much greater problem, one that had existed in England for centuries, a problem that had resisted the efforts of many humanitarians and reformers to find an adequate solution: there were too many poor in England, too many idle hands, too many homeless beggars, too many orphans on the streets of London, too many debtors in prison, too many capital crimes requiring too many executions of simple thieves, and so many condemned felons that they were being transported by the hundreds to the American colonies. Oglethorpe's solution—to establish a colony in America for the idle poor, indebted prisoners, and homeless of English cities—was not original, though the way he went about accomplishing his dream was different from earlier plans and attempts. Oglethorpe's dream—to eliminate poverty and imprisonment for poverty in England by establishing a colony in America where the yeomen farmer could enjoy hard work, landownership, lack of debt, self-sufficiency, and equality among people—led to the founding of Georgia.[1]

In 1732, King George II granted a charter creating a corporation for the establishment of the colony of Georgia. The stated goal of the colony was "that many of Our poor Subjects are, through Misfortunes, and Want of

Employment, reduced to great Necessity, insomuch as by their Labour they are not able to provide a Maintenance for themselves and Families: and if they had Means to defray their Charges of Passage, and other Expences incident to new Settlements, they would be glad to settle in any of Our Provinces in America; where, by cultivating the Lands at present waste and desolate, they might not only gain comfortable Subsistance for themselves and Families, but also strengthen Our Colonies, and increase the Trade, Navigation and Wealth of these our Realms."[2]

Such were the stated reasons for British colonies in general; Georgia, the last of the 13 colonies, was to be founded for the same purposes of relieving the poor population of the realm, rendering them serviceable to England, and establishing a thriving colony that would benefit England's economy and help provide a continued strategic hold on part of North America thereby increasing England's power in respect to other countries.

The person most responsible for establishing the province of Georgia, James Oglethorpe, was appointed a trustee of the province by George II. Oglethorpe ensured that the province would be founded for humanitarian reasons; that it would benefit the impoverished of England; that it would be open to all people (even Jews and Quakers, but not Roman Catholics) to exercise freedom of conscience; that it would not establish the institution of negro slavery; and that it would be a colony for the yeomen farmer, simultaneously encouraging a middling lifestyle of small, productive farms, rather than allowing the very rich to own huge acreages of land, and working to prevent a class of impoverished, dependent people.

Initially indentured servants were the only form of bound labor in Georgia. This was in keeping with the prolific nature of indentured servitude in other southern colonies: Maryland, Virginia, North Carolina, and South Carolina. When North Carolina was founded in 1663, the proprietors, who were supporters of Charles II, restored to power in 1660, set themselves up as feudal lords charged with peopling the colony; servants were to serve dutifully on the land of the liege lord. The proprietors encouraged immigrants to bring servants to North Carolina in return for 80 acres of land per person; in addition, the proprietors granted indentured servants 40 acres upon the end of their term of service. When South Carolina was settled in 1669, initially many of the settlers arrived from Barbados, where white servitude was extensive. In the passenger list for the ship, *Carolina*, for example, sailing from England for South Carolina in 1669, were 63 servants. South Carolina proprietors in 1670 allowed for 100 acres for every servant brought into the colony. An example was Millicent How, who traveled on the *Carolina*. Her indenture indicates that she was a "spinster" from London; she was 1 of 10 woman servants on board the ship. Upon agreeing to serve in South Carolina, her indenture was sold from Captain Joseph West of London to Will Bowman. When the *Carolina* went to Barbados and returned to South

Carolina in 1670 she brought back another 10 servants—nine males to serve as sawyers, carpenters, and planters, and one woman, Joan Burnet, to serve three years.[3]

The proprietors of South Carolina, as indicated in the *Fundamental Constitutions* establishing the colony, provided for a feudal society, as in North Carolina, with the proprietors holding one-fifth of the land, the landed gentry another fifth, and the people the rest. As a condition for keeping their land, the proprietors and gentry had to bring people, many of them servants. The promoters of both colonies, North and South, continued this emphasis on bringing white servants to their lands, even as chattel slavery increasingly dominated labor in the 18th century. John Peter Purry, a Swiss promoter and author of *A Description of the Province of South Carolina, Drawn Up at Charles Town, in September, 1731*, wrote that when South Carolina became a royal colony, "His Majesty . . . grants to every European Servant, whether Man or Woman, 50 Acres of Land free of all Rents for 10 Years, which shall be distributed to them after having served their Master for the Time agreed on." He claimed further that "persons may grow rich in *Carolina* without being at much Expence or Labour, by planting white Mulberry Trees for feeding of Silk-worms, there being perhaps no Country in the World where those Trees grow better, nor where the Silk is finer than in *Carolina*." Purry, attempting to transport 600 Swiss free-willers, proposed: "Those who are desirous to go as Servants must be Carpenters, Vineplanters, Husbandmen, or good Labourers," and they must be agreeable to work for three years. Purry tried to ensure that these redemptioners would have sufficient funds to set themselves up in the colony. This demand for white servants continued into the 18th century; while slaves worked on rice plantations, white servants worked growing indigo and serving as craftsmen and artisans in towns, villages, and plantations. Servants were prolific workers in North and South Carolina. One master advertised his chimney sweep to clean the chimneys of other people. Other servants were bakers, barkeeps, blacksmiths, bricklayers, butchers, cabinet makers, carpenters, joiners, boat builders, ship carpenters, collectors, coopers, farmers, farmhands, planters, fencing masters, file cutters, gardeners, masons, millers, nail makers, painters, wig makers, printers, rope makers, saddlers, sailors, boat pilots, sawyers, scriveners, teachers, shoemakers, stone cutters, barber-surgeons, surgeons, tailors, weavers, and wheelwrights.[4]

Such a prolific need for labor, skilled and unskilled, augured well for the new colony south of the Savannah River. Oglethorpe's dream was egalitarian, focused on as much equality among humans as possible, therefore making chattel slavery unavailable for Georgia planters. Some of his contemporaries were supportive of this view. One author, Benjamin Martyn, who published *Reason's for Establishing the Colony of Georgia, with Regard to the Trade of Great Britain, the Increase of Our People, and the Employment and Support It Will Afford to Great Numbers of Our Own Poor*, in 1733 in London, argued: "It is undoubtedly a self-evident Maxim, that the Wealth of a Nation consists in the Number of her People. But this holds true so far only, as Employment is, or can be found for them; if there be any Poor, who do not, or cannot add to the Riches of their Country by Labour, they must lie a dead Weight on the Publick; and as every wise Government, like the Bees, should not suffer any Drones in the State, these Poor should be situated in such Places, where they might be easy themselves, and useful to the Commonwealth." He added, "If this can be done by transplanting such as are necessitous and starving here . . . it is incumbent on us, at this Time more particularly, to promote and enlarge our Settlements abroad with unusual Industry." Martyn agreed with Oglethorpe that Georgia represented an asylum for the destitute of England, especially those in debtor's prisons. Men and their families rotting in prison with little chance of liberty were wasteful and unmerciful; these people deserve compassion and our help. Moreover, there are thousands of sturdy idle poor, who live on charity, or reside in workhouses, who will never change unless they have the chance. To this end, George II had "given a large Tract of Land (call'd Georgia) near Carolina, in Trust. The Management of it is in the Hands of several Noblemen and Gentlemen, who give up their Time and Assistance to the Improvement of it, without any View to their own Interest." Martyn lauded the trustees for selecting people to go to Georgia who were not taking away needed crafts and arts from England, not leaving behind dependents, not escaping debt, rather people looking for a new opportunity in life. Martyn's conviction that Georgia provided hope for the dispossessed of England grew in eloquence, as he argued for the humanitarian reasons for the colony: "How many never gain a sufficient Settlement in the World? Here they may be sure of one. How many, after they have gain'd it, fail by various Misfortunes? Here they may recover, and forget them. How many may be saved hereby from begging and perishing in our Streets by Want? How many from the Gallows, to which, Necessity and Idleness lead the Way? How many may now live to be useful, who are destroyed by their Parents at their very Birth, lest they should be a Burthen too great for their Support; and whose Light is extinguish'd the very Hour they receive it? How many more would see the Light, by the Marriage of those, who are prevented now by the Fear of Want? And how many may be preserved from languishing out a miserable Life in a Prison, to the Loss of their Families, and the Publick, and the Scandal of a country of Liberty?"[5]

England's success in establishing 12 other colonies along the North American coast was despite poor planning; lack of resources and funds; squabbling and in-fighting; religious, political, and commercial disputes; and ignorance about the land and its peoples. Martyn pointed out that the Georgia trustees were making every effort this 13th time around to ensure success without the many pitfalls that had hindered previous colonial efforts. "The Poor," he wrote, "who are sent to Georgia on the Charity, have all the Expences of their

Passage defrayed, have likewise all Conveniencies allowed them in their Passage: And great Care is, (as I hear) and will be taken not to croud too many of them in a Ship for fear of Illness. When they are set down in Georgia, the Trustees supply them with Arms for their Defence, Working-Tools for their Industry, Seeds of all Kinds for their Lands, and Provisions for a Year, or 'till the Land can yield a Support." The trustees wished to ensure that landholding would be equitable, without extremes of rich and poor, and towns would be well planned. The colony was to conform to English law, to guarantee "Civil Liberty" in part by disallowing "Slavery, not even in Negroes; by which means, the People being oblig'd to labour themselves for their Support, will be, like the old Romans, more active and useful for Defence of their Government." The Republican freedom extended to religion as well, although the corporation sent a representative of the Society for Propagating the Gospel to inculcate religious values.[6]

Upon arriving at the Savannah River in January 1733, Oglethorpe and the colonists of Georgia established the new settlement of Savannah. Oglethorpe was a hands-on leader who tried to ensure that the colony would succeed according to the expectations of the trustees. Rum and other intoxicating liquors were not allowed; everyone in the colony, according to reports, worked together and cheerfully. The trustees, concerned for the treatment of Protestants in Germany, had encouraged immigration from Salzburg; these people arrived at the Savannah River in 1734, founding the town of Ebenezer. Scottish highlanders from Inverness also made the voyage to Georgia, where they established the town of Darien. Other poor families embarked from England in company with missionaries led by John Wesley.[7]

Even skeptics at the time believed that Georgia had a bright future before it. Many thought of the land, with fertile soil and a wonderful climate—"the Air healthy, always serene, pleasant and temperate, never subject to excessive Heat or Cold, not to sudden Changes"—as something of an "Earthly Paradise." Moreover, there was a sense of optimism that Georgia "could not fail of succeeding when the Nation was so bountiful, the King so gracious, the Trustees so disinterested and Honourable, who had, for the Benefit of Mankind, given up that Ease and Indolence to which they were entitled by their fortunes . . . ; and withal being able, by seeing the Mistakes and Failures of other Colonies, both to avoid and rectify them."[8]

Unfortunately, the colony of Georgia never met those laudable objectives outlined by the trustees. It would have indeed been something of a paradise to find a southern colony in British America that was generally egalitarian, without extremes of rich and poor, that did not support slavery, with inhabitants not depending on intoxicating beverages with the evils consequent upon their abuse. One of the biggest challenges facing the colony was its location between the southernmost British colony, South Carolina, and the Spanish colony of Florida. Within 10 years of the colony's founding, war occurred with Spain, involving attacks on Spanish holdings in Florida and an attempted Spanish invasion of Georgia. Another problem was the prohibition on rum. Of course, smuggling occurred, so that those who wanted rum might have it. Others supported relaxing the restriction on rum, which would be useful for the colony's trade; besides, they believed that hard-working laborers needed to slack their thirst; and that rum, mixed with water, became a wholesome drink. In addition, the uncertain government of Georgia, in which trustees in England were making long distance decisions, led to questionable leadership, arbitrary decisions, and undue influence among individuals who were not representatives of the people.[9]

The most significant threat to the pastoral ideal of Oglethorpe and the other Georgia trustees was slavery. The "malcontents" were the most vociferous group arguing forcefully for the repeal of Georgia's law against slavery. These critics of the trustees published, in 1748, *A True and Historical Narrative of the Colony of Georgia in America, from the First Settlement Thereof until This Present Period: Containing the most Authentick Facts, Matters and Transactions Therein; Together with His Majesty's Charter, Representations of the People, Letters, &c. and a Dedication to His Excellency General Oglethorpe.* In this tract, the authors argued that the climate of Georgia and the kind of work required were too great a burden upon white servants, to the detriment of their masters and of the colony in general. In "Hoeing the Ground" servants were "exposed to the sultry Heat of the Sun, insupportable; and it is well known, that this Labour is one of the hardest upon the Negroes, even though their Constitutions are much stronger than white People, and the Heat no way disagreeable nor hurtful to them; but in us it created *inflammatory Fevers* of various kinds both *continued* and *intermittent, wasting* and *tormenting Fluxes, most excruciateing Cholicks,* and *Dry-Belly-Aches; Tremors, Vertigoes, Palsies,* and a long Train of *painful* and *lingring nervous Distempers*; which brought on to many a Cessation both from Work and Life; especially as Water without any Qualification," such as rum, "was the Chief Drink, and *salt Meat* the only Provisions that could be had or afforded: And so general were these Disorders that during the hot Season, which lasts from *March* to *October,* hardly one half of the Servants and working people were ever able to do their Masters or themselves the least Service; and the yearly Sickness of each Servant, generally speaking, cost his Master as much as would have maintained a Negroe for *four* Years."[10]

Such was the argument—based on some real differences between white servants and black slaves, though exaggerated— put forth by whites encouraging and justifying the establishment and continuance of slavery throughout the entire South for 150 years. Though some whites supported the trustees in their prohibition of slavery, many others did not, and the force and frequency of their arguments finally won the day. Increasingly the trustees received petitions, such as the following from citizens of Savannah, complaining "that the great Want of *Servants* in this Town and Country, doth render the Freeholders thereof incapable of proceeding with proper Vigour in the Cultivating their Lands; and as the honourable *James Oglethorpe*, Esq did generously promise, that your Honours would be pleas'd to give this Colony continual Assistance, by sending over Servants to the said Freeholders at reasonable Rates: *Therefore*, we do, with all Humility, lay before your Honours the great and general Want of Servants in this Town and Country." The petitioners of Savannah supported their request with evidence "That the Inhabitants of this Town and County are at a vast Expence in time of Sickness, especially they who have most Servants; it being a general Misfortune, that during the *hot* Season of the Year, hardly one half of the Servants are able to do their Masters any Work, by reason of the *violent* Sicknesses; which hath very much prevented the Inhabitants from making Improvements." This and other such petitions resulted, after 1750, in slavery expanding and spreading throughout colonial Georgia, making white servitude less prevalent, less important. Contrary to the wishes of the Georgia trustees, an egalitarian society of modest yeomen farmers was supplanted by a plantation economy of very large farms and very rich masters.[11]

William Ewen's life is a tale of rags to riches from the perspective of indentured servitude in colonial Georgia. A native of England, Ewen arrived in Georgia in 1734, bound as a servant to the trustees; he was assigned to serve magistrate Thomas Causton for two years. At the end of his service the trustees granted Ewen 50 acres on Skidaway Island, south of Savannah, where he tried farming, without success. In a petition directed to the Georgia trustees in 1741, Ewen claimed that he had two servants working with him to improve the land but the yield "was not Sufficient to mentain my Servants in provisions; Exclusive'd of Cloaths; Sickness; tools &c: Thus seeing poverty Approching in the mids[t] of Industry," Ewen received permission from James Oglethorpe to return his servants to the colony store. Around this time, he attached himself to the household at Captain Jacob Matthews, serving Matthews as majordomo. William Stephens, an on-again, off-again friend of Ewen's, referred to him as "Ad omnia paratus," that is, involved in everything. Ewen joined with others in opposing the trustee's proscriptions against slavery and rum; the trustees considered him a leader of the "malcontents." At one point Ewen opposed actions by the Savannah trustee-appointed storekeeper, Thomas Jones, with whom he had many conflicts; Ewen accused Jones of attempting "to introduce soldiers into the town" to "enslave the people." Ewen's proclivity to oppose authority for the sake of what he considered to be his rights and the rights of others like himself (white planters) enabled him, as the years passed, to become an opposition leader to other policies directed toward Georgia colonists, in this case, policies of Parliament.[12]

As the years passed Ewen became a local and provincial leader in Georgia. He was a member of the colonial assembly and a justice of the peace. He used his positions of respect, and changes in Georgia's laws, to garner land. Ewen took advantage of the change in policy toward owning slaves, in which the provincial government encouraged large plantations worked by slaves. He petitioned the Council of Georgia in 1760, stating that "he was possessed of five Negroes for whom he had never obtained a Grant of Land"; therefore, he requested "five hundred Acres on the Savannah River"; the Council granted his request. A decade later, Ewen became an important colonial leader against king and Parliament; he was a member of the provincial congress in 1775. As the revolutionary crisis reached a head in 1775, Ewen joined the Committee of Intelligence followed by the Council of Safety, of which he became president.[13]

Perhaps Ewen's humble beginnings and years of serving others drove him forward to be like one of those Georgians he knew in the 1730s and 1740s—masters to others, in charge of his own affairs. If he felt uncomfortable as a servant to a master, he made sure that he would, in the future, be a master to servants. He readily adopted the Whiggish tone of the mid-18th century about rights and liberties in contrast to tyranny and arbitrary rule. But like so many southern revolutionaries, he hesitated to bring his Whig ideals to the logical conclusion of the rights and liberties of all humans regardless of race.

Notes

1. Thaddeus M. Harris, *Biographical Memorials of James Oglethorpe: Founder of the Colony of Georgia* (Boston: printed by author, 1841); *New Georgia Encyclopedia*: "James Oglethorpe, 1696–1785." http://www.georgiaencyclopedia.org/articles /history-archaeology/james-oglethorpe-1696-1785

2. Quoted in *A True and Historical Narrative of the Colony of Georgia in America, from the First Settlement Thereof until This Present Period: Containing the Most Authentick Facts, Matters and Transactions Therein; Together with His Majesty's Charter, Representations of the People, Letters, &c. and a Dedication to His Excellency General Oglethorpe.* http://quod.lib.umich.edu/e/evans/N03913.0001.001/1:4?rgn=div1;vi ew=fulltext

3. John S. Ballagh, *Slavery and Servitude in the Colony of North Carolina* (Baltimore: Johns Hopkins, 1896), 78, 79; Warren B. Smith, *White Servitude in Colonial South Carolina* (Columbia: University of South Carolina Press, 1961), 3–4, 6, 7.

4. Smith, *White Servitude,* 7, 19, 20–26; *A Description of the Province of South Carolina, Drawn Up at Charles Town, in September, 1731* (Washington: Peter Force, 1837), 4, 14–15.

5. Benjamin Martyn, *Reason's for Establishing the Colony of Georgia, with Regard to the Trade of Great Britain, the Increase of Our People, and the Employment and Support It Will Afford to Great Numbers of Our Own Poor* (London: Meadows, 1733), 3, 18, 19, 20, 23, 24–25.

6. Ibid., 28, 29, 30.

7. Harris, *Biographical Memorials*, 56–57, 60–61, 81–82, 115–116, 121–122.

8. *True and Historical Narrative of the Colony of Georgia*, 25–26

9. Ibid., 28–29.

10. *True and Historical Narrative of the Colony of Georgia*, 31.

11. Ibid., 46–47. See Timothy J. Lockley, *Lines in the Sand: Race and Class in Lowcountry Georgia, 1750–1860* (Athens: University of Georgia Press, 2001), ch. 1.

12. George White, *Historical Collections of Georgia* (New York: Pudney and Russell, 1855), 16; Allen D. Candler, *Colonial Records of the State of Georgia*, vol. 23 (Atlanta: Chas. P. Byrd, 1914), 39, 97, 295; "A Brief Account of the Causes That Have Retarded the Progress of the Colony of Georgia in America" (London: 1743), in *Collections of the Georgia Historical Society*, vol. 2 (Savannah: Georgia Historical Society, 1842), 144.

13. Allen D. Candler, *Colonial Records of the State of Georgia*, vol. 8 (Atlanta: Franklin-Turner, 1907), 385, 629; White, *Historical Collections*, 41, 46, 65, 72, 96, 200.

CHAPTER TEN

The Prisoners of Culloden

Human bondage in its many forms is an expression of one person in control of another, one group controlling another: hence, human bondage is about power. One human or group of humans having the self-perceived right backed with the power of enforcement to place another human or group of humans in bondage, is a rudimentary form of the exertion of strength and will, one upon another, one animal overwhelming another animal. Such is the natural way of life among all creatures, and humans are little different. What is different is that humans think that they are elevated among other creatures—elevated in reason, sense of right, and ability to know and prac- tice the good. But in the end, as the centuries of war, of one human killing and imprisoning another and of one human capturing and enslaving another reveal, humans are brutal creatures indeed.

No better example of human brutality is found than in the wars that dis- rupted England during the century from the 1640s to the 1740s. During this time, political conflict between those supporting the Stuart monarchy, which included the Scots, and those supporting Parliamentary control and, after the Glorious Revolution, the Hanover monarchy, resulted in a variety of con- flicts during the 1640s, 1650s, 1680s, 1710s, and 1740s. One of the last of these conflicts occurred at the Battle of Culloden, during which the pretender to the English throne, Charles Stuart, led a force of Scottish Highlanders against the English forces led by the Duke of Cumberland. Charles Stuart, known as Bonnie Prince Charlie, was the grandson of James II, who had been ousted from the English throne in the Glorious Revolution of 1688. James, his son, and his grandson had long attempted to regain the throne. This time, in 1745 and 1746, Charles Stuart had the support of the Scots and the French when he attempted to raise a force that could stand up to the Eng- lish. The two armies met at Culloden, a broad moor south of Moray Firth in northeastern Scotland. At Culloden, the Scottish Highlanders were routed, destroyed, murdered, imprisoned; Bonnie Prince Charlie would spend months on the run. Such was the memory of the horror of that day, April 16, 1746, that Thomas Paine, in one of his issues of *The American Crisis*, used the example of the vengeful British at Culloden as indicative of what the British, had they been victorious, would have done to the Americans. "Success and power are the only situations in which clemency can be shewn," Paine wrote, "and those who are cruel, because they are victorious, can, with the same facility, act any other degenerate characters." Paine's source for the battle, Tobias Smollett, elaborated: "The glory of the victory was sullied by the barbarity of the soldiers. They had been provoked by their former disgraces to the most savage thirst of revenge. Not contented with the blood which was so profusely shed in the heat of action, they traversed the field after the battle, and massacred those miserable wretches who lay maimed and expiring." This was especially astonishing since in 1689 the English, in their Glorious Revolution, proclaimed the rights of humankind, including life and liberty, and the rule of law. The Duke of Cumberland followed up the victory by ranging about the highlands killing, destroying, and imprisoning. In time, "all of the jails of Great-Britain, from the capital northwards, were filled with those unfortunate captives; and great numbers of them were crowded together in the holds of ships, where they perished in the most deplorable manner, for want of necessaries, air, and exercise." Some of these men never left their prison aboard ship until it reached America, for scores were sent to the "plantations" to labor as servants. One prisoner, William Jack, recalled that he and 157 others were kept aboard a prison ship for nine months before they were shipped out to labor in Barbados. Hundreds of prisoners were transported to the 13 American colonies. One of these, William Lawson, a native of Montrose on the eastern coast of Scotland, was a teenage boy of 15 when the Duke of Cumberland and his troops ranged about Scotland arresting supposed Jacobites, that is, supporters of the pretender Bonnie Prince Charlie. Imprisoned in the north of England, William was one of many who were shipped from Liverpool aboard the *Gildart*, arriving in Maryland in 1747. William became servant to a Virginia planter, serving about a year before running away. He ended up in Virginia, where he married, raised a family, farmed, and eventually fought the English at the Battle of King's Mountain during the American War of Independence.[1]

The forced bondage in America upon the prisoners of Culloden was not the exception. American Indian captives from the Pequot War and King Philip's War, as well as Dutch captured during the Second Anglo-Dutch War, were sentenced to servitude or banished for the same purpose. The English routinely sentenced political prisoners who had escaped the hangman's noose to the 13 colonies or the British Caribbean. After the Jacobite Uprising of 1715, in which James II's son, James Stuart, claimed and attempted to control Great Britain, hundreds of his followers, upon defeat, were transported to

Virginia, South Carolina, Antigua, Barbados, and Jamaica. Hundreds of prisoners taken in Monmouth's Rebellion, in 1685, were transported for 10-years of servitude to America—the precise whereabouts unknown. One captive, Henry Pitman, was taken to Barbados and wrote about his experiences in *A Relation of the Great Sufferings and Strange Adventures of Henry Pitman, Chyrurgion to the late Duck of Monmouth*, published in 1689. Pitman's master treated him cruelly; Pitman escaped with four others, making their way to the northern colonies, then back to England, where he became an apothecary. Another prisoner, John Coad, was sent to Jamaica aboard a ship that had all types of sickness as well as inadequate food and water; but, through faith and perseverance, he survived and was released when the Glorious Revolution occurred. The published *Account of the Proceedings Against the Rebels, and Other Prisoners, Tried before the Lord Chief Justice Jefferies, and Other Judges in the West of England, in 1685, for Taking Arms under the Duke of Monmouth* provides numerous lists of "Prisoners convicted for High Treason, . . . to be Transported." These prisoners were often condemned for 10 years and, if they tried to escape, were branded as a "Fugitive Traitor," an "FT." A few years earlier, in 1679, a rebellion by Scottish Convenanters willing to die for their Presbyterian beliefs was concluded at the Battle of Bothwell Bridge; 52 of those Scots captured were transported to Virginia.[2]

During the English Interregnum, or Commonwealth, Charles in exile, the son of the deposed and executed king, conspired with royalists in England to win back his throne. One group of conspirators, known as the "Sealed Knot," launched an attempted coup in 1655, afterward known as the Penruddock Uprising. The conspiracy failed; some conspirators were arrested and executed, while others were transported. Two men who were transported, who claimed to have not been involved in the conspiracy and to have been falsely accused and arrested, were Marcellus Rivers and Oxenbridge Foyle. They, along with "three score and ten more freeborn people of this nation," were sold into slavery in Barbados. They were kept aboard a ship in Plymouth harbor for two weeks before the ship sailed for Barbados. During the five-and-a-half week voyage "the captive prisoners being all the way locked up under decks, . . . amongst horses, that their souls, through heat and steam, under the tropic, fainted in them; and they never till they came to the island knew whither they were going." Arriving in May 1656, the prisoners were sold "for one thousand five hundred and fifty pound weight of sugar a-piece, more or less, according to their working faculties." Notwithstanding their age and capacity, rank and status, they were alike put to work "grinding at the mills and attending at the furnaces, or digging in this scorching island; having nought to feed on (notwithstanding their hard labour) but potatoe roots, nor to drink, but water with such roots washed in it, besides the bread and tears of their own afflictions; being bought and sold still from one planter to another, or attached as horses and beasts for the debts of their masters, whipped at the whipping-posts (as rogues,) for their masters' pleasure, and sleeping in sties worse than hogs in England, and many other ways made miserable, beyond expression or Christian imagination."[3]

The English Civil War, and the defeat of the Royalists at Dunbar and Worcester, in particular, by the Parliamentarians under Cromwell, resulted in many political prisoners who were transported to the colonies. After Parliament beheaded Charles I in 1649, his son and potential successor, Charles II, attempted on several occasions to regain power with the help of the Scots, of whom he was still king, and the French, who were always willing to capitalize on English civil conflicts. But Charles was defeated by Oliver Cromwell, the Lord Protector of the Commonwealth that replaced the English monarchy. At the Battle of Dunbar, east of Edinburgh, in 1650, Cromwell was successful in defeating the Scots under David Leslie. Thousands of prisoners were taken; hundreds were kept at Durham Cathedral. The prisoners suffered from a variety of diseases, such as dysentery, and their numbers quickly declined—upward of 1,600 died. Of those who survived, the victors divided them to be sent to various locales, such as Ireland, the Caribbean, and the American colonies; 150 were put aboard the *Unity*, bound for New England. The voyage was a good one in terms of speed, six weeks, but the men were weak, many were sick, and about 50 died on the voyage. Those who survived were sold as servants throughout New England. The man in charge of the prisoners at Durham, Samuel Haselrig, shipped up to 900 to Virginia. A year later in 1651 at Worcester, in western England, Cromwell again outmanned and outgeneraled Charles. Several thousand Scots were taken prisoner, then transported the following year to America. They were kept in London while they awaited transport. Over 1,600 prisoners found themselves bound to Virginia. Some of these prisoners found their way to New England aboard the *John and Sara*. They landed in Charlestown and were put under the charge of Thomas Kemble, a merchant who had interests in Massachusetts, New Hampshire, and Maine.[4]

John Cotton of Boston wrote Oliver Cromwell in 1651 about the arrival of these captives, saying that the colonists were "desirous (as we could) to make their yoke easy. Such as were sick of the scurvy or other diseases have not wanted physic and chirurgery. They have not been sold for slaves to pertpetuall servitude, but for 6 or 7 or 8 yeares, as we do our owne" servants. The two men with the responsibility to transport the captives, John Beck (or Becx) and Joshua Foote, brought about two dozen to the Piscataqua valley on the Maine/New Hampshire border. Here they were apparently sold to different masters on both the New Hampshire and Maine sides of the Piscataqua River. Some were set to work at the remains of mills erected 20 years before by Ambrose Gibbons on behalf of John Mason along the Newichawannock River, revived and owned by Richard Leader; Leader soon sold the mills to Beck and a couple of his associates. The men, upon eventual freedom, stayed in Maine, living in what became Berwick, named for a town in Scotland near Dunbar. Others servants were sold to masters who lived north of Kittery, eventually settling a place called, appropriately, Scotland. Many Scottish captives found a better life in America; often they became landowners, and themselves purchased servants.[5]

Of the Scotch prisoners from Dunbar, 62 were sent to the town of Lynn, north of Boston, where they were put to work in the iron works at Saugus. John Winthrop Jr. had originally founded the ironworks with financing and workmen from England on the Saugus River in 1646. The iron works were run by a servant himself, Richard Leader, who, according to historian Lawrence Towner, "signed an indenture, as any bound servant did, for seven years. He was to get one hundred pounds per year plus passage for wife, children and three servants. A house was to be built for him, and land was to be available for his horses and cows. Today (and then too, at times) he would be called a factor or agent. Yet he was bound, and he illustrates the flexibility of the institution of servitude." The servant Richard Leader, followed by his successor, another servant, John Gifford, took charge of the bound servants from Scotland. The newcomers were treated surprisingly well. During the two-day march from Boston to the ironworks, they received ample food and had a physician look after them. Upon arrival, they settled into small houses that accommodated four each; their masters supplied them with stockings, shirts, shoes, and "skines for making the cloathes, Hatts, and Bands," and tobacco as well. The men had a garden; they worked three days for master, four for themselves: "as soon as they can repay the money laid out for them he will set them at liberty." Their tasks were those associated with ironworks. Some served as colliers mining for ore; others chopping wood for charcoal; some worked the forge; others employed their skills as smiths; still others worked on the ironworks farm.[6]

The historical record provides a mixed report on how well these Scots fared. The Scots' Charitable Society was organized in 1657 to help the destitute Scots of the Cromwellian wars. The Scots' Charitable Society was similar to a London society founded during the reign of Charles II (Royal Scottish Corporation). Both were dedicated to helping the sick, burying the impoverished dead, and providing food and shelter. One Scot, John Stewart, petitioned Governor Edmund Andros many years later, in 1688, that "your poor petitioner was in service in five battles under the noble Marquis of Montrose, in Scotland, for His Majesty, King Charles the First, and thereby suffered and received many dangerous wounds, having escaped with his life through mercy." He was sold into servitude for eight years at the Saugus ironworks, but a town leader of Springfield, Massachusetts, John Pynchon, bought his contract and services as a blacksmith for three years. Pynchon was active in purchasing indentured servants; he would then turn around and sell their contract to another townsperson in Springfield. One Scottish servant, Hugh

Dudley, contracted for five years with Pynchon who then sold him to Henry Smith, who was to support Dudley to the tune of "three pounds and ten shillings per yeare, to find him apparell: and to endevor at the end of his tyme to provide him a convenient allottment of land." Duncan Stewart was another with the name of the royal family who was transported to America. He was born in 1623 in the Scottish Highlands, captured by Cromwell's men, and sent to America. He ended up in Ipswich, near Lynn, married, and eventually moved north to Newbury and became a farmer.[7]

Captives of the English Civil War—as well as other wars in which the English were victorious—ended up in other places in the Americas: such as Barbados, Bermuda, and the island of St. Christopher. A German soldier fighting for Charles, Heinrich von Uchteritz, was captured at the Battle of Worcester; he was subsequently transported to Barbados. He was one among many from the Battle of Dunbar and Battle of Worcester that Cromwell and his advisers sent to the English Caribbean. Von Uchteritz was a minor German nobleman who owned a manor in Meissen in what is today eastern Germany on the Elbe River. He claimed that his reason for fighting in the English Civil War was for "knightly virtue," but he was in reality a mercenary fighting for Charles. He joined Charles's cause in 1650, probably after the Battle of Dunbar, and felt confident that the Scottish army, stronger than Cromwell's, would carry the day. Lackluster leadership—Von Uchteritz called it cowardice—resulted in Cromwell's victory. Von Uchteritz was made a prisoner and questioned by Cromwell. He was kept in London for months until finally he and hundreds of others were transported to Barbados in 1652. Barbados is a small island in the Lesser Antilles; the English had sugar plantations for which they needed a large labor force. The planter to whom Von Uchteritz was sold, a man named Whittaker, owned "one hundred Christians, one hundred Negroes, and one hundred Indians as slaves." Perhaps the Indians were native islanders, though some tribes from the northern British American colonies, such as the Pequot, had been condemned for servitude in the British Caribbean isles. Von Uchteritz, little better than a slave, slept in one of "the slaves' small houses. These are made of inferior wood, look almost like dog-houses, and are covered with the leaves of trees," which "are quite wide. They are almost reed-like, and they serve well against the rain." Masters acquired slaves for agricultural labor: cotton, tobacco, ginger, and primarily, sugar. Slave diet was, Von Uchteritz proclaimed, "very bad and consisted only of roots. One such root called *batatas*, is cooked in large pots and tastes almost like chestnuts. The other root is called cassava from which a small, but fruitless, tree grows." Slaves were not allowed meat, and their drink was water, with a bit of lemon and sugar added, unlike the "gentry," who "make a drink from the potato root," the *batatas*—nothing intoxicating was allowed for the slave laborers. These laborers were divided into Christian and pagan; the latter, Indian and Negro pagans, were "completely naked except for a cloth tied around their privities"; and, they spoke native dialects. Christians spoke English and wore "light linen clothes which are finely made." Christians were "Calvanists [sic]," befitting Cromwell and the English Commonwealth. "There are a number of churches and ministers, and their church services are not different from those performed in England." The pagans, of course, "pray to the Devil."[8]

Von Uchteritz was, unlike the other imprisoned captives from Dunbar and the Indian and Negro slaves, eventually ransomed. Having spent about four-and-a-half months in "miserable bondage," his prayers for deliverance, he believed, were answered. Apparently Master Whittaker was a reasonable man who, when he learned that Von Uchteritz was himself a landowner of noble birth, agreed to allow him to buy his freedom for 800 pounds of sugar, the price he paid. The master approached German merchants in Barbados and informed them of this opportunity to free Von Uchteritz. Fortunately, the merchants knew Von Uchteritz's cousin, a famous merchant and traveler named Hans Christoph Von Uchteritz. They were unconvinced that Heinrich Von Uchteritz was indeed who he said he was, so they contrived a test. They had with them a copy of a book, *Description of Travels in the Orient*, that included a picture of several travelers, including Hans Christoph. The merchants covered the names and ask Heinrich to select his cousin, whom he did not know from sight, but made a lucky guess! That settled, the merchants paid the ransom, and Von Uchteritz obtained his freedom. The merchants also bought some clothes for him, so that he could dress his rank. The problem was that his rank was not equaled by his fortune, and Von Uchteritz did not know whether or not his family could pay such an exorbitant ransom. The merchants decided, however, to swallow the cost themselves in hopes that Hans Christoph Von Uchteritz would someday do them a favor. Von Uchteritz now boarded a ship for Amsterdam, and he successfully reached home, and redemption.[9]

Among all of the stories of catastrophe and suffering of war captives sold into servitude are stories of hope and redemption. One comes from a captive of Culloden, Alexander Stewart, who was transported along with many others to the Chesapeake region in 1747. Stewart left behind an account of his experiences. Upon arriving at their destination, the captain of the ship "came and sat down on the trap that came down between dakes and discours'd us, and asked us what we was to doe now when we was near our journey's end. So we told him we was to depend on God's providence and him, for which he said he would make all the int[e]rest for us that in his power lay." Indeed, upon reaching the custom house, the captain ordered a carpenter to strike off their irons. That evening, the supercargo of the ship told the men that they had arrived at a fine country, that they would serve seven years, be well treated, then freed with tools and clothes. Stewart claimed that he first, then others, refused the offer: "I would sign non for no man that ever was born, though they should hang me over the yard arms." The captain, in response, wrote letters to "Roman Catholick gentlemen" to see if they would come to the ship to view the prisoners, which they did on July 22, 1747. These men paid the purchase price of "all the eightie eight that was aboarde of our ship except thre or four that went with two of the common buckskins, them that are born in the countrie, for so they are called." Stewart and the others were free; Stewart made his way back to Scotland in 1748.[10]

Meanwhile, other Scots were going a different direction, leaving Scotland for America. Particularly in the 18th century, Highland Scots emigrated to America in greater numbers. Many of these immigrants to America settled along the frontiers, especially in the southern colonies. At the conclusion of the American War of Independence, Highland Scots arrived in British Canada, especially in Upper Canada (Ontario). Lowland Scots also arrived in America, often settling in cities on the coast. Scots, like others in the British Isles and Europe, left for America because of war and famine. Many saw their journey as an opportunity for redemption, for freedom, to possess rather than to be dispossessed. Yet others, like Alexander Stewart, after their American experience, only wanted to go home.[11]

Notes

1. Thomas Paine, *The American Crisis* (London: Carlile, 1819), 151; Tobias Smollett, *The History of England from the Revolution to the Death of George the Second*, vol. 3 (London: Cadell and Baldwin, 1785), 168, 169, 174; Hugh G. Allison, *Culloden Tales: Stories from Scotland's Most Famous Battlefield* (Edinburgh: Mainstream Publishing, 2007); David Dobson, *Scottish Emigration to Colonial America, 1607–1785* (Athens: University of Georgia Press, 1994), 96; Bill Porter, "Lawson, William—A Scottish Rebel." http://www.electricscotland.com/webclans/minibios/l/lawson_william.htm

2. J. D. Butler, "British Convicts Shipped to American Colonies," *American Historical Review* 2 (1896): 12–33; Abbot E. Smith, *Colonists in Bondage: White Servitude and Convict Labor in America, 1607–1776* (New York: W. W. Norton, 1947), 190, 193, 195–196, 198; *An Account of the Proceedings against the Rebels, and Other Prisoners, Tried before the Lord Chief Justice Jefferies, and Other Judges in the West of England, in 1685, for Taking Arms under the Duke of Monmouth*, 3rd ed. (London: Andrew Bell, 1716). http://quod.lib.umich.edu/e/ecco/004840465.0001.000?rgn =main;view=fulltext; Philip A. Bruce, *Economic History of Virginia in the Seventeenth Century* (New York: Macmillan, 1907), 611; Peter Rushton, "'Barbados'd'— The Transportation of Convicts," in *Convict Voyages: A Global History of Convicts and Penal Colonies.* http://convictvoyages.org/expert-essays/caribbean

3. Rushton, "Barbados'd'"; *Diary of Thomas Burton, Esq. Member in the Parliaments of Oliver and Richard Cromwell, from 1656 to 1659*, vol. 4 (London: Henry Colburn, 1828), 255–257.

4. Peter Reese, *Cromwell's Masterstroke: The Battle of Dunbar, 1650* (South Yorkshire: Pen and Sword Books, 2006), 105; Michael Tepper, ed., *New World Immigrants: A Consolidation of Ship Passenger Lists and Associated Data from*

Periodical Literature, vol. 1 (Baltimore: Genealogical Publishing, 1979), 138ff; Smith, *Colonists in Bondage*, 154–155.

5. *New World Immigrants*, 145, 148, 149; Richard Candee, *Merchant and Millwright: The Water Powered Mills of the Piscataqua*, 153–154. *New England Bulletin of the Society for the Preservation of New England Antiquities*. 1968; "The Scottish Prisoners of 1650," Old Berwick Historical Society. http://oldberwick.org/index .php?option=com_content&view=article&id=261:the-scottish-prisoners-of -1650&catid=53:historical-events&Itemid=72; Smith, *Colonists in Bondage*, 157.

6. Alison C. Simcox and Douglas L. Heath, *Breakheart Reservation* (Charleston, SC: Arcadia Publishing, 2013), 8, 21; Lawrence W. Towner, *A Good Master Well Served: Masters and Servants in Colonial Massachusetts* (New York: Taylor and Francis, 1998), 49; *New World Immigrants*, 154; Reese, *Cromwell's Masterstroke*, 105; "Scots Prisoners and Their Relocation to the Colonies, 1650–1654." https:// www.geni.com/projects/Scots-Prisoners-and-their-Relocation-to-the-Colonies -1650-1654/3465

7. *The Constitution and By-Laws of the Scots' Charitable Society of Boston* (Cambridge: Wilson, 1878). The information on Duncan Stewart comes from *Sprague's Journal of Maine History* 8 (1920): 151–152; Sprague was uncertain whether Stewart was captured at Worcester or Dunbar. Information on John Stewart and Hugh Dudley comes from Stephen Innes, *Labor in a New Land: Economy and Society in Seventeenth Century Springfield* (Princeton, NJ: Princeton University Press, 1983), 9, and *New World Immigrants*, 144. It is not clear whether Dudley was captured at Dunbar or Worcester.

8. "A German Indentured Servant in Barbados in 1652: The Account of Heinrich Von Uchteritz," ed. and trans. by Alexander Gunkel and Jerome S. Handler, *Journal of the Barbados Museum and Historical Society* 33 (1970): 91–93. http://jeromehandler.org/1970/01/a-german-indentured-servant-in-barbados -in-1652-the-account-of-heinrich-von-uchteritz/

9. Ibid., 94–96.

10. "Narrative of Alexander Stewart," *Maryland Historical Magazine*, 1 (1906): 349–352.

11. Dobson, *Scottish Emigration*, 6.

CHAPTER ELEVEN

John Harrower and Servitude in the Colonial South

Highlanders and Lowlanders who sought to voyage to America from Scotland in search of opportunity sometimes never arrived. Two hundred and sixty Lowland Scots from Leith on the Firth of Forth on their way to North Carolina in 1773 were unavoidably detained from reaching their destination. The ship, taking the northern and western route around Scotland, experienced problems, and the vessel was driven toward the Shetland Islands. The captain and crew attempted to put into Vela Sound on the west coast, but winds or tide drove the ship onto shoals and damaged it. Many of the passengers were sick with smallpox; small children who had easily become ill in the crowded midships had been cast into the grave of the sea. The survivors were desperate, sick, and impoverished. The people of this region of the Shetlands hosted and cared for them, so that after a time many were able to return home to Leith—never to go to America.[1]

John Harrower was a Shetland Islander who had once experienced prosperity, to whom time and chance had brought about a change in fortunes, though he had the drive and desire for something more. Harrower lived on the east coast of the islands in the town of Lerwick. From here, on December 6, 1773, he departed "on board a sloop ready to saile for Leith" at the Firth of Forth. Harrower kept a diary, which has survived time, by which we know of his experiences. Harrower "left my house and family" early in the morning, sailing with a north wind; he was never to return. He left three children and a wife, Annie, who was from an important Shetland family, her brother being a merchant. Harrower assumed without asking her brother, James Craigie, that he would help his sister get by in her husband's absence. He asked his wife to keep his departure a secret, apparently because he was on the brink of financial ruin, brought about, it appears, in part by poor health, and wished to escape for a time to earn some money to repair his fortunes. John Harrower was poor, and poorly equipped for traveling, with just a few pence in his pocket; the most valuable item he owned were some Shetland stockings, which were worth £3—"a small value indeed to traviel with." It is possible (though not certain) that Harrower had been a dealer in stockings, and wished to find opportunities in Scotland, England, and the Netherlands. Perhaps because he could not afford the passage to Leith, he got off at Montrose on the east coast between Aberdeen and Dundee. Harrower took to the road, walking close to 30 miles to Dundee on the River Tay. He spent a fortnight at Dundee, apparently "in search of business"—precisely what kind of business he did not say. Harrower was a member of the Freemasons, an organization known for its solicitousness toward the poor; brother masons doubtless provided hospitality to the newcomer during his stay. He enjoyed watching masons from three local lodges reveling about the streets of the town on December 27. The next day, he spontaneously thought to board a brigantine bound for North Carolina, which idea he reconsidered because "the thoughts of being so far from my family prevented me." Harrower lived as economically as possible, dining on cheese, bread, meat, and ale before leaving Dundee for Newcastle, England, on the Tyne River. He took ship in "the sloop Williams" and after midnight on Thursday, December 30, the ship passed the bar at the mouth of the river and sailed up the Tyne to Newcastle. Here, Harrower tried to find a passage for the Netherlands, but failed; he heard that Sunderland, to the south on the River Wear, was the best place to pick up such a ship. He journeyed to Sunderland by foot and spent several nights there. He lived off of the proceeds of stockings that he sold. He finally found and boarded a ship apparently bound for the Netherlands. The brigantine, called the *Nancy*, set sail on January 7. The cold weather kept the ship close to the English shore; for several days they sailed south, finally coming to Portsmouth on the southeastern coast. The captain of the ship entertained Harrower, who though poor appeared as something of a gentleman, and provided bed and board at no cost. Harrower departed from Portsmouth on January 12 making his way by land for London. He had hardly any money, and wrote: "I pray, May God provide more for me and for all who are in strait." On the road he was able to sell more stockings, which provided a bit of money to live on. He stayed at various places along the road, at one point writing some verses of consolation:

My absent friends God bless, and those,
My wife and Children dear;
I pray for pardon to my foes,
And for them sheds a tear.
At Epsom here this day I ly,

Repenting my past sins;
Praying to Jesus for his mercy,
And success to my friends.[2]

Harrower reached London on January 18. He "was like a blind man without a guide, not knowing where to go being freindless [sic] and having no more money but fifteen shilling and eight pence farthing a small sum to enter London with." He put on fresh clothes and began making calls to prospects for business and employment—without any success. He tried to get a position as a "steward of a ship bound to Maryland," but failed. Meanwhile he did a lot of sight-seeing and lived on bare necessities. Disconsolate, Harrower turned again to melancholy verses:

Now at London in a garret room I am,
Here frendless and forsaken;
But from the Lord my help will come,
Who trusts in him are not mistaken.
When freinds on earth do faint and faile,
And upon you their backs do turn;
O Truly seek the Lord, and he will
Them comfort that do m[o]urn.
I'll unto God my prayer make,
To him my case make known;
And hopes he will for Jesus sake,
Provide for me and soon.[3]

The situation in London for the unemployed and impoverished, Harrower discovered, was dire. Many people were "sterving [sic] for want of employment, and many good people are begging." Harrower had experience in business and tried to get positions as a clerk or steward, but to no effect. Down to his "last shilling" on January 26, Harrower "was obliged to engage to go to Virginia for four years as a schoolmaster for Bedd, Board, washing and five pound during the whole time." He wrote a letter to his wife explaining his situation and decision, and "went on board the Snow Planter." One Alex Stuart from the Shetland Islands, to Harrower's surprise, was also on board; Stuart had been a servant to one of the landed lords of the islands, and had left his service to try America. Other servants came on board as the ship made ready to depart. Two Lowlanders from Edinburgh and Glasgow, and another Scot, as well as a fellow from Yorkshire, joined Harrower in slinging their hammocks amidships. The captain of the ship, one Bowers, was himself from a town called Aberbothick, in Scotland, though he had not been there for years, ever since he had become a seaman in the Atlantic trade. Every day, until February 4, when the ship "fell down the river with the tide there being no wind," more "good tradesmen of all kinds," bound for America, came on board. Harrower, feeling that his future was set, purchased "a penknife, a paper Book, and some paper and pens."[4]

Vessels on their way from London to the English Channel stopped at Gravesend; Captain Bowers made anchor so that a merchant, physician, and clerk could come on board, fill out indentures for 75 men, and certify their health. All the servants were indentured to the captain "for four Years"; Harrower was indentured as "Clerk and Bookeeper." While the ship took on supplies, a few servants were released because of sickness. The snow got under way, made the mouth of the Thames, and under a west-north-west wind rounded Margate into the Strait of Dover, where they anchored at Deal to purchase gin. Proceeding south on February 13th, "at noon the Indented servants was like to mutiny against the Cap[tain] for putting them to Allowance of bread and Maté,[5] but it was soon quelled," in part because Harrower and his Scottish mates refused to join in. The captain took this as a sign of alliance, and while he went ashore for supplies asked Harrower to stand with the mate against trouble. As the ship continued south and west toward the Isle of Wight, several men took sick, one of whom died of dysentery.[6]

Winter in the North Atlantic is often treacherous, with towering waves and cold, strong wind. The crew and passengers of the *Planter* experienced such weather, and the servants were not prepared for such a voyage. On March 11, the conditions were such that the men were terrified, some vomiting, others "Blasting their leggs and thighs," others cursing "Father, Mother, Sister, and Brother." Harrower, perhaps because of his Shetland background, fared well. Some servants continued mutinous, but a time in irons would curb their tongues. By the end of March, most (50) of the servants were ill, including some of the Scots, even Stuart, who was, Harrower wrote, "so high in the fever that I sat up with him all night." The crew prepared chicken soup for the sick. One of the crew had some medical knowledge; he prescribed blistering for Stuart, in which the skin was purposefully raised by heat or mustard so that pus and blood would be released—part of the old humoral theory of medicine. The chief mate, one Jones, prescribed a unique medicinal therapy for a cabin boy: he asked Harrower to give the boy an emetic to make him vomit, then to place a handkerchief next to his chest with the following lines written on a piece of paper therein:

When Jesus saw the Cross he trembled,
The Jews said unto him why tremblest thou,
You have neither got an Ague nor a fever.
Jesus Answered and said unto them
I have neither got an Ague nor a fever
But whosoever keepeth my words
Shall neither have an Ague nor a fever.

Harrower himself needed the therapy a few days later when he developed the same illness.[7]

Harrower recovered by the time they made Cape Henry at the entrance of Chesapeake Bay on Wednesday, April 27. It had been a good voyage for the Shetland Islander; he had earned Captain Bowers's trust such that he kept the log while the mate was sick. The morning of April 28, anchored at Hampton Roads at the mouth of the James River, the captain "employ'd" him "in Making out a Clean list of the servants names and Business and age." The captain auctioned off one servant, a boat-builder. From Hampton Roads the ship sailed north to the mouth of the Rappahannock River, which they proceeded up toward Fredericksburg. Along the way Harrower saw five ships from Glasgow, with perhaps similar cargos to Captain Bowers's ship. At Leedstown "there was a ship from London lying with Convicts" ready to be auctioned. The valley of the Rappahannock revealed the type of life and culture Harrower would now experience: "Woods in the blossom, Gentlemens seats and Planters houses." An "old German" succumbed to the effects of his journey and was buried on shore in the woods. May 10, on the tide they reached Fredericksburg.[8]

The Virginia to which Harrower arrived in 1774 was much more heavily reliant upon slaves than servants. Planters growing cash crops such as tobacco depended upon intensive labor, for which the Virginians, after having relied largely on white servants in the 17th century, had come to depend upon black slaves in the 18th century. The number of servants sent to labor-hungry Virginia in the 17th century included indentured, convicts, and prisoners of war. After the Restoration of Charles II, some of the prisoners sent to Virginia under Cromwell had encouraged the rumblings of white servants, resulting in "a villainous plot," in the words of Robert Beverley, "to destroy their masters, and afterwards to set up for themselves." On the eve of the rebellion, however, one of the servants, Birkenhead, lost his nerve, and informed his master; the militia was called out and the conspiracy fell apart; many of the servants escaped; the ringleaders were executed. Such episodes involving prisoners and convicts led the House of Burgesses in 1670 to pass a law to restrict "the great numbers of Felons and other desperate villaines sent hither from the several prisons of England." A few years later, a similar situation to the Birkenhead incident occurred, during Bacon's Rebellion. The apparent rebellious nature of some white servants, especially those brought to Virginia against their will, led Virginia plantation owners, toward the end of the 17th century, to opt for more black slaves than white servants.[9]

One contemporary, Robert Beverley, believed that notwithstanding such episodes as Bacon's Rebellion, in general servants were well treated in Virginia. "Because I have heard," he wrote, "how strangely cruel and severe the service of this country is represented in some parts of England, I can't forbear affirming, that the work of [Virginia] servants and slaves is no other than what every common freeman does; neither is any servant required to do more in a day than his overseer; and I can assure you, with great truth, that generally their slaves are not worked near so hard, nor so many hours in a day, as the husbandmen, and day laborers in England." Whereas female servants were put to work in domestic activities, "male servants, and slaves of both sexes, are employed together in tilling and manuring the ground, in sowing and planting tobacco, corn &c." Beverley emphasized that provincial law protected the rights of servants; courts had the power to relieve cruel masters of their servants; parish churchwardens were also allowed to step in on the servant's behalf, if needed. Courts oversaw any agreements between masters and servants and protected the property rights of servants. Freedom dues, according to Beverley, included "ten bushels of corn, (which is sufficient for almost a year,) two new suits of clothes, both linen and woolen, and a gun, twenty shillings value." The freed servant "then becomes as free in all respects, and as much entitled to the liberties and privileges of the country"— including the "right to take up fifty acres of land, where he can find any unpatented," or unappropriated.[10]

Notwithstanding Beverley's optimistic appraisal of servitude, there were sufficient numbers of servants who were dissatisfied with their situation that the House of Burgesses had to pass laws to address the situation. In 1658, for example, in a law "Against Runnaway Servants," the House declared that runaways have their time of service doubled for the amount of time absent; recalcitrant runaways would have an R branded on their shoulder. As with all human societies, there were in colonial Virginia enough examples of cohabitation among men and women, free as well as servants, that the House of Burgesses declared a law against "ffornication" in 1662. In this law, a person so charged owed their parish a fine of 500 pounds of tobacco; if the person was a servant, the master had to pay the fine but the servant had to serve extra time for the master; if the master refused to pay, the servant was whipped. "If it happen a bastard child to be gotten in such ffornication then the woman if a servant in regard of the losse and trouble her master doth sustaine by her having a bastard shall serve two yeares after her time by indenture is expired."[11]

That servants could still be punished very severely, even tortured, in Harrower's time, is revealed in his journal. "Daniel Turner, a serv[ant] returned onb[oard] from Liberty so drunk that he abused the Cap[t]. and chief Mate and Boatswan to a very high degree, which made to be horse whip[t] put in Irons and thumb screwed. [O]n[e] houre afterward he was unthumbscrewed, taken out of the Irons, but then he was hand cuffed, and gagged all night." A further example that could have frightened any servant aboard ship awaiting a master occurred on May 16, when "two Soul drivers" came on board. These "are men who make it their business to go onb[oard] all ships who have in either Servants or Convicts and buy sometimes the whole and sometimes a parcel of them as they can agree, and then they drive them through the Country like a parcel of Sheep until they can sell them to advantage." Fortunately, the captain either refused to deal with such men or could not come to terms.[12]

For the next week Harrower waited as more of the servants on board were sold to masters. On the 23rd, at a local fair, a tent was erected and the servants put on display for sale; some were purchased. Harrower had made the acquaintance of a local merchant, one Anderson, who sought on his behalf to find a situation for Harrower "as a Clerk or bookeeper if not as a schoolmaster" among his friends. Colonel William Daingerfield agreed with Anderson that Harrower would make an excellent tutor for his children, so purchased his indenture for four years.[13]

Harrower had gained for himself an admirable situation. The colonel gave him money to clean his clothes and purchase some supplies, then sent for him by horseback. The school where Harrower was to teach was also his apartment. The plantation, called Belvidera, was a half dozen miles below Fredericksburg on the Rappahannock. The colonel and his lady were part of the Virginia elite and sometimes dined with the Washingtons. Harrower's school was a stone's throw from the river. Harrower's pupils were the three sons of the colonel, aged eight, six, and four, as well as the children of the colonel's neighbors. For each additional scholar, Harrower was allowed to charge "five shillings currency per Quarter." He was to teach them arithmetic, spelling, and writing. In time he enrolled a student in his school who was "deaf and dum"; Harrower "consented to try what I cou'd do with him." He also, either by his own accord or at the colonel's request, kept a night school for "a small Congregation of Negroes, learn[in]g their Catechisim [sic] and hearing me read to them." The colonel owned several dozen slaves, who worked in the field and in his house; perhaps these were the students.[14]

Harrower clearly missed his family, as revealed in a series of verses he wrote on the first Sabbath of his new situation; in his prayerful rhymes he asked that his family be cared for and preserved from harm and that he might afford to send them money. He soon found the means to send letters to his wife by the hands of Fredericksburg merchants. In his letters he informed his wife of his situation and how he had "no Occasion to spend a farthing on myself every shill[in]g I make shall be carefully remitted to you, for your support and my Dear Infants." He also intended to send for his family to make a new life in America. "But I must be some time here before any thing can be done, for you know every thing must have a beginning." Harrower informed his wife of his dining habits, how he ate at the master's table, of the fine foods and elegant conversation. There was unfortunately no tea to drink, as the Virginia planters had joined others up and down the coast in protesting the British Tea Act. The colonel shared his newspapers with Harrower, who learned of the problems between the colonies and the Parliament—"and I'm afraid if the Parli[a]ment do not give it over it will cause a revolt as all the North Americans are determined to stand by one another, and resolute on it that they will not submit."[15]

The uncertainty of the post in the Shetland Islands ensured that Harrower had still not received a letter from his wife in early December when he wrote to her on the anniversary of his departure for America. He again inquired what she thought of removing to America and outlined how it could be done. He discussed his school and the students, such as the deaf and dumb teenager with whom Harrower had succeeded well enough that "he can write mostly for anything he wants and understands the value of every figure and can work single addition a little." He was also teaching an adult carpenter on evenings and weekends. The colonel's children were learning as well. The eldest "is now reading verry distinctly in the Psalter according to the Church of England and the other two boys ready to enter into it." The colonel and wife liked Harrower well enough to have named their newborn fourth child, a boy, John, after their servant. Harrower wrote a newsy letter for his wife, even if he was unsure if and when she would receive it. He informed her of the Battle of Point Pleasant of Lord Dunmore's War and of the continuing disagreement between the American colonists and the British. He described in great detail the effects of the Boston Port Bill on Boston and how other colonists were rallying around Boston in support. His own master Colonel Daingerfield sent "fifty Bushels of wheat and One Hundred Bushels of Indian Corn, By which ye may Judge of the rest" of contributions from the colonies. Harrower asked his wife for an account of his children, Jack, George, and Bettie, hoping that the two boys were still in school—"I beg of you to strain every nerve to keep them at it until I am able to assist you, for he who has got education will always gain Bread and to spare, and that in a genteel way in some place or other of the World." He requested also of his wife that Betts be kept hard at work domestically in sewing, "and do not bring her up to Idleness or play or going about from house to house which is the first inlet in any of the sex to laziness and vice." He said to his wife, "I yet hope please God, if I am spared, some time to make you a Virginian Lady among the woods of America which is by far more pleasent than the roaring of the raging seas abo't Zetland." A fortnight later Harrower dreamed that his wife arrived in America, though she had left their three children behind.[16]

In the ensuing months Harrower did not hear from his wife, Annie, though he was quite busy with school, helping the colonel in a variety of tasks, and keeping up with political news of the growing tension between the American colonies and the British. In May, a letter arrived from Mrs. Harrower ending the suspense of over a year and a half. She and the children were well. Her brother, merchant James Craigie, helped (financially, no doubt) and advised the single mother and her children. But the suspense of the conflict between England and her colonies was making Harrower's plan to bring his family to America seem more and more distant. He wrote his wife in August 1775, telling her that he had written to her brother about "assisting to you, until such time as the ports are open for trade betwixt Britain and the Collonies and the disputes made up betwixt them, for untill that is done there is no such thing as remitting money or goods from any part of America to Britain"—in other words, while the conflict continued there was little chance that his family could come to America. Harrower still held out a glimmer of hope: should she or her brother learn that a ship in the Lerwick harbor be bound for Virginia or Maryland, "I wou'd have you at all events Make your Brother apply for your Passage with the Children and a servant and imediatly dispose of every article in the house your Feather Bedds Bedding and Cloaths excepted," and "write me imediatly on your Aravell here by post and I shou'd soon be with you." It was not to happen.[17]

Harrower the same day (August 28) wrote to James Craigie, eating crow because of the apparent subterfuge and folly of his actions—abandoning his wife and children on an uncertain errand to earn money, ending up in America as an indentured servant with no legal ability to return. "I did not intend," he wrote his brother-in-law, "going further than Holland, or even London cou'd I have found business there to my liking but not finding that, and the frost being strong in Holland, I was determined to see what I cou'd do in this Western World." He continued: "I have now wrote Annie to advise with you with respect to her moving to this Country with the Children." The problem, of course, was money: "Until the disputes betwixt Government and the Collonies are settled there is no such thing as getting any remittance made to any part in Britain; Hostilities being already begun at Boston and three Engagements already fought betwixt the British troops and the provincials the last of which on the 17th June last at Charleston near Boston, when the Provincialls gained the day as they did of the other two. . . . How or when these differences will [end] God only knows, But the Americans are determined to stand by one another to the last man and all exports and imports are intirely stopt also planting of Tobacco." A little over a fortnight later Harrower again wrote his wife, directing that the letter be sent through New York because of the "Nonimportation and Nonexportation Acts of the Continental Congress." Annie Harrower had indicated in her letter the previous spring that she desired to come to America, joking (perhaps) that otherwise her husband might find a "Virginian Lady." Harrower assured her such was not the case, and the reason for his inability to bring her to America, and send money to help her, was the dispute between England and her colonies. He assumed that the dispute would not be long lasting, and told Annie that she might not hear from him until the conflict was resolved.[18]

Harrower's position and his natural decorum, concern for dress and demeanor, and ability to converse with the most elegant English person allowed him to become almost a part of the Daingerfield family. He dined with them and often joined them at common entertainments. He was intimate with the children as well. Harrower accidentally became involved in a Daingerfield family dispute wherein the colonel expected him to "correct," that is, whip, his children when they acted incorrectly, but Mrs. Daingerfield resented him for it. Indeed, she referred to him as "Old Harrower," which the servant considered a mark of disrespect. Also disrespectful was the mother of one of his students, a Mrs. Richards, wife of a plantation overseer, who was "really a Wolf cloathed with a lambs skin and the greatest Mischief maker I have seen in all my Travels." Her mischief included spreading rumors of an alliance between Harrower and a housekeeper named Lucy Gaines. Harrower assumed, however, that those among his acquaintances who mattered would realize that such a story was false. Perhaps Mrs. Richards saw that Harrower and Lucy had quite a mutual respect, including giving each other gifts—on Harrower's part, because of "her readiness to do any little thing for me." Perhaps the concerns of the war, of his absent family, of rumors and innuendo, led to temptations, one of which was drink. Having previously bragged that he had not had any hard liquor while in America, Harrower broke down on November 15 and "drank a small dram of rum made thick with brown suggar for the cold, it being the first dram I have drunk since I lived on the Plantation." A month later, he wrote a poem of confession:

Both the last nights quite drunk was I,
Pray God forgive me the sin;
But had I been in good company,
Me in that case No man had seen.
Plac'd by myself, without the camp,
As if I were unclean—
No friendly soul does my floor tramp,
My greiff to ease, or hear my moan.
For in a prison at large I'm plac't,
Bound to it, day and night;
O, grant me patience, god of grace.
And in thy paths make me walk right.
This day alone, at home I am,
Repenting sadly and full sore
That ever the like unto me came.
When this I see, the cause I will repent for ever more.[19]

The political and military crisis, rather than lessening, sunshine breaking through clouds, worsened, and so, too, did Harrower's despair. A fortnight after he penned his sorrowful rhyme he heard of the town of Norfolk, Virginia, being set ablaze, "reduced to ashes," by Lord Dunmore, the former colonial governor. His teaching responsibilities grew during the first half of

1776, but rather than a cessation in the conflict Harrower learned, on July 10, "that there was great rejoicings in Toun on Acco[un]t of the Congress having declared the 13 United Colonys of North American Independent of the Crown of great Britain."[20]

As John Harrower witnessed, from his partially removed position as a plantation school teacher the growing conflict between America and England, he appears to have felt a growing empathy with the Americans, perhaps because of the long history of conflict between the English and Scottish. In September 1775, he witnessed a company of 70 Virginia militia marching to Williamsburg "for the defence of the rights and liberties of this Coll[on]y in particular and of North American in Generall." The last entry of the diary, Thursday, July 25, reads: "I imployed this morn[in]g and forenoon getting Lead off Snowcreek house"—lead for the purpose of making bullets. Harrower, it seems, became a part of the American effort to gain independence. Harrower died soon after, in late 1776 or early 1777. Colonel Daingerfield kindly wrote to Harrower's widow, Annie, who lamented her husband's death but praised the colonel's generosity.[21]

John Harrower was one of many impoverished, desperate people who lived in the British Isles, Europe, and elsewhere over the course of many centuries who abandoned all—family, security, love—for the sake of journeying to America to find abundance and a new life or, in John Harrower's case, a lonely death.

Notes

1. "Diary of John Harrower, 1773–1776," *American Historical Review* 6 (1900): 66.

2. Ibid., 66–69, 99.

3. Ibid., 70–71.

4. Ibid., 71–72.

5. Perhaps Yerba Maté, a South American caffeinated beverage.

6. Ibid., 73.

7. Ibid., 73–75; Ira Rutkow, *Seeking the Cure: A History of Medicine in America* (New York: Scribner, 2010), 39.

8. "Diary of John Harrower," 75–76.

9. Edmund S. Morgan, *American Slavery, American Freedom* (New York: W. W. Norton, 2003); Marcus W. Jernegan, *Laboring and Dependent Classes in Colonial America, 1607–1783* (New York: Frederick Ungar, 1965), 48; Robert Beverley, *The History of Virginia: In Four Parts* (London: 1722; revised ed., Richmond, VA: Randolph, 1855), 55–56.

10. Beverley, *History of Virginia*, 219–222.

11. Quoted in http://www.encyclopediavirginia.org/_Against_Runaway _Servants_1657-1658, and http://www.encyclopediavirginia.org/_Against_ffor nication_1661-1662

12. "Diary of John Harrower," 76–77.

13. Ibid., 77–78.

14. Ibid., 78–83.

15. Ibid., 83–84.

16. Ibid., 88–92.

17. Ibid., 92–99.

18. Ibid., 99–102.

19. Ibid., 98, 101, 103–105.

20. Ibid., 105–107.

21. Ibid., 103, 107; Alan Gallay, ed., *Voice of the Old South: Eyewitness Accounts, 1528–1861* (Athens: University of Georgia Press, 1994), 122–123.

CHAPTER TWELVE

New England Apprentices

Family was the bedrock institution of colonial society, and yet economic necessity often resulted in its undermining. Early American families were primarily agricultural; even so, arable land often became scarce in some colonies, and large families were sometimes hard put to find land for their sons and husbandmen for their daughters. The institution of apprenticeship had developed in England as a means to train young people in crafts that were regulated by guilds. But no such guilds existed in the colonies, hence apprenticeship became more of a system to provide vocational education for children, or even more, to feed and clothe and educate extra mouths for which the nuclear family struggled to provide. In England, apprenticeship was the means by which an individual could become a freeman with civic rights; in America apprenticeship was the means by which an individual could learn a trade that would allow him or her to participate as an informed and independent citizen in society. Apprenticeship, therefore, performed the same function in colonial America that public education would perform in the 19th, 20th, and 21st centuries.[1]

But unlike the often distant relationship between public school teacher and pupil, the master and apprentice had a close, even familial relationship. Although an indenture or contract regulated the relationship between apprentice and master, nevertheless in practice, over the space of many years, the master was as a father figure to the apprentice, who was treated as part of the family. Indentures required the master to feed, clothe, shelter, and educate apprentices—the master assumed the personal responsibility of correcting the apprentice as well, which meant the master used the same disciplinary rules, including corporeal punishment, as a father on a son or daughter.[2]

In England, the laws regulating the relationship between master and apprentice were systematized by the Statute of Artificers in 1562 and the Poor Law of 1601. These laws provided guidance to colonial authorities in how to deal with the poor, particularly poor children. The practice of the indentured contract continued; colonials followed the English standard of apprenticeship for seven years or until a boy was 24 and a girl 21. In 17th-century Boston, apprentices had to serve this seven-year period if they expected to be accepted as journeymen in their crafts.[3]

Unlike during the 19th century, when in England the guild system disappeared and in America the contractual system of apprenticeship declined in the wake of the demand for industrial labor, there were certain legal safeguards protecting the rights of the apprentice in the colonial system. The indenture was a legal contract recognized as binding by magistrates in the 13 colonies. Typically, there existed a distinction between an indenture regulating a labor arrangement (the traditional form of indentured servitude) from an indenture regulating an apprenticeship, wherein the master agreed to furnish a youth with years of training in a skill. But often the arrangement was not clear, as in the case of the indenture agreed upon between Mary Hobson and Latham Clarke in May 1668, in Portsmouth, Rhode Island. Mary Hobson was the daughter of Mary Hobson of Newport and the late Henry Hobson; she was apparently already indentured to Elizabeth Conagrave, upon what terms or capacity is unknown. She now, "vallentaryly . . . Indenture Covinant and binde my selfe unto Latham Clarke Seny[r] of Rhoad Island for the space of five yeares, duringe which time I doe promis and ingage unto my said master to searve him trewly and faithfully, in any Servis of imployment as my said master or his assignes shall See good to imploy me about which is lawfull duringe the said time of my Searvis." Mary promised not to neglect her master, engage in debased behavior, or entertain "unCivell Company." The master, in his turn, agreed, upon "Consideration of the said apprentis trew and lawfull performance," "to finde hur meate drinke and aparill sutable for such a servant, for the space of five yeares"; the master also agreed to provide Mary, upon the end of her term, "one New Sutte of aparrille suttable to weare one hollidayes or other dayes." But the indenture, although it called Mary an "apprentice," did not specify that she would learn anything in particular. Often girls were taught to read and write, or the intricacies of housekeeping, but this indenture was silent. Likewise, an indenture from 1721 Boston contracted an Indian youth, James Bryant, to a master, Thomas Hathaway, for seven years. Hathaway did not, however, agree to train Bryant in a skill; rather, Hathaway agreed to provide Bryant's mother with a sheep and a cash payment of 20 shillings.[4]

A straightforward indenture providing for the mutual benefit of master and apprentice is found in the records of New Hampshire for 1676. Nathan Knight agreed with Samuel Whidden of Portsmouth, New Hampshire, to serve for "twelve years and five months, . . . during which time the said apprentice his said master faithfully shall serve, his lawful secrets shall keep, and commands shall gladly do, damage unto his said master he shall not do, nor see to be done of others, but to the best of his power shall give timely notice thereof to his said master. Fornication he shall not commit, nor contract matrimony within the said time. The goods of his said master, he shall not spend or lend. He shall not play cards, or dice, or any other unlawful game, whereby his said master may have damage in his own goods, or others, taverns, he shall not haunt, or from his master's business absent himself by day or by night, but in all things shall behave himself as a faithful apprentice ought to do." The master, in turn, agreed to "teach and instruct" his apprentice "in the art and mystery as mason," besides finding him adequate food, shelter, clothing, lodging, and education: "to go to school to write."[5]

If Nathan Knight or any other apprentice should break the indenture by loose living, disobedience, or running away, they paid a heavy penalty. Alexander Maxwell found this out in 1653 Plymouth, when he was "publicly whipped for abusing his master." Another apprentice, John Cooke of Salem, was "severely whipped" and had "a shackle put upon his leg for resisting his master's authority." Thomas Manchester of Connecticut, "servent to Mr. Perry, being accused by his master for being drunk, and for giving his master uncomely language, for which his master having given him some correction, the Court (only) caused him to be sett in the stocks for a certain time." Will Mendlue of Plymouth, in 1635, was "whipped for attempting uncleanes with the maid serv[an]t of" of his master, Will Palmer, "& for running away from his master being forcibly brought againe by Penwatechet a Manomet Indian." In the 17th century, Connecticut magistrates ordered female servant Ruth Acie to be whipped for "stubornes, lyeing, stealing from her Mrs. and yeilding to filthy dalliance with Will Harding." Servants could be whipped for playing cards, abusive language, and stealing as well. The early laws of Connecticut, the "Blue Laws," granted to magistrates the right of correcting children and servants who "shall bee convicted of any stuborne, or rebellious carriage against their parents or governors"; magistrates could "committ such person or persons to the House of Correction; and there to remaine under hard labour, and severe punnishment so long as the Courte, or the major parte of the Magistrates, shall judge meete." Runaway apprentices were liable for extra service in the colonies. The Connecticut Blue Laws demanded that escaped servants, upon recapture, "shall serve theire said masters, as they shall be apprehended or retained, the treble term, or three fold time of theire absence in such kinde." In 1639, Plymouth, the apprentice Simon agreed to serve two years for every occasion that he ran away from his master. John Robinson, in 1653 Salem, had to serve an extra year besides being whipped for running away. Apprentices very often, it seems, tried to escape by ship. The government of Massachusetts responded in 1694 with the following act: "Every Apprentice or covenant servant who shall unlawfully absent himself from his master and enter himself on any ship or vessel as aforesaid, with intent to leave his master's service, or continue there more than the space of twenty-four hours, and be thereof convicted before their majesties' justices in general sessions of the peace within the same county, *shall forfeit unto his master such further service*, from and after the expiration of the term which his said master had in him at the time of his departure, as the said court shall order, not exceeding one year." Even with such penalties, colonial newspapers had frequent advertisements placed by masters who were seeking escaped servants. One example of many comes from the *Massachusetts Spy*, January 1797: "Two Pence Half Penny Reward: Ran away from the subscriber, on the 15th of this month Simon Remington, an indented lad, 16 years of age, about five feet eight inches high, slender built, dark brown hair; had on when he went away a cinnamon coloured coat, Jane waistcoat and overalls, and a round hat. Who ever will take up the said runaway, and return him to his master shall receive the above reward."[6]

That the master might loan a young apprentice/servant to another is found in a cryptic comment in a letter from Mather Byles Jr. to his father, in 1765. Byles, a Harvard graduate and clergyman, served as pastor of the New London, Connecticut, congregational church from 1757 to 1768. He was married and had children and required domestic assistance, an indentured servant. Initially he contracted with a boy, who left after his indenture was finished, upon which he contracted with a maid. Who exactly this girl was, and under what terms she served, is unclear from his letters. Byles wrote his father in December 1765: "My Negroe Girl I have sent back to Roxbury. She was so intolerably troublesome that I could by no means keep her any longer." This letter implies that the girl was a servant on loan from a friend in Roxbury, a town next to Boston, and that because she was not able to perform her duties according to Byles's specifications, the loan was returned.[7]

This young black girl found herself in an institution that so many thousands of young blacks, Indians, and whites experienced, in which their parents—if they were still alive—abandoned them to a public legal system whereby they were bought and sold, traded and used as commodities. The adults who were responsible for the system had their consciences mollified by the tender sermons of pastoral leaders who blessed such institutions with godly and scriptural authority. Adults taught children duty rather than love—and this duty was, following the Fifth Commandment, to be given not only to parents and relations but to masters, teachers, and other authority figures. "When my Father and my Mother forsake me, then the Lord will take me up," counseled one English minister, quoting Psalm 27.

Words full of Consolation to all God's faithful Servants; who, by doing his Will, and living in Obedience to his Laws, are entitled to the Benefit of them, in whatever Calamities they may happen to be in this Life. And considering the Uncertainty and insufficiency of all worldly Comforts, it is happy for them, that they have this assurance, since nothing else can give them any firm and solid hope of Security in a *Prosperous*, or of redress and support in an *Adverse* State. All other Dependences are too weak and unstable to build any Confidence upon; and whatever visible Assistances we can propose to our Selves, are so deficient and frail, that they *may*, and probably *will*, fail and shrink from us when stand most in need of them. The natural Affection and Tenderness of Parents, how deep and strong soever the Impressions of it are, is not always to be relied upon. *A Woman*, the Lord tells us by his Prophet, *may forget her sucking Child*, so as *not to have compassion of the Son of her Womb*, Isai. XLIX. 15. And *Fathers* and *Mothers* abandon and *forsake* their own Offspring, as *David* here intimates, and History and Experience attest. What then can we securely repose our selves on, and have recourse to for Protection and Support, in case of Danger and Distress?

The answer, of course, is God, the sermonizer, the Rev. John Waugh, said this day of August 24, 1713, in London. Waugh preached before 1,400 apprentices and servants about their duty. These children had admittedly been placed in difficult circumstances. In some cases, the father had taken to drink and was unable to support his child. A mother might "withdraw" her affection "for weak and trivial Causes." But, of course, in Defoe's London in the early 18th century, oftentimes "parents are constrained to leave their Children destitute and helpless, for want of Ability to relieve them; when neither their Estate, nor their Industry, can furnish them with a sufficient Maintenance for themselves and their Family. In such indigence as this, not happening through any default of the *Parent*, the Providence of God is engaged to take Care of the Children." Providence, said Rev. Waugh, had "put into the Hearts of your Benefactors, whom He hath made his Instruments in Supplying your Wants, to provide those who might teach you to Read, and Work; to instruct you in the Principles of the Christian Religion, and initiate you in the Practice of all those Duties that relate to *God*, and your *Neighbour*; to inure you betimes to Labour and Industry; and afterwards to place you out Apprentices to some honest Trade and Imployment, in order to your getting a comfortable Subsistence in this world, and securing eternal Bliss in the next." Children who were servants and apprentices, therefore, owed a "*Duty to God*" by willingness "to demean your Selves, every one in the Station wherein God hath placed you, and according to the Abilities He hath given you." Duty to God implied duty to "your *Masters according to the Flesh*." Scripture itself demanded that it be "incumbent upon Apprentices and Servants" to obey "the Commands of their Masters." Rev. Waugh knew that youths would sometimes be put in service in places that were disagreeable, to masters who were unfair, doing work that was "mean and servile." But the servant must abide by "the Custom of the Place you live in." The loyal servant must patiently submit to all censures and reproofs of the master. A young servant must be faithful, and never lie, or else they might earn "their portion in the Lake which burneth with Fire and Brimstone."[8]

An American clergyman, Jeremy Belknap, given to such sermons, found himself, ironically, in the situation described by Rev. Waugh, of a parent unable to provide adequately for a family, and as a result must consider apprenticing a child. Belknap was a congregational minister who lived in Dover, New Hampshire. He and wife Ruth had to care for six children during a time, the American War of Independence, when Belknap found it difficult to keep "the belly and back from grumbling and the kitchen-fire from going out." Belknap as a result had "to plant my own bread-corn . . . , and expect to handle the hoe as a common laborer, as my wife is forced to do the wheel, to the great injury of her health, and the neglect of the other necessary business of the famly." The people in his parish in the small town of Dover, situated on the Cochecho River, found it similarly difficult to make ends meet; Belknap was like most New England clergymen on a fixed income; his parishioners found it burdensome to make their annual obligation to the pastor. Besides, inflation was making currency worthless, and the purchase price of items exorbitant.[9]

By war's end, the financial situation of neither the parish nor their pastor had improved significantly. Belknap's father Joseph, a Boston craftsman, had afforded Harvard College for his only son. But Jeremy had several sons and daughters, none of whom could he afford to educate in the way he preferred. Indeed, during the war he had tutored his children, as Dover had neither the will nor the means to hold a public school. By June 1783, Belknap, knowing that he could not send Joseph (Jo), his oldest, to Harvard, decided the next best thing would be to apprentice Jo in a trade that would be a means for a useful, remunerative career in adulthood. Belknap was a writer and historian, who was negotiating the terms to print his *History of New-Hampshire* with a Philadelphia printer, Robert Aitken. Belknap was using his friend Ebenezer Hazard as negotiator of terms with Aitken. In a letter written on June 10, he asked Hazard, of Aitken: "Does he want an apprentice? I have a lively boy in his 14th year whom I would wish to put under such a master as I think he is." He asked Hazard to approach Aitken with the idea, but to write the printer's response on a separate piece of paper enclosed to Belknap: "You will not perhaps see the reason of this at once; but after you have been married sixteen years, if you need it, I will tell you."[10]

Robert Aitken responded favorably to the idea of having Joseph Belknap journey to Philadelphia to serve as a printer's apprentice. Belknap was agreeable as well, though, he wrote in July, two matters stood in the way. One was "maternal fondness," which "strongly plead that he should go under the care of some very trusty person, and one whom he has some knowledge of." The second problem, was that Jo had never been inoculated for the smallpox, and Philadelphia was reputedly a city where the disease was frequent and prevalent. Belknap was at a loss how to get the boy inoculated. If a solution could be found to this issue, Belknap thought to send his son to Philadelphia in September, where he and the master, Aitken, could have "*a time on trial* before any indentures pass." Belknap hoped that the agreement would involve some schooling for his son, which during wartime Dover had been nonexistent. Ruth Belknap, the mother, "wishes to know how often during his apprenticeship she may expect the pleasure of a visit from him? which may also conduce to the convenience of fitting him with clothing, linen, &c."[11]

During the waning months of the summer of 1783, Belknap, his wife, and his son waited to see whether or not Robert Aitken was agreeable, Jo was agreeable, and it seemed the best thing to do in the current economic situation. By September 1, everyone involved were in agreement, and Belknap told his friend Hazard that he "shall now do the best I can to prepare him for his voyage, and desire my friends in the sea-port towns to look out for him a good opportunity of conveyance, and some careful person with whom I may trust him." Three weeks later Belknap wrote, "I cannot yet hear of a passage for Jo. The tailors are fitting him up for his voyage." A week passed and Belknap had heard that "the seaport towns are very sickly, and we hear Philadelphia is remarkably so, which makes us concerned about Jo, though no passage presents as yet." Another week passed and the parents' anxiety increased: "We hear of a great sickness in Philadelphia and the places adjacent: if this be so, it may be best for Mr. Aitken not to have an addition to his family, nor for Jo to be absent from home, till it is abated." Meanwhile, Ebenezer Hazard wrote Belknap to tell him that "Mr. Aitken has lately refused an apprentice, and is anxiously expecting Josey's arrival, as he now wants him." Hazard was friends with a physician, Geraldus Clarkson, who offered to inoculate Jo, upon arrival at Philadelphia, gratis. At the same time, however, Belknap had heard from "a gentleman of character, whose information seemed direct," that the "epidemical sickness" in Philadelphia was the "yellow spotted fever, and that great numbers had died." Such alarming "accounts, you may well think, have affected the minds of parents concerned for a son whom they are about sending thither." Hazard nonchalantly replied, "You seem to hear more of sickness in Philadelphia than we do who live here." Belknap, writing from Portsmouth on October 27, reported that "it is a vexatious circumstance to me that I have not yet been able to get a passage for my son. There has not that I can learn a vessel sailed from hence for Philadelphia since July." Changing plans, "I must now convey Josey to Boston, and let him wait there, to get a passage, which there is a much better chance for there than there can be here." Then, four days later, Belknap learned that a ship was to sail to Philadelphia from Portsmouth. But "the slow and uncertain movement of our Pascataqua [Piscataqua] merchants and ship-masters" eventually made Belknap realize that he must travel to Boston, which he did in the first week of November, where, "to my great joy, found my desire accomplished. The sloop on board of which he will go is to sail on Sunday, and I have agreed with the master (or rather owner) for his passage, he to live on the ship's provisions, at the price of eight dollars." Belknap packed in "Jo's chest two English guineas, one French one, and ten crowns," to pay for the passage, as well as "for a Bible, book of Arithmetic, and Entick's Spelling Dictionary," for Jo's use. Belknap wrote four days later that Jo "sailed from this place [Boston] yesterday on board the sloop 'Caroline,' Moses Killsa master, for Philadelphia. She is a fine new large vessel, laden with rum and flaxseed; and I had the very great pleasure of finding that there was a young gentleman named Myrick, a passenger on board, who was so very kind as to let Josey have part of his cabbin and mattress on the voyage. . . . If I hear of his safe arrival at Philadelphia, my desires will be crowned." The parents had to wait a full month to hear of Jo's safe arrival.[12]

Jo's apprenticeship with printer Aitken began well. Belknap was horrified to learn, however, that Aitken "laments exceedingly Josey's want of education." The problem was, Belknap explained, the town of Dover, which during, and so far after, the war paid no attention to public education. As a result, "a sense of duty to him, and a regard to his interest, in conjunction with my other children, have led me to a determination, as soon as ever they are of sufficient age, to put them out of this place. It is not in my power to place them at public schools where their board must be paid for; but if I can get them into some good family in the rank of apprentices, in places where they may have some opportunities of profiting by evening schools, and at the same time be learning some trade to get their future living in the world, it is all that I can do for them." Belknap continued, "I believe that a lad of tolerable good sense, who sets out in the world with such views as these, and has the opportunity for good instruction in a decent way to get his bread, has really a better prospect before him, and is more likely to turn out well, than one who places his dependence on a paternal inheritance." Hazard, writing from Philadelphia the first week of January 1784, wrote that Aitken "does not know what is in him, but the folks downstairs (the workmen) like him, and the folks upstairs (the family) like him." Jo seemed to like his situation quite well and began to learn the craft. This pleased Belknap such that he responded, "If Mr. A[itken] thinks he can make Josey a profitable apprentice, and you will take the trouble to act in my stead to bind him, please to send me the proper form of a letter of attorney for the purpose, and also the form of the indenture which is used in such cases." Months passed. By March, Belknap sent Hazard the "power of attorney, drawn agreeable to your form, with the addition of the precise age of my son, that there may be no misunderstanding on that head." Belknap asked his friend Hazard to speak privately to Jo, once "the ceremony of binding Jos is performed, . . . to comment upon the several articles in the indenture, that he may have his duty fixed in his mind, and remember that each part of the covenant is a condition on his part of the fulfilment of the stipulation of his master."[13]

As time passed, Jo became a part of the family, such that Aitken felt that he could correct Jo the same way he corrected his own children. After three years, Jo resented the correction, and Aitken resented the resentment, and master and apprentice began to fall out. Indeed, by May 1787, "I find the breach is grown so wide that they *both* desire a separation. A[itken], *by his* own account, has made a very free use of 'the fist' and the 'knotted cord,' both very bad instruments of reformation in the hands of a perfervid Caledonian" (that is, passionate Scotsman). Once, Jo had such "a blow received from his master's fist, on the Sunday noon at dinner, which gave him a black eye, and unfitted him for a *decent* appearance in any worshipping assembly." Jo further told his father that Aitken "has had six apprentices, and that but *one* ever served his time out, and that he has shown him marks of the old man's cruelty." Jo consulted a friend and Philadelphia physician, Dr. Clarkson, who agreed that Jo must separate. Jo returned home to Dover and was immediately apprenticed to another printer, John Mycall of Newburyport, Massachusetts. Unfortunately, Jo's experience with his new master was little better. The master and apprentice did not get along and frequently quarreled. The master threatened to request an end to the relationship, which would threaten Jo's ability to find work as a journeyman printer upon the conclusion of his apprenticeship. With his father's constant advice and counsel, Jo patiently endured to the end. "Remember my Son," Belknap counseled at one point, "the great Dr. Franklin," himself an apprentice, "set out to get his living in the world with much less than you will have."[14]

Jeremy Belknap was a middle-class minister, a local leader, a respected writer, and a historian, who was involved in the creation of successful government out of the chaos of revolution. Yet, through Jo's apprenticeships with Robert Aitken and John Mycall, even the respectable clergyman Jeremy Belknap could experience what so many humans had experienced in America: the necessity and negativism of bondage. Belknap was conservative—in politics he was a Federalist—who became adamantly opposed to any restriction on human rights. He was an early abolitionist in New Hampshire and Massachusetts, seeking an end to slavery and to guarantee equal rights for blacks. Even before the American Revolution, Belknap was a vocal opponent of slavery, writing to the *Boston Evening Post*, in November 1772, that Scripture does not condone the enslavement of a people's entire posterity. The African people, he wrote, are under no curse from God. They were unjustly driven from the home continent. Europeans, and Americans, "have no more right to make Slaves of the Africans than they have to make Slaves of us."[15]

Jeremy Belknap and others like him who experienced the American War of Independence from 1775 to 1783, and took to heart the words of freedom and liberty upon which Americans professed to fight and die, found the contradiction of bondage staring them in the face.

Notes

1. Robert F. Seybolt, *Apprenticeship & Apprenticeship Education in Colonial New England & New York* (New York: Columbia University, 1917).

2. Ibid., 14.

3. Ibid., 22, 25–26.

4. Richard B. Morris, *Government and Labor in Early America* (New York: Harper and Row, 1946), 364–365; *Early Records of the Town of Portsmouth* (Portsmouth, RI: E. L. Freeman and Sons, 1901), 409–410; "Witness to an Indenture, 9 October, 1721," *Miscellaneous Manuscripts*, Massachusetts Historical Society.

5. Quoted in Seybolt, *Apprenticeship*, 29.

6. Ibid., 30–32; *Blue Laws of Connecticut. The Code of 1650; Being a Compilation of the Earliest Laws and Orders of the General Court of Connecticut* (Cincinnati: U. P. James, n. d.), 30, 66, 108, 112.

7. Mather Byles Jr. to Catherine Byles, 12/8/1765, *Byles Family Papers*, Massachusetts Historical Society.

8. John Waugh, *A Sermon Preach'd at the Parish Church of St. Bridget, alias Bride, August 24th, 1713, Being the Festival of St. Bartholomew; At a Meeting of about 1400 Persons of Both Sexes* (London: Strahan and Downing, 1713).

9. Jeremy Belknap to Ebenezer Hazard, 10/23/1783, Belknap Papers, *Collections of the Massachusetts Historical Society (CMHS)*, ser. 5, vol. 2 (Boston: Massachusetts Historical Society, 1877), 267; Jane Belknap Marcou, *Life of Jeremy Belknap, D. D. The Historian of New Hampshire* (New York: Harper, 1847), 120.

10. Belknap to Hazard, 6/10/1783, *CMHS*, ser. 5, vol. 2, 215.

11. Belknap to Hazard, 7/14/1783, *CMHS*, ser. 5, vol, 2, 230–232.

12. Belknap to Hazard, 9/1/1783, 9/20/1783, 9/29/1783, 10/4/1783, 10/12/1783, 10/27/1783; Hazard to Belknap, 10/8/1783, 10/22/1783, 10/31/1783, 11/7/1783, 11/11/1783, 12/17/1783, *CMHS*, ser. 5, vol. 2, 245, 250, 257, 259, 260–261, 266, 269–271, 273–275, 286.

13. Belknap to Hazard, 12/21/1783, 1/13/1784; Belknap to Hazard, 3/18/1784; Hazard to Belknap, 1/7/1784, 1/16/1784, *CMHS*, ser. 5, vol. 2, 287, 289–290, 293, 298–299, 320.

14. Belknap to Hazard, 4/29/1787, 5/18/1787, *CMHS*, ser. 5, vol. 2, 473, 478–479; Jeremy Belknap to Joseph Belknap Jr., 10/6/1790, *Belknap Papers*, New Hampshire Historical Society.

15. *Supplement to the Boston Evening Post*, November 30, 1772.

CHAPTER THIRTEEN

Servants and the American Revolution

One of the great ironies in American history is that the British Americans of the 17th and 18th centuries—at the same time that they professed human rights (the Glorious Revolution of 1689 and the American Revolution of 1776) and embraced Protestant Christianity as the dominant bases for belief and culture—countenanced, invited, encouraged, and allowed human bondage in its most humiliating and cruel forms. A disregard for human rights, for the teachings of Jesus of Nazareth, has continued in America long after those words were penned in recognition of "the laws of Nature and Nature's God," that "all men are created equal, endowed by their Creator with certain unalienable rights, that among these are life, liberty, and the pursuit of happiness." Poverty, inequality, bondage: are these the real inheritance of previous human society and culture? Although Jesus predicted that "you will always have the poor," he nevertheless called upon his followers to cherish the impoverished, the helpless, the meek, the fatherless, and the widowed. Yet his followers in British America turned a blind eye to Jesus and exploited, harmed, imprisoned, starved, and neglected other humans, ignoring his teachings. What kind of society professes great ideas but refuses to act upon them? America was built upon an idea; and perhaps no other people in history have been so beguiled by great ideas than the Americans.

The French writer and philosopher J. Hector St. John de Crevecoeur, having resided in America for many years before and during the American Revolution, and notwithstanding the injustices he witnessed in the South, could still enthusiastically exclaim, in *Letters from an American Farmer*, written in 1782, that America is "the asylum of freedom, . . . the cradle of future nations and the refuge of distressed Europeans." Crevecoeur, a European American writing for Europeans, believed that the immigrants who crossed the Atlantic

Ocean to America were changed by the wide-open wilderness environment and the social and cultural institutions peculiar to Americans. The European became a "new man" in America. The European immigrant who had experienced the sameness and degeneration of European peasantry found in America a frontier environment conducive to feelings of liberty and opportunity. Land was available for those with the courage and energy to build farms from the forest. There was a profound sense of equality among the poor and middle-class farm immigrants. America was not a land for aristocrats, those with privileges of inherited wealth and power, but rather for the poor and downtrodden, the seekers and discoverers. The American, in short, according to Crevecoeur, was a new human living in a new society that, like youth, was filled with purity, potential, and energy—unlike the Old World society of Europe, stuck in the old ways and prejudices of a traditional society.[1]

Many of the images and concepts by which we best know America—such as the Statue of Liberty and its proclamation "Give me your tired, your poor, Your huddled masses yearning to breathe free, The wretched refuse of your teeming shore. Send these, the homeless, tempest-tost to me, I lift my lamp beside the golden door!"; the American dream of economic independence; the ideal of American democracy; the words of the Declaration of Independence: "We hold these truths to be self-evident, that all men are created equal"—give weight to the contention that America is still a New World inhabited by Crevecoeur's "New Man" who lives according to freedom, liberty, and opportunity. Americans have seen themselves as the defenders of freedom and the open society throughout the world.

The American is most often identified with the idea of democracy, which promises much, though the reality always falls short. The promise is of wide participation in government, free and open competition among diverse groups, and self-determination. Democracy offers the vision of individuals working together to achieve their own particular goals, using similar means to accomplish collectively individual wealth and freedom. History offers few examples of really successful democracies, success being defined as actual structures of government and society that make concrete the image that the word *democracy* conjures up. *Democracy*—like *liberty, freedom, equality*—is elusive, visualized in the mind and a part of one's dreams yet never quite fulfilled. Another French observer of America, Alexis de Tocqueville, who traveled throughout America in the 1820s, observed, in *Democracy in America*, that, respecting 19th-century American society, the typical American was without pretense to birth or social rank, engaged in lifelong entrepreneurship. The American commoner was restless, hardworking, always seeking something, especially a satisfactory amount of wealth, which was typically just out of reach. Such characteristics formed the backbone not only of American capitalism but of American democracy as well. The aggressiveness of the American in business spilled over to local assemblies, state legislatures, and courthouses. Ideas of American justice, morality, and law had a pragmatic, businesslike approach. The American democracy, like American business, involved controversy rather than conciliation, anger and argument rather than acceptance and apathy. Even in the 20th century, in the wake of World War I and World War II, when traditional values were being challenged everywhere and democracy was under attack from the left and the right, it was diversity rather than sameness, relativism rather than absolutism, that strengthened American democracy.

Thomas Paine, in *Common Sense*, seems to have identified the general sense of self-perception of the people of North America when he wrote in 1776 that it contradicted nature and reason that a small island thousands of miles away should rule over a vast country where existed freedom and opportunity rather than stagnation and despair. Liberty and freedom were watchwords of American republicanism during the age of revolution.

One of the most famous revolutionaries, Thomas Jefferson, had a lifelong dream die on Independence Day, 1826. The epitaph that he composed to mark his passing highlighted the three great achievements of his life: creating the Declaration of Independence, penning the Statute of Religious Freedom, and founding the University of Virginia. These three trumped, in his mind, his other achievements: president of the United States, vice president of the United States, minister to France, governor of Virginia, secretary of state. The focus of Jefferson's life, as he reflected on it during his final years, was "human freedom." Jefferson thought radically about human freedom, even as he contradicted his grand ideas by participating in the enslavement of other humans. Jefferson owned slaves for 50 years after he penned the words: "We hold these truths to be self-evident, that all men are created equal." His dream of a society that fully promoted individual freedom, of individuals such as himself being willing to take extreme actions for the sake of human freedom, was unfulfilled upon his death. But Jefferson believed, despite his personal failings, as well as the failings of the United States in regard to human freedom, that the actions of revolutionaries, marked by the Declaration of Independence in 1776, would someday fulfill the promise of the American Revolution, which transcended his life and the lives of his contemporaries. Jefferson believed, as he wrote in 1818 to his old friend John Adams, that with their passing, even so, the phenomenon that they had created, the American Revolution, was far from over.

Jefferson was one of the most radical of the Founding Fathers. He clearly seems to have been ahead of his time, although the many years since his death have failed to realize his dream of the unshackling of the individual from the constraints of the standards and institutions of modern society and culture. To be sure, multicultural awareness, the emergence of women and people of diverse racial and ethnic backgrounds as political forces, expanding suffrage, the democratization and integration of education and public facilities, points to expanded individual freedoms. But this conclusion is only true if one's definitions of "revolution" and "freedom" are limited to an external, institutional, structural meaning. There is a more fundamental meaning to these two concepts, one that transcends the normal meaning assigned by historians and politicians. Revolution has several standard definitions: a cycle or rotation; a successful colonial revolt; a violent political change; or a novel and dramatic change that completely supplants the past. Revolution usually means an event that occurs over a specific time period with a clearly defined end. Jefferson's use of the word "revolution," however, implies an ongoing process without end.

The American Revolution never ended, Jefferson believed. The idea seems a bit absurd, but consider it. The idea of an ongoing revolution implies that revolution is made anew by each person who is willing to formulate, believe, and express his or her own singular experiences and ideals. The idea implies that revolution is not bound by war, government, or time, but is a more spiritual, amorphous phenomenon. It implies much about the time of the actual American War of Independence—that the people of the time had a personal experience. Below the surface lies a burning passion for freedom, for liberty of thought and conscience, for personal knowledge unencumbered by traditions, standards, and institutions. One's "glorious cause," to use the phrase of the American patriots, is personal knowledge and liberty. Oppression comes in a variety of different forms: in the past it was the oppression of an imperialistic government; today it is the oppression of a well-meaning government built on a brilliant document, the Constitution, that was meant to provide order and stability more than freedom and liberty.

The perspective of history tells us that America has come closest to accomplishing freedom and liberty than any government of all time. Perhaps it is impossible to have a government that grants complete freedom. Indeed, as Thomas Paine noted two centuries ago, government and individual liberty are at odds. Government is often perceived as a "necessary evil"—necessary to prevent the chaos generated by rampant liberty. But deep inside, doesn't the individual yearn to break from the oppression that forestalls complete freedom? It is there within us, this sense of wanting to do anything in one's power to overcome oppression so to breathe free, unimpeded, unstructured air. Freud figured that such a sense of freedom, if realized, would yield random acts of sexual and abusive terror. Indeed, there have been those in American history who view liberty through pessimistic eyes. The Hamiltonians among us seek freedom as granted through government rather than *government granted through freedom*. No wonder Jefferson distrusted the Constitution, which was created while he was in France, in 1787. For it countered his meaning of revolution.

The great error of Madison, Washington, Adams, and Hamilton (the Federalists) was to make government an end in itself, rather than a means to an end—the means to the "end" of government. The wise parent who raises the child to be independent knows that the consequence is complete and utter independence. The best teacher teaches the student to be an independent learner. The old cliché, "the government that governs best governs least," should perhaps be reworked to conform to the philosophy of Jefferson: "government should govern itself out of existence." John Adams once wrote that he studied politics so that his sons and grandsons could study architecture, music, and art. But he clearly failed. His son John Quincy Adams lived his life in government and politics, as did his grandson Charles Francis Adams. Adams should have studied politics so that politics would never again exist.

The American Revolution first implemented the humanistic ideals of the European Renaissance and the 18th-century Enlightenment. Renaissance thinkers, reaching the limitations on freedom of thought imposed by Aristotelian logic and Medieval Scholasticism, argued that individual experience was the cornerstone to knowledge, and the government that promoted this individual quest for knowledge would gain the greatest allegiance of its citizens. Such was the "civic humanism" of Renaissance city-states. Machiavelli's *other* great work, the *Discourses*, argues precisely this point. The poet and orator Petrarch, not a statesman but the leader of the Italian literati, developed a historical perspective that established the uniqueness of a given historical epoch—and the uniqueness of the individual as well. Michel de Montaigne, the 16th-century French essayist, though a conservative thinker who resisted political change, nevertheless fought to retain the sanctity of personal knowledge and free thought. Montaigne was an intellectual revolutionary who fought battles against oppression from the library of his Bordeaux chateau. But was he therefore any less a revolutionary than Jefferson? The battle for the ideas of freedom of conscience are most grimly fought within one's own mind. It is an easy thing to give in to the ways of culture, to the standards and trends of another's choosing, not one's own. The great challenge of human existence is to formulate one's own views independent of one's times, then to live accordingly.

Montaigne wrote a series of *essais* exploring life, self, and time. One of his most compelling is *Of Cannibals*. Montaigne was fascinated by the discovery of the New World and its peoples and tried to find out as much as he could about the customs and institutions of the Indians. He learned that their way of life was completely different from the "civilized" Europeans. The Indians wore the skins of animals—if they wore clothes at all. They sometimes practiced cannibalism. They did not know the techniques of metalworking. They did not practice Christianity. They lived in huts and skin dwellings, hunted and gathered for at least part of the year, practiced brutality against their enemies, had no use for money, were not concerned with private ownership of land, and painted and tattooed their bodies with all sorts of strange images and colors. But more, Montaigne learned that they lived and fought by codes of valor and honor; they lived in accommodation to the natural environment rather than tried to mold it artificially; they practiced a simple lifestyle accepting what nature and fate had given them. At the conclusion of his essay Montaigne argued that the Indians were more civilized and less savage than the Europeans, whose constant greed required them to acquire more and more of everything and build as many artificial structures and institutions as they could. Europeans could not accept and be content with what they had; hence, they were the true savages and barbarians. Montaigne, a representative European aristocrat, knew that he spent a life that was artificially raised above the peasants who tilled the soil on his estate. In such essays as *Of Cannibals*, Montaigne was yearning for the simplicity of life of the European peasant and American Indian. These were lives of inherent equality based on the acceptance of life without pretension. This was "to live appropriately," Montaigne concluded.

The Frenchman Crevecoeur 300 years later in America reached the same conclusion. The soil of America, he wrote, "feeds, . . . clothes us; from it we draw even a great exuberancy, our best meat, our richest drink; the very honey of our bees comes from this privileged spot. No wonder we should thus cherish its possession; no wonder that so many Europeans who have never been able to say that such portion of land was theirs cross the Atlantic to realize that happiness." Crevecoeur, like Montaigne, fascinated with birds, learned from these creatures, as well as a host of others, that "the whole economy of what we proudly call the brute creation is admirable in every circumstance; and vain man, though adorned with the additional gift of reason, might learn from the perfection of instinct how to regulate the follies and how to temper the errors" that are consequences of the use of reason. America was the place by which the ungovernable passions, the unyielding excesses, of humans could be tempered, leveled, brought close to the undiscriminating rich soil of the fertile landscape.

This place described by Montaigne, by Crevecoeur, by Jefferson, this ideal place America, was on the verge of history. Indian and black servants and slaves as well as the white indentured servants, free-willers, and transported prisoners of war and felons came to America, on their own accord or against their will, in the colonial period, to a place caught between the institutions of the past, which included bondage in all of its forms, and the humanistic traditions that were being expressed in the present as Enlightenment ideas of freedom and liberty.

In this verge of time, 1776, was found the complexity of the idea of the revolution, freedom, liberty, in a land built in part by bondage, servitude, slavery—and indeed even when war is fought for these great principles and victory achieved, and government is built on these principles, still bondage, servitude, and slavery exist. Notwithstanding the great numbers of people who voluntarily or involuntarily immigrated in bondage during the colonial period, during and after the American War of Independence, the enslavement of blacks, the continuing immigration of free-willers, indentured servitude, debt imprisonment, and apprenticeship continued for years afterward. Examples are many. Jefferson wrote a French correspondent that even in the time that he wrote, 1786, "so desirous are the poor of Europe to get to America, where they may better their condition, that being unable to pay their passage, they will agree to serve two or three years on their arrival there, rather than not to go." Jefferson had personal experience in this regard. In a letter, preserved at the Library of Congress, from Jefferson to James Madison, April 19, 1809, Jefferson outlined a contract in which he sold the indenture of one John Freeman to Madison for $400. The original indenture for Freeman, perhaps a free black, was for 11 years; he had about 6.5 years remaining when he was sold to Madison. Other servants in the wake of the American Revolution were immigrants, such as "John Hesselbach and Anna Elizabetha his wife." In December 1784, the couple "bound themselves Servants to Frederick Boulange of the city of Philadelphia, Merchant, to Serve him four years to have customary Freedom Suits." The same couple four years later in 1788 bound themselves out again to John Edwards for four years. In Maryland, in August 1800, "John Andrew Maurer his wife Anna Barbary, Son John Andrew and Daughters Anna Barbara and Catherine Elizabeth, have bound themselves to Samuel Ringgold Esq'r in the State of Maryland, to serve him Four years, the son to have two quarters' schooling, and each of them to have customary Freedom Suits." Seventeen years later, another couple, Landelin Stregel and Anna Maria Stregel, bound themselves for three years to Parkes Boyd; they were to receive "Fifteen Dollars per year in lieu of Apparel and no Freedom suit." Four years later, in Philadelphia, "Eva Wagner with consent of her father" was bound "to John M. Brown of the Northern Libertyes, Phila. County, Riger, for five years, to have six months' schooling and at the end of the term Two complete suits of clothes, one of which to be new, also one Straw bed, one bedstead, one Blanket, one pillow and one sheet." The same year, 1824, 25 redemptioners arrived on board the *Jane*: the health officer declared "that none of them are superannuated, impotent or otherwise likely to become chargeable to the Public, but all of them sound, without any defect in mind or body."[2]

Many people feel that there continues in 21st-century America a kind of bondage to government and financial institutions—the order imposed by the Constitution on a liberty-loving people. Examples of bondage in the wake of the colonial period are ubiquitous. Poorhouses dotted this land of freedom throughout the 19th century. One example among many comes from the *Buffalo* (New York) *Medical Journal* for 1855, in which the editors reported that "the whole policy of the Poorhouse is niggardly and mean. Cheap provisions, cheap doctors, cheap nurses, cheap medicines, cheapness everywhere is the rule, forgetting that higher policy which finds true economy in a humane liberality." In the Erie County poorhouse, "lying-in women have died of fever, leaving their children, and the numerous found-lings brought to the house, to die of starvation together. Brought there as bright, healthy infants, these little offsprings of misfortune and crime have scarcely an average of four weeks of life in this great lazar house. Other child[r]en become idiotic, dwarfed, inanimate; and men and women die from a hundred diseases, written down upon the case-book, with Latin names, but which might be better called starvation—starvation of God's air and the fruit of God's earth."[3] Others chimed in with their descriptions of the despair of the poor: Charles Loring Brace's *The Dangerous Classes of New York*; Jacob Riis's *How the Other Half Lives*; Upton Sinclair's *The Jungle*; Stephen Crane's *Maggie: A Girl of the Streets*, all described in horrifying detail the suffering of the poor in a land of liberty and freedom. Although blacks suffered in the post–Civil War South because of the Jim Crow laws and the continuing seg-regation of blacks and whites throughout much of the 20th century, poverty in America tended to be color blind, as witnessed by the economic privation and virtual enslavement to the factory of the proletariat of the post–Civil War North; the contradictions in the loss of freedom experienced by immi-grants in the late 19th and early 20th centuries; the lack of freedoms experi-enced by orphans and slum-dwellers (such as in the Bowery) during the same time period at the turn of the century; the despair and loss of rights of the dispossessed workers and farmers experienced during the Great Depres-sion; and the dispossessed natural rights of the mentally ill and emotionally disabled, especially the growing numbers of the elderly, during the whole of American history.

What did the Declaration of Independence really mean for Americans: whites, blacks, Indians, immigrants? Was there life, liberty, and the pursuit of happiness? What does America stand for? Freedom, liberty—from bond-age? What kind of liberty? What did the Revolution really mean?

When Jefferson, in the draft of the Declaration of Independence, accused the king of allowing slavery to exist in America, he condemned George III for waging "cruel war against human nature itself, violating its most sacred rights of life and liberty in the persons of a distant people who never offended him, captivating and carrying them into slavery"; further, George excited "those very people" in bondage "to rise in arms among us, and to purchase that liberty of which *he* had deprived them, by murdering the people upon whom *he* also obtruded them: thus paying off former crimes committed against the *liberties* of one people, with crimes which he urges them to com-mit against the *lives* of another." Jefferson's implication was that the bondage of people, not just blacks but whites and Indians as well, by depriving them of liberty and freedom, ensured that these people in bondage would rise up against their oppressors—which was exactly what the Americans as a whole were doing against the British Empire. Bondage, deprivation of freedom, dispossession of liberty, will hardly proceed without consequence. The Revolution, in short, was waged by all sorts of people—free and not so free—to guarantee what bound immigrants had always sought: the simple right to life, liberty, and pursuit of happiness. These people—Scots, Irish, English servants, redemptioners, Indian and black servants, and slaves—had experienced oppression from England and wanted redress.

Freedom and liberty can be ideas that are mesmerizing, intoxicating: These ideas brought many people to America in search of them; many of them failed; but the ideas were there, tantalizing, that America was such a place. The ideas still tantalize us. People still expect America to be a place where bondage, and the results of bondage, should not exist, even if it does. There is an idealism at work here, an idealism that makes America something special. John Harrower mentioned it. The German redemptioners sought it. Daniel Defoe expressed it. Many indentured servants firmly believed it to have come hither. America still attracts people throughout the world. Crevecoeur sensed it. America would change a person, make them new, make them free.

Many years ago, Edmund S. Morgan wrote a persuasive book, *American Slavery, American Freedom*, in which he argued that the American Revolution came about in part because white planters in the South daily saw the consequences of slavery, and hence knew the benefits of freedom, and were willing to fight and die for it. The English initially disbelieved in slavery, Morgan wrote, and thought they were better than the Spanish who enslaved Indians; but as colonization occurred the English began to see that Indians were different—they thought inferior—and that the Indians could therefore be enslaved. White servants were also considered chattel. Bacon's Rebellion threatened the ruling class with the large number of servants and freedmen who wanted rights, so the ruling class purposefully began to import slaves, and began to argue that these black slaves were inferior to whites, in this way getting the lower- and middle-class whites to see eye to eye with the upper class. The unification of whites in opposition to blacks allowed ideas of republicanism (for whites) to develop with the blacks as the unequal, enslaved ones. Freedom was cherished. Morgan's thesis applies to servitude as well, and not just in the South. Throughout the American colonies there was the experience of master and servant; sometimes the servant became a master in turn. Bondage was ubiquitous and was forever before the eyes of people who feared its consequences.[4]

It is not too far of a stretch of the imagination to consider that revolutionary ideals were appealing to many—to the patriots, to slave owners like Thomas Jefferson and George Washington, to radicals like Thomas Paine, to former servants like Charles Thomson and Matthew Lyon, and to the children of servants who crossed the Atlantic such as John and James Sullivan—such as to universalize sentiments of freedom and liberty, to unite together into a *Cause*, not just for themselves, but for all humankind. Charles

Thomson emigrated from Ireland along with his father and brothers aboard a vessel bound for Philadelphia; his father died at sea and the Thomson boys, penniless, were redeemed to indentured labor by the captain of the ship. Thomson eventually became a signer of the Declaration of Independence and secretary of the Continental Congress. Matthew Lyon, also from Ireland, left home as a teenaged boy to serve as a cabin boy in a ship bound for New York; the duplicitous captain of the ship, however, sold him as a servant upon arriving in America. Lyon eventually served as a soldier during the war and in the U.S. Congress. General John Sullivan and Governor James Sullivan were the sons of an Irish immigrant who had to redeem his passage to America through indentured labor; his sons became a Revolutionary War general and a Revolutionary statesman, respectively. They believed that their beliefs—in the necessity of the cause, the support of history, the validity of the will of the people, the sanction of God—were self-evident for all humans.[5]

Some of the dispossessed who came to America were able, upon liberty, to pursue happiness, and succeed. George Taylor was such a person. He was an Irishman, son of a clergyman, but poor; he traveled to America as an indentured servant to the owner of an ironworks. Taylor did menial work with the furnaces, but in time became a clerk, and eventually the proprietor of the ironworks. He became involved in provincial politics and eventually was sent to the Continental Congress, signing the Declaration of Independence.[6] Such people grasped the opportunity to better themselves, to be free from the constraints of order and the economy, to be their own free agents. What would it take to drive a person to journey across the ocean leaving all behind? It would take desperation, yes, but also, as Moll Flanders argued to her husband, a desire to achieve, to build one's own life, to accomplish something, to be free. George Taylor came of his own free will; the fictional Moll Flanders, like thousands of real people, did not. Even these people were presented with the chance to go to a new place, to experience, potentially, freedom. They were, to be sure, prisoners, quasislaves, and many of them died. But they had the opportunity to go to a new land to experience something completely different from the old: new institutions, new opportunities, wide-open spaces. No wonder some people thrived. They embraced their destiny and achieved. Some did not, but their progeny did. As John Harrower believed, if one accepted what happened, accepted God's will, then a person might find a route to peace and contentment in this new world.

Of Jefferson's three great truths—life, liberty, and the pursuit of happiness—oftentimes the first one, life, is taken for granted. But it is, of course, the prerequisite for the other two. It is after all the essential foundation, the first blessing. One might not have liberty but have life and still have blessings. One might not be able to pursue happiness in all its forms, though life might be sufficient for happiness. The greatest tragedy is the taking of life, more than liberty or happiness, because one can have liberty without happiness, or happiness without liberty, but neither happiness nor liberty can be experienced without life—it is the sine qua non of existence. Life is the first blessing, the first freedom. If life is terminated, then liberty and happiness have no value, are inconsequential. Hence is it absurd to speak of liberty without life, or of happiness without life.

The lexicographer Samuel Johnson in 1769, in one of his glib, self-righteous comments, referring to the American colonists, proclaimed: "Sir, they are a race of convicts, and ought to be thankful for anything we allow them short of hanging." In retrospect, Johnson's comment is absurd. But it reveals the uncertainty that many Europeans had about the Americans and their hodge-podge origins and indeterminate existence on the verge of European civilization. More accurate than Johnson's was the comment, 70 years ago, by the historian Abbot Emerson Smith: "There was a speedy winnowing of the vast influx of riffraff which descended on the settlements; the residue, such as it was, became the American people."[7] The answer to Crevecoeur's question—*What is the American?*—is simple: a survivor who, upon sustaining life, eventually found liberty, and continues to pursue happiness.

Notes

1. J. Hector St. John de Crevecoeur, *Letters from an American Farmer and Sketches of Eighteenth-Century America* (New York: Penguin Books, 1981), 37.

2. John P. Foley, ed., *The Jefferson Cyclopedia* (New York: Funk and Wagnalls, 1900), 414; "Sales Contract between Thomas Jefferson and James Madison for an Indentured Servant's Remaining Term, 19 April 1809," Carter G. Woodson Collection, Library of Congress. http://memory.loc.gov/cgi-bin/query/h?ammem/mcc:@field(DOCID+@lit(mcc/060)); Karl F. Geiser, *Redemptioners and Indentured Servants in the Colony and Commonwealth of Pennsylvania* (New Haven, CT: Yale Publishing, 1901), 114–117.

3. Austin Flint and S. B. Hunt, eds., *Buffalo Medical Journal and Monthly Review of Medical and Surgical Science* (Buffalo, NY: Thomas and Lathrops, 1855), 185–186, 380–381.

4. Edmund S. Morgan, *American Slavery, American Freedom* (New York: W. W. Norton, 2003).

5. Lewis Harley, *The Life of Charles Thomson: Secretary to the Continental Congress and Translator of the Bible from the Greek* (Philadelphia: George W. Jacobs, 1900), 20; James F. McLaughlin, *Matthew Lyon, the Hampden of Congress: A Biography* (New York: Wynkoop Hallenbeck Crawford, 1900), 40–41; "Master John Sullivan, Margery Sullivan, and Their Remarkable Family, Berwick, Maine." http://www.oldberwick.org/index.php?option=com_content&view=article&id=518&Itemid=285

6. Charles A. Goodrich, *Lives of the Signers to the Declaration of Independence* (New York: Thomas Mather, 1837), 296–297.

7. Abbot E. Smith, *Colonists in Bondage: White Servitude and Convict Labor in America, 1607–1776* (New York: W. W. Norton, 1947), 306.

Afterword

There is much debate in the United States today as to whether America is a *Christian* country—that is, formed by the Judeo-Christian heritage. There are so many arguments for and against, and so much political and ideological invective used in this so-called debate, that it is a muddy morass that one should hesitate to wade into. Facts speak louder than theories, and evidence, rather than belief and opinion, is the solid ground to build upon. The facts, relating to servitude and servants in Colonial America, are that the British American colonies built their systems of law and order on the English common law and, even further back, on ancient law codes that seemed to make sense and be in accord with God's will. It is absurd to assume that the British Americans of the 16th, 17th, and 18th centuries were not Christians, devoted to what they considered to be God's will and the strictures and laws of Holy Scripture. The Bible, the Old and New Testaments, were not official law codes, though the Decalogue of the Old Testament laid down the Hebrew understanding of the Law of Moses, and the New Testament elucidates the moral codes about which Jesus of Nazareth taught. The Book of Leviticus, Chapter 25, establishes the code of servitude among the Hebrews: "And if your brother becomes poor beside you, and sells himself a slave; he shall be with you as a hired servant and as a sojourner." In other words, a person of your own people shall not be enslaved but, rather, shall be placed into temporary service. The only people who could be enslaved were those who were foreigners—"strangers who sojourn with you." Typically, in the ancient world, such people would be the casualties of war.

British Americans established laws relating to servitude and slavery on English law as well as the Law of Moses. The Massachusetts Body of Liberties plainly states, "There shall never be any bond slaverie, villinage or Captivitie amongst us unles it be lawfull Captives taken in just warres, and such strangers as willingly selle themselves or are sold to us. And these shall have all the liberties and Christian usages which the law of god established in Israell concerning such persons doeth morally require." The English Statute of Artificers from Elizabeth I's reign allowed magistrates to impose a term of service or apprenticeship upon young men or women with cause, typically that these people were unemployed, unmarried, begging, or disrupting the peace. But these people never had servitude for life imposed upon them. The general standard for servitude is again expressed in the Massachusetts Body of Liberties: "Servants that have served deligentlie and faithfully to the benefitt of their maisters seaven years, shall not be sent away emptie. And if any have bene unfaithfull, negligent or unprofitable in their service, notwithstanding the good usage of their maisters, they shall not be dismissed till they have made satisfaction according to the Judgement of Authoritie."

Often these laws were misconstrued, and frequently people were abused and dispossessed of their basic rights, but that is, after all, the story of civilization, in which humans attempt to live ordered lives, attempt to erect an ideal of law and order, the reality of which always falls short. But there is always this goal, as expressed in the Massachusetts Body of Liberties: "The free fruition of such liberties Immunities and priveledges as humanitie, Civilitie, and Christianitie call for as due to every man in his place and proportion without impeachment and Infringement hath ever bene and ever will be the tranquillitie and Stabilitie of Churches and Commonwealths. And the denial or deprival thereof, the disturbance if not the ruine of both."

The challenge for a society in which freedom of movement and liberty depends so much on the availability of earned income and the ability to acquire wealth is to ensure that those who fail in this regard—the poor, the debtor, the hungry, the homeless—do not become de facto servants to others, whether they be employers or creditors or landlords or the local, state, and federal government. The Massachusetts Body of Liberties, almost 400 years ago, addressed what should be the basic rights of all people living in a common region: "No mans life shall be taken away, no mans honour or good name shall be stayned, no mans person shall be arested, restrayned, banished, dismembred, nor any wayes punished, no man shall be deprived of his wife or children, no mans goods or estaite shall be taken away from him, nor any way indammaged under colour of law, or Countenance of Authoritie, unless it be by vertue or equitie of some expresse law of the Country waranting the same, established by a generall Court and sufficiently published, or in case of the defect of a law in any partecular case by the word of God."

There are dispossessed in all societies. But these people have one hope: by coming to know, by gaining an insight into, what is real, *they shall know the truth, and the truth shall set them free.*

Appendix:
Documents in the History of
Colonial American Servitude

1. Statute of Artificers, 1563

The Statute of Artificers, legislated in the early years of the reign of Elizabeth Tudor, provided the legal foundation for laws and customs relating to servitude in England as well as in the 13 British American colonies. An abridged version follows:

An Act Touching Divers Orders For Artificers, Labourers, Servants Of Husbandry And Apprentices, 1563.

I. Although there remain in force presently a great number of statutes concerning . . . apprentices, servants and labourers, as well in husbandry as in divers other . . . occupations, yet partly for the imperfection and contrariety . . . in sundry of the said laws, and for the variety and number of them, and chiefly for that the wages and allowances limited in many of the said statutes are in divers places too small . . . respecting the advancement of prices . . . the said laws cannot conveniently without the greatest grief and burden of the poor labourer and hired man be put in due execution; and as the said statutes were at the time of the making of them thought to be very good and beneficial . . . , as divers of them yet are, so if the substance of as many of the said laws as are meet to be continued shall be digested and reduced into one sole law, and in the same an uniform order prescribed . . . , there is good hope that it will come to pass that the same law, being duly executed, should banish idleness, advance husbandry and yield unto the hired person both in the time of scarcity and in the time of plenty a convenient proportion of wages: Be it therefore enacted. . . . That as much of the statutes heretofore made as concern the hiring, keeping, departing, working, wages or order of servants, workmen, artificers, apprentices and labourers . . . shall be from and after the last day of September next ensuing repealed. . . .

II. No person . . . shall be retained, hired or taken into service to work for any less time than for one whole year in any of the sciences . . . or arts of clothiers, woollen cloth weavers, tuckers, fullers, cloth workers, shearmen, dyers, hosiers, tailors, shoemakers, tanners, pewterers, bakers, brewers, glovers, cutlers, smiths, farriers, curriers, sadlers, spurriers, turners, cappers, hat-makers or feltmakers, bowyers, fletchers, arrowheadmakers, butchers, cooks, or millers.

III. Every person being unmarried and every other person being under the age of thirty years . . . , and having been brought up in any of the said arts . . . or that hath exercised any of them by the space of three years or more, and not having lands, tenements . . . copyhold or freehold of an estate of inheritance . . . , not being retained with any person in husbandry or in any of the aforesaid arts . . . nor in any other art, nor in household or in any office with any nobleman, gentleman or others, . . . nor having a convenient farm or other holding in tillage whereupon he may employ his labour, shall . . . upon request-made by any person using the art or mystery wherein the said person so required hath been exercised as is aforesaid, be retained and shall not refuse to serve according to the tenor of this Statute upon the pain and penalty hereafter mentioned.

IV. No person which shall retain any servant shall put away his said servant, and no person retained according to this Statute shall depart from his master, mistress or dame before the end of his term, upon the pain hereafter mentioned, unless it be forborne reasonable cause to be allowed before two Justices of Peace, or one at the least, or before the mayor or other chief officer of the city, borough or town corporate wherein the said master . . . inhabiteth, to whom any of the parties grieved shall complain; which said justices or chief officer shall have the hearing and ordering of the matter between the said master . . . and servant, according to the equity of the cause; and no such master . . . shall put away any such servant at the end of his term, or any such servant depart from his said master . . . at the end of his term, without one quarter warning given . . . upon the pain hereafter ensuing.

V. Every person between the age of 12 years and the age of 60 years not being lawfully retained nor apprentice with any fisherman or mariner haunting the seas, nor being in service with any carrier of any corn, grain or meal for provision of the city of London, nor with any husbandman in husbandry, nor in any city . . . in any of the arts . . . appointed by this Statute to have apprentices, nor being retained . . . for the digging . . . melting . . . making of any silver . . . , nor being occupied in the making of any glass, nor being a gentleman born, nor being a student or scholar in any of the universities or in any school, . . . nor being otherwise lawfully retained according to the true meaning of this Statute, shall . . . by virtue of this Statute be compelled to be retained to serve in husbandry by the year with any person that keepeth husbandry and will require any such person so to serve.

VII. None of the said retained persons in husbandry or in any of the arts or sciences above remembered, after the time of his retainer expired, shall depart forth of one city, town or parish to another nor out of the . . . hundred nor out of the county where he last served, to serve in any other city . . . or county, unless he have a testimonial under the seal of the said city or of the constable or other head officer and of two other honest householders of the city, town or parish where he last served, declaring his lawful departure, . . . which testimonial shall be delivered unto the said servant and also registered by the parson of the parish where such master . . . shall dwell. . . .

IX. All artificers and labourers being hired for wages by the day or week shall . . . be at their work at or before 5 of the clock in the morning, and continue at work until betwixt 7 and 8 of the clock at night, except it be in the time of breakfast, dinner or drinking, the which times at the most shall not exceed above 2 1/2 hours in the day . . . upon pain to forfeit one penny for every hour's absence to be deducted out of his wages. . . .

XI. And for the declaration what wages servants, labourers and artificers, either by the year or day or otherwise, shall receive, be it enacted, That the justices of the peace of every shire . . . within the limits of their several commissions . . . and the sheriff of that county if he conveniently may, and every mayor, bailiff or other head officer within any city . . . wherein is any justice of peace, within the limits of the said city . . . calling unto them such discreet and grave persons of the said county or city as they shall think meet, and conferring together respecting the plenty or scarcity of the time and other circumstances necessary to be considered, have authority within the limits of their several commissions to rate and appoint the wages as well of such of the said artificers . . . or any other labourer, servant or workman whose wages in time past hath been by any law rated and appointed, as also the wages of all other labourers, artificers . . . which have not been rated, as they shall think meet to be rated . . . by the year or by the day, week, month or other wise, with meat and drink or without meat and drink, and what wages every workman or labourer shall take by the great for mowing, reaping or threshing . . . , and for any other kind of reasonable labours or service, and shall yearly, . . . certify the same . . . to all persons . . . straitly to observe the same, and to all Justices . . . to see the same duly and severely observed . . .; upon receipt whereof the said Sheriffs, Justices . . . shall cause the same proclamation to be entered of record . . . and shall forthwith in open markets upon the market days . . . cause the same proclamation to be proclaimed . . . and to be fixed in some convenient place . . .

XV. Provided that in the time of hay or corn harvest the Justices of Peace and also the constable or other head officer of every township upon request . . . may cause all such artificers and persons as be meet to labour . . . to serve by the day for the mowing . . . or inning of corn, grain and hay, and that none of the said persons shall refuse so to do, upon pain to suffer imprisonment in the stocks, by the space of two days and one night. . . .

XVII. Two justices of peace, the mayor or other head officer of any city . . . and two aldermen or two other discreet burgesses . . . if there be no aldermen, may appoint any such woman as is of the age of 12 years and under the age of 40 years and unmarried and forth of service . . . to be retained or serve by the year or by the week or day for such wages and in such reasonable sort as they shall think meet; and if any such woman shall refuse so to serve, then it shall be lawful for the said justices . . . to commit such woman to ward until she shall be bounden to serve as aforesaid.

XVIII. And for the better advancement of husbandry and tillage and to the intent that such as are fit to be made apprentices to husbandry may be bounden thereunto, . . . every person being a householder and having half a ploughland at the least in tillage may receive as an apprentice any person above the age of 10 years and under the age of 18 years to serve in husbandry until his age of 21 years at the least, or until the age of 24 years as the parties can agree . . . .

XIX. Every person being an householder and 24 years old at the least, dwelling in any city or town corporate and exercising any art, mistery or manual occupation there, . . . retain the son of any freeman not occupying husbandry nor being a labourer and inhabiting in the same or in any other city or town incorporate, to be bound as an apprentice after the custom and order of the city of London for 7 years at the least, so as the term of such apprentice do not expire afore such apprentice shall be of the age of 24 years at the least.

XX. Provided that it shall not be lawful to any person dwelling in any city or town corporate exercising any of the misteries or crafts of a merchant trafficking into any parts beyond the sea, mercer, draper, goldsmith, ironmonger, embroiderer or clothier that doth put cloth to making and sale, to take any apprentice or servant to be instructed in any of the arts . . . which they exercise, except such servant or apprentice be his son, or else that the father or mother of such apprentice or servant shall have . . . lands, tenements . . . of the clear yearly value of 40s. of one estate of inheritance or freehold at the least. . . .

XXI. . . . it shall be lawful to every person being an householder and 24 years old at the least and not occupying husbandry nor being a labourer dwelling in any town not being incorporate that is a market town . . . and exercising any art, mistery or manual occupation . . . to have in like manner to apprentices the children of any other artificer not occupying husbandry nor being a labourer, which shall inhabit in the same or in any other such market town within the same shire, to serve as apprentices as is aforesaid to any such art . . . as hath been usually exercised in any such market town where, such apprentice shall be bound.

XXIII. . . . it shall be lawful to any person exercising the art of a smith, wheelwright, ploughwright, millwright, carpenter, rough mason, plaisterer, sawyer, lime-burner, brickmaker, bricklayer, tiler, slater, healyer, tilemaker, linenweaver, turner, cooper, millers, earthen potters, woollen weaver weaving housewives' or household cloth only and none other, cloth-fuller otherwise called tucker or walker, burner of ore and wood ashes, thatcher or shingler, wheresoever he shall dwell, to have the son of any person as apprentice . . . albeit the father or mother of any such apprentice have not any lands, tenements or hereditaments.

XXIV. . . . it shall not be lawful to any person, other than such as now do lawfully exercise any art, mistery or manual occupation, to exercise any craft now used within the realm of England or Wales, except he shall have been brought up therein seven years at the least as apprentice in manner abovesaid, nor to set any person on work in such occupation being not a workman at this day, except he shall have been apprentice as is aforesaid, or else having served as an apprentice will become a journeyman or be hired by the year; upon pain that every person willingly offending shall forfeit for every default 40s. for every month. . . .

XXVI. Every person that shall have three apprentices in any of the said crafts of a cloth-maker, fuller, shearman, weaver, tailor or shoemaker shall keep one journeyman, and for every other apprentice above the number of the said, three apprentices one other journeyman, upon pain of every default therein, 10£.

XXVIII. If any person shall be required by any householder having half a ploughland at the least in tillage to be an apprentice and to serve in husbandry, or in any other kind of art before expressed, and shall refuse so to do, then upon the complaint of such housekeeper made to one Justice of Peace of the county wherein the said refusal is made, or of such householder inhabiting in any city, town corporate, or market town to the mayor, bailiffs or head officer of the said city . . . they shall have full power to send for the same person so refusing; and if the said Justice or head officer shall think the said person meet to serve as an apprentice in that art . . . the said Justice or head officer shall have power . . . to commit him unto ward, there to remain until he will be bounden to serve . . . and if any such master shall evil entreat his apprentice . . . or the apprentice do not his duty to his master, then the said master or apprentice being grieved shall repair unto one Justice of Peace within the said county or to the head officer of the place where the said master dwelleth, who shall . . . take such order and direction between the said master and his apprentice as the equity of the case shall require; and if for want of good conformity in the said master the said Justice or head officer cannot compound the matter between him and his apprentice, then the said Justice or head officer shall take bond of the said master to appear at the next sessions then to be holden in the said county or within the said city . . . and upon his appearance and hearing of the matter . . . if it be thought meet unto them to discharge the said apprentice, then the said Justices or four of them at the least, whereof one to be of the quorum, or the said head officer, with the consent of three other of his brethren or men of best reputation within the said city shall have power . . . to pronounce that they have discharged the said apprentice of his apprenticehood . . .: and if the default shall be found to be in the apprentice, then the said Justices or head officer, with the assistants aforesaid, shall cause such due punishment to be ministered unto him as by their wisdom and discretions shall be thought meet.

XXIX. Provided that no person shall by force of this Statute be bounden to enter into any apprenticeship, other than such as be under the age of 21 years.

XXX. And to the end that this Statute may from time to time be . . . put in good execution . . . be it enacted, That the Justices of Peace of every county, dividing themselves into several limits, and likewise every mayor or head officer of any city or town corporate, shall yearly between the feast of St. Michael the Archangel and the Nativity of our Lord, and between the feast of the Annunciation of our Lady and the feast of the Nativity of St. John Baptist . . . make a special and diligent inquiry of the branches and articles of this Statute and of the good execution of the same, and where they shall find any defaults to see the same severely corrected and punished without favour . . . or displeasure. . . .

Source: *English Economic History: Select Documents*. Compiled and Edited by A. E. Bland, P. A. Brown, and R. H. Tawney. New York: Macmillan, 1919.

2. The Liberties of the Massachusets Collonie in New England, 1641

The Body of Liberties established by the colony of Massachusetts Bay in 1641 provides a remarkable record of civil and criminal law respecting all inhabitants, free and bound, in Massachusetts. The Body of Liberties derives from the English legal heritage as well as the heritage of the ancient Hebrews, as revealed in the Old Testament of the Bible. (Original spelling retained.)

The free fruition of such liberties Immunities and priveledges as humanitie, Civilitie, and Christianitie call for as due to every man in his place and proportion without impeachment and Infringement hath ever bene and ever will be the tranquillitie and Stabilitie of Churches and Commonwealths. And the deniall or deprivall thereof, the disturbance if not the ruine of both.

We hould it therefore our dutie and safetie whilst we are about the further establishing of this Government to collect and expresse all such freedomes as for present we foresee may concerne us, and our posteritie after us, And to ratify them with our sollemne consent.

Wee doe therefore this day religiously and unanimously decree and confirme these following Rites, liberties and priveledges concerneing our Churches, and Civill State to be respectively impartiallie and inviolably enjoyed and observed throughout our Jurisdiction for ever.

1. No mans life shall be taken away, no mans honour or good name shall be stayned, no mans person shall be arested, restrayned, banished, dismembred, nor any wayes punished, no man shall be deprived of his wife or children, no mans goods or estaite shall be taken away from him, nor any way indammaged under colour of law or Countenance of Authoritie, unlesse it be by vertue or equitie of some expresse law of the Country waranting the same, established by a generall Court and sufficiently published, or in case of the defect of a law in any parteculer case by the word of God. And in Capitall cases, or in cases

concerning dismembring or banishment according to that word to be judged by the Generall Court.

2. Every person within this Jurisdiction, whether Inhabitant or forreiner shall enjoy the same justice and law, that is generall for the plantation, which we constitute and execute one towards another without partialitie or delay.

3. No man shall be urged to take any oath or subscribe any articles, covenants or remonstrance, of a publique and Civill nature, but such as the Generall Court hath considered, allowed and required.

4. No man shall be punished for not appearing at or before any Civill Assembly, Court, Councell, Magistrate, or Officer, nor for the omission of any office or service, if he shall be necessarily hindred by any apparent Act or providence of God, which he could neither foresee nor avoid. Provided that this law shall not prejudice any person of his just cost or damage, in any civill action.

5. No man shall be compelled to any publique worke or service unlesse the presse be grounded upon some act of the generall Court, and have reasonable allowance therefore.

6. No man shall be pressed in person to any office, worke, warres or other publique service, that is necessarily and suffitiently exempted by any naturall or personall impediment, as by want of yeares, greatnes of age, defect of minde, fayling of sences, or impotencie of Lymbes.

7. No man shall be compelled to goe out of the limits of this plantation upon any offensive warres which this Comonwealth or any of our freinds or confederats shall volentarily undertake. But onely upon such vindictive and defensive warres in our owne behalfe or the behalfe of our freinds and confederats as shall be enterprized by the Counsell and consent of a Court generall, or by authority derived from the same.

8. No mans Cattel or goods of what kinde soever shall be pressed or taken for any publique use or service, unlesse it be by warrant grounded upon some act of the generall Court, nor without such reasonable prices and hire as the ordinarie rates of the Countrie do afford. And if his Cattle or goods shall perish or suffer damage in such service, the owner shall be suffitiently recompenced.

9. No monopolies shall be granted or allowed amongst us, but of such new Inventions that are profitable to the Countrie, and that for a short time.

10. All our lands and heritages shall be free from all fines and licenses upon Alienations, and from all hariotts, wardships, Liveries, Primer-seisins, yeare day and wast, Escheates, and forfeitures, upon the deaths of parents or Ancestors, be they naturall, casuall or Juditiall.

11. All persons which are of the age of 21 yeares, and of right understanding and meamories, whether excommunicate or condemned shall have full power and libertie to make there wills and testaments, and other lawfull alienations of theire lands and estates.

12. Every man whether Inhabitant or fforreiner, free or not free shall have libertie to come to any publique Court, Councel, or Towne meeting, and either by speech or writeing to move any lawfull, seasonable, and materiall question, or to present any necessary motion, complaint, petition, Bill or information, whereof that meeting hath proper cognizance, so it be done in convenient time, due order, and respective manner.

13. No man shall be rated here for any estaite or revenue he hath in England, or in any forreine partes till it be transported hither.

14. Any Conveyance or Alienation of land or other estaite what so ever, made by any woman that is married, any childe under age, Ideott or distracted person, shall be good if it be passed and ratified by the consent of a generall Court.

15. All Covenous or fraudulent Alienations or Conveyances of lands, tenements, or any heriditaments, shall be of no validitie to defeate any man from due debts or legacies, or from any just title, clame or possession, of that which is so fraudulently conveyed.

16. Every Inhabitant that is an howse holder shall have free fishing and fowling in any great ponds and Bayes, Coves and Rivers, so farre as the sea ebbes and flowes within the presincts of the towne where they dwell, unlesse the free men of the same Towne or the Generall Court have otherwise appropriated them, provided that this shall not be extended to give leave to any man to come upon others proprietie without there leave.

17. Every man of or within this Jurisdiction shall have free libertie, notwithstanding any Civill power to remove both himselfe, and his familie at their pleasure out of the same, provided there be no legall impediment to the contrarie.

Rites Rules and Liberties concerning Juditiall proceedings.

18. No mans person shall be restrained or imprisoned by any authority whatsoever, before the law hath sentenced him thereto, If he can put in sufficient securitie, bayle or mainprise, for his appearance, and good behaviour in the meane time, unlesse it be in Crimes Capitall, and Contempts in open Court, and in such cases where some expresse act of Court doth allow it.

19. If in a general Court any miscariage shall be amongst the Assistants when they are by themselves that may deserve an Admonition or fine under 20 sh. it shall be examined and sentenced amongst themselves, If amongst the Deputies when they are by themselves, It shall be examined and sentenced amongst themselves, If it be when the whole Court is togeather, it shall be judged by the whole Court, and not severallie as before.

20. If any which are to sit as Judges in any other Court shall demeane themselves offensively in the Court, the rest of the Judges present shall have power to censure him for it, if the cause be of a high nature it shall be presented to and censured at the next superior Court.

21. In all cases where the first summons are not served six dayes before the Court, and the cause breifly specified in the warrant, where appearance is to be made by the partie summoned, it shall be at his libertie whether he will appeare or no, except all cases that are to be handled in Courts suddainly called, upon extraordinary occasions, In all cases where there appeares present and urgent cause any assistant or officer apointed shal have power to make out attaichments for the first summons.

22. No man in any suit or action against an other shall falsely pretend great debts or damages to vex his adversary, if it shall appeare any doth so, The Court shall have power to set a reasonable fine on his head.

23. No man shall be adjudged to pay for detaining any debt from any Creditor above eight pounds in the hundred for one yeare, And not above that rate proportionable for all somes what so ever, neither shall this be a coulour or countenance to allow any usurie amongst us contrarie to the law of god.

24. In all Trespasses or damages done to any man or men, If it can be proved to be done by the meere default of him or them to whome the trespasse is done, It shall be judged no trespasse, nor any damage given for it.

25. No Summons pleading Judgement, or any kinde of proceeding in Court or course of Justice shall be abated, arested or reversed upon any kinde of cercumstantiall errors or mistakes, If the person and cause be rightly understood and intended by the Court.

26. Every man that findeth himselfe unfit to plead his owne cause in any Court shall have Libertie to imploy any man against whom the Court doth not except, to helpe him, Provided he give him noe fee or reward for his paines. This shall not exempt the partie him selfe from Answering such Questions in person as the Court shall thinke meete to demand of him.

27. If any plantife shall give into any Court a declaration of his cause in writeing, The defendant shall also have libertie and time to give in his answer in writeing, And so in all further proceedings betwene partie and partie, So it doth not further hinder the dispach of Justice then the Court shall be willing unto.

28. The plantife in all Actions brought in any Court shall have libertie to withdraw his Action, or to be nonsuited before the Jurie hath given in their verdict, in which case he shall alwaies pay full cost and chardges to the defendant, and may afterwards renew his suite at an other Court if he please.

29. In all actions at law it shall be the libertie of the plantife and defendant by mutual consent to choose whether they will be tryed by the Bench or by a Jurie, unlesse it be where the law upon just reason hath otherwise determined. The like libertie shall be granted to all persons in Criminall cases.

30. It shall be in the libertie both of plantife and defendant, and likewise every delinquent (to be judged by a Jurie) to challenge any of the Jurors. And if his

challenge be found just and reasonable by the Bench, or the rest of the Jurie, as the challenger shall choose it shall be allowed him, and tales de cercumstantibus impaneled in their room.

31. In all cases where evidences is so obscure or defective that the Jurie cannot clearly and safely give a positive verdict, whether it be a grand or petit Jurie, It shall have libertie to give a non Liquit, or a spetiall verdict, in which last, that is in a spetiall verdict, the Judgement of the cause shall be left to the Court, and all Jurors shall have libertie in matters of fact if they cannot finde the maine issue, yet to finde and present in their verdict so much as they can, If the Bench and Jurors shall so suffer at any time about their verdict that either of them cannot proceede with peace of conscience the case shall be referred to the Generall Court, who shall take the question from both and determine it.

32. Every man shall have libertie to replevy his Cattell or goods impounded, distreined, seised, or extended, unlesse it be upon execution after Judgement, and in paiment of fines. Provided he puts in good securitie to prosecute his replevin, And to satisfie such demands as his Adversary shall recover against him in Law.

33. No mans person shall be arrested, or imprisoned upon execution or judgment for any debt or fine, If the law can finde competent meanes of satisfaction otherwise from his estaite, and if not his person may be arrested and imprisoned where he shall be kept at his owne charge, not the plantife's till satisfaction be made: unlesse the Court that had cognizance of the cause or some superior Court shall otherwise provide.

34. If any man shall be proved and Judged a commen Barrator vexing others with unjust frequent and endlesse suites, It shall be in the power of Courts both to denie him the benefit of the law, and to punish him for his Barratry.

35. No mans corne nor hay that is in the feild or upon the Cart, nor his garden stuffe, nor any thing subject to present decay, shall be taken in any distresse, unles he that takes it doth presently bestow it where it may not be imbesled nor suffer spoile or decay, or give securitie to satisfie the worth thereof if it comes to any harme.

36. It shall be in the libertie of every man cast condemned or sentenced in any cause in any Inferior Court, to make their appeale to the Court of Assistants, provided they tender their appeale and put in securitie to prosecute it, before the Court be ended wherein they were condemned, And within six dayes next ensuing put in good securitie before some Assistant to satisfie what his Adversarie shall recover against him; And if the cause be of a Criminall nature for his good behaviour, and appearance, And everie man shall have libertie to complaine to the Generall Court of any Injustice done him in any Court of Assistants or other.

37. In all cases where it appeares to the Court that the plantife hath wilingly and witingly done wronge to the defendant in commenceing and prosecuting an

action or complaint against him, They shall have power to impose upon him a proportionable fine to the use of the defendant or accused person, for his false complaint or clamor.

38. Everie man shall have libertie to Record in the publique Rolles of any Court any Testimony given upon oath in the same Court, or before two Assistants, or any deede or evidence legally confirmed there to remaine in perpetuam rei memoriam, that is for perpetuall memoriall or evidence upon occasion.

39. In all actions both reall and personall betweene partie and partie, the Court shall have power to respite execution for a convenient time, when in their prudence they see just cause so to doe.

40. No Conveyance, Deede, or promise whatsoever shall be of validitie, If it be gotten by Illegal violence, imprisonment, threatening, or any kinde of forcible compulsion called Dures.

41. Everie man that is to Answere for any criminall cause, whether he be in prison or under bayle, his cause shall be heard and determined at the next Court that hath proper Cognizance thereof, And may be done without prejudice of Justice.

42. No man shall be twise sentenced by Civill Justice for one and the same Crime, offence, or Trespasse.

43. No man shall be beaten with above 40 stripes, nor shall any true gentleman, nor any man equall to a gentleman be punished with whipping, unles his crime be very shamefull, and his course of life vitious and profligate.

44. No man condemned to dye shall be put to death within fower dayes next after his condemnation, unles the Court see spetiall cause to the contrary, or in case of martiall law, nor shall the body of any man so put to death be unburied 12 howers unlesse it be in case of Anatomie.

45. No man shall be forced by Torture to confesse any Crime against himselfe nor any other unlesse it be in some Capitall case, where he is first fullie convicted by cleare and suffitient evidence to be guilty, After which if the cause be of that nature, That it is very apparent there be other conspiratours, or confederates with him, Then he may be tortured, yet not with such Tortures as be Barbarous and inhumane.

46. For bodilie punishments we allow amongst us none that are inhumane Barbarous or cruel.

47. No man shall be put to death without the testimony of two or three witnesses or that which is equivalent thereunto.

48. Every Inhabitant of the Countrie shall have free libertie to search and veewe any Rooles, Records, or Regesters of any Court or office except the Councell, And to have a transcript or exemplification thereof written examined, and signed by the hand of the officer of the office paying the appointed fees therefore.

49. No free man shall be compelled to serve upon Juries above two Courts in a yeare, except grand Jurie men, who shall hould two Courts together at the least.

50. All Jurors shall be chosen continuallie by the freemen of the Towne where they dwell.

51. All Associates selected at any time to Assist the Assistants in Inferior Courts, shall be nominated by the Townes belonging to that Court, by orderly agreement amonge themselves.

52. Children, Idiots, Distracted persons, and all that are strangers, or new comers to our plantation, shall have such allowances and dispensations in any cause whether Criminal or other as religion and reason require.

53. The age of discretion for passing away of lands or such kinde of herediments, or for giveing, of votes, verdicts or Sentence in any Civill Courts or causes, shall be one and twentie yeares.

54. Whensoever any thing is to be put to vote, any sentence to be pronounced, or any other matter to be proposed, or read in any Court or Assembly, If the president or moderator thereof shall refuse to performe it, the Major parte of the members of that Court or Assembly shall have power to appoint any other meete man of them to do it, And if there be just cause to punish him that should and would not.

55. In all suites or Actions in any Court, the plaintife shall have libertie to make all the titles and claims to that he sues for he can. And the Defendant shall have libertie to plead all the pleas he can in answere to them, and the Court shall judge according to the intire evidence of all.

56. If any man shall behave himselfe offensively at any Towne meeting, the rest of the freemen then present, shall have power to sentence him for his offence. So be it the mulct or penaltie exceede not twentie shilings.

57. Whensoever any person shall come to any very suddaine untimely and unnaturall death, Some assistant, or the Constables of that Towne shall forthwith sumon a Jury of twelve free men to inquire of the cause and manner of their death, and shall present a true verdict thereof to some neere Assistant, or the next Court to be helde for that Towne upon their oath.

Liberties more peculiarlie concerning the free men.

58. Civill Authoritie hath power and libertie to see the peace, ordinances and Rules of Christ observed in every church according to his word. so it be done in a Civill and not in an Ecclesiastical way.

59. Civill Authoritie hath power and libertie to deale with any Church member in a way of Civill Justice, notwithstanding any Church relation, office or interest.

60. No church censure shall degrade or depose any man from any Civill dignitie, office, or Authoritie he shall have in the Commonwealth.

61. No Magestrate, Juror, Officer, or other man shall be bound to informe present or reveale any private crim or offence, wherein there is no perill or danger to this plantation or any member thereof, when any necessarie tye of conscience binds him to secresie grounded upon the word of god, unlesse it be in case of testimony lawfully required.

62. Any Shire or Towne shall have libertie to choose their Deputies whom and where they please for the Generall Court. So be it they be free men, and have taken there oath of fealtie, and Inhabiting in this Jurisdiction.

63. No Governor, Deputy Governor, Assistant, Associate, or grand Jury man at any Court, nor any Deputie for the Generall Court, shall at any time beare his owne chardges at any Court, but their necessary expences shall be defrayed either by the Towne or Shire on whose service they are, or by the Country in generall.

64. Everie Action betweene partie and partie, and proceedings against delinquents in Criminall causes shall be briefly and destinctly entered on the Rolles of every Court by the Recorder thereof. That such actions be not afterwards brought againe to the vexation of any man.

65. No custome or prescription shall ever prevaile amongst us in any morall cause, our meaneing is maintaine anythinge that can be proved to be morrallie sinfull by the word of god.

66. The Freemen of every Towneship shall have power to make such by laws and constitutions as may concerne the wellfare of their Towne, provided they be not of a Criminall, but onely of a prudential nature, And that their penalties exceede not 20 sh. for one offence. And that they be not repugnant to the publique laws and orders of the Countrie. And if any Inhabitant shall neglect or refuse to observe them, they shall have power to levy the appointed penalties by distresse.

67. It is the constant libertie of the free men of this plantation to choose yearly at the Court of Election out of the freemen all the General officers of this Jurisdiction. If they please to dischardge them at the day of Election by way of vote. They may do it without shewing cause. But if at any other generall Court, we hould it due justice, that the reasons thereof be alleadged and proved. By Generall officers we meane, our Governor, Deputy Governor, Assistants, Treasurer, Generall of our warres. And our Admirall at Sea, and such as are or hereafter may be of the like generall nature.

68. It is the libertie of the freemen to choose such deputies for the Generall Court out of themselves, either in their owne Townes or elsewhere as they judge fitest. And because we cannot foresee what varietie and weight of occasions may fall into future consideration, And what counsells we may stand in neede of, we decree. That the Deputies (to attend the Generall Court in the behalfe of the Countrie) shall not any time be stated or inacted, but from Court to Court, or at the most but for one yeare, that the Countrie may have an Annuall libertie to do in that case what is most behoofefull for the best welfare thereof.

69. No Generall Court shall be desolved or adjourned without the consent of the Major parte thereof.

70. All Freemen called to give any advise, vote, verdict, or sentence in any Court, Counsell, or Civill Assembly, shall have full freedome to doe it according to their true Judgements and Consciences, So it be done orderly and inofensively for the manner.

71. The Governor shall have a casting voice whensoever an Equi vote shall fall out in the Court of Assistants, or generall assembly, So shall the presedent or moderator have in all Civill Courts or Assemblies.

72. The Governor and Deputy Governor Joyntly consenting or any three Assistants concurring in consent shall have power out of Court to reprive a condemned malefactour, till the next quarter or generall Court. The generall Court onely shall have power to pardon a condemned malefactor.

73. The Generall Court hath libertie and Authoritie to send out any member of this Comanwealth of what qualitie, condition or office whatsoever into forreine parts about any publique message or Negotiation. Provided the partie sent be acquainted with the affaire he goeth about, and be willing to undertake the service.

74. The freemen of every Towne or Towneship, shall have full power to choose yearly or for lesse time out of themselves a convenient number of fitt men to order the planting or prudentiall occasions of that Towne, according to Instructions given them in writeing, Provided nothing be done by them contrary to the publique laws and orders of the Countrie, provided also the number of such select persons be not above nine.

75. It is and shall be the libertie of any member or members of any Court Councell or Civill Assembly in cases of makeing or executing any order or law, that properlie concerne religion, or any cause capitall, or warres, or Subscription to any publique Articles or Remonstrance, in case they cannot in Judgement and conscience consent to that way the Major vote or suffrage goes, to make their contra Remonstrance or protestation in speech or writeing, and upon request to have their dissent recorded in the Rolles of that Court. So it be done Christianlie and respectively for the manner. And their dissent onely be entered without the reasons thereof, for the avoiding of tediousnes.

76. Whensoever any Jurie of trialls or Jurours are not cleare in their Judgements or consciences conserneing any cause wherein they are to give their verdict, They shall have libertie in open Court to advise with any man they thinke fitt to resolve or direct them, before they give in their verdict.

77. In all cases wherein any freeman is to give his vote, be it in point of Election, makeing constitutions and orders or passing sentence in any case of Judicature or the like, if he cannot see reason to give it positively one way or an other, he shall have libertie to be silent, and not pressed to a determined vote.

78. The Generall or publique Treasure or any parte thereof shall never be exspended but by the appointment of a Generall Court, nor any Shire Treasure, but by the appointment of the freemen thereof, nor any Towne Treasurie but by the freemen of that Towneship.

Liberties of Women.

79. If any man at his death shall not leave his wife a competent portion of his estaite, upon just complaint made to the Generall Court she shall be relieved.

80. Everie marryed woeman shall be free from bodilie correction or stripes by her husband, unlesse it be in his owne defence upon her assalt. If there be any just cause of correction complaint shall be made to Authoritie assembled in some Court, from which onely she shall receive it.

Liberties of Children.

81. When parents dye intestate, the Elder sonne shall have a doble portion of his whole estate reall and personall, unlesse the Generall Court upon just cause alleadged shall judge otherwise.

82. When parents dye intestate haveing noe heires males of their bodies their Daughters shall inherit as copartners, unles the Generall Court upon just reason shall judge otherwise.

83. If any parents shall wilfullie and unreasonably deny any childe timely or convenient mariage, or shall exercise any unnaturall severitie towards them, such childeren shall have free libertie to complaine to Authoritie for redresse.

84. No Orphan dureing their minoritie which was not committed to tuition or service by the parents in their life time, shall afterwards be absolutely disposed of by any kindred, freind, Executor, Towneship, or Church, nor by themselves without the consent of some Court, wherein two Assistants at least shall be present.

Liberties of Servants

85. If any servants shall flee from the Tiranny and crueltie of their masters to the howse of any freeman of the same Towne, they shall be there protected and susteyned till due order be taken for their relife. Provided due notice thereof be speedily given to their maisters from whom they fled. And the next Assistant or Constable where the partie flying is harboured.

86. No servant shall be put of for above a yeare to any other neither in the life time of their maister nor after their death by their Executors or Administrators unlesse it be by consent of Authoritie assembled in some Court or two Assistants.

87. If any man smite out the eye or tooth of his man-servant, or maid servant, or otherwise mayme or much disfigure him, unlesse it be by meere casualtie, he shall let them goe free from his service. And shall have such further recompense as the Court shall allow him.

88. Servants that have served deligentlie and faithfully to the benefitt of their maisters seaven yeares, shall not be sent away emptie. And if any have bene unfaithfull, negligent or unprofitable in their service, notwithstanding the good usage of their maisters, they shall not be dismissed till they have made satisfaction according to the Judgement of Authoritie.

Liberties of Forreiners and Strangers.

89. If any people of other Nations professing the true Christian Religion shall flee to us from the Tiranny or oppression of their persecutors, or from famyne, warres, or the like necessary and compulsarie cause, They shall be entertayned and succoured amongst us, according to that power and prudence, god shall give us.

90. If any ships or other vessels, be it freind or enemy, shall suffer shipwrack upon our Coast, there shall be no violence or wrong offerred to their persons or goods. But their persons shall be harboured, and relieved, and their goods preserved in safety till Authoritie may be certified thereof, and shall take further order therein.

91. There shall never be any bond slaverie, villinage or Captivitie amongst us unles it be lawfull Captives taken in just warres, and such strangers as willingly selle themselves or are sold to us. And these shall have all the liberties and Christian usages which the law of god established in Israell concerning such persons doeth morally require. This exempts none from servitude who shall be Judged thereto by Authoritie.

Off the Bruite Creature.

92. No man shall exercise any Tirranny or Crueltie towards any bruite Creature which are usuallie kept for man's use.

93. If any man shall have occasion to leade or drive Cattel from place to place that is far of, so that they be weary, or hungry, or fall sick, or lambe, It shall be lawful to rest or refresh them, for competant time, in any open place that is not Corne, meadow, or inclosed for some peculiar use.

94. *Capitall Laws.*

(Deut. 13. 6, 10. Dut. 17. 2, 6. Ex. 22.20)
If any man after legall conviction shall have or worship any other god, but the lord god, he shall be put to death.

(Ex. 22. 18. Lev. 20. 27. Dut. 18. 10.)
If any man or woeman be a witch, (that is hath or consulteth with a familiar spirit,) They shall be put to death.

(Lev. 24. 15,16.)
If any person shall Blaspheme the name of god, the father, Sonne or Holie Ghost, with direct, expresse, presumptuous or high handed blasphemie, or shall curse god in the like manner, he shall be put to death.

(Ex. 21. 12. Numb. 35. 13, 14, 30, 31.)
If any person committ any wilfull murther, which is manslaughter, committed upon premeditated malice, hatred, or Crueltie, not in a mans necessarie and just defence, nor by meere casualtie against his will, he shall be put to death.

(Numb. 25. 20, 21. Lev. 24. 17)
If any person slayeth an other suddaienly in his anger or Crueltie of passion, he shall be put to death.

(Ex. 21. 14.)
If any person shall slay an other through guile, either by poysoning or other such divelish practice, he shall be put to death.

(Lev. 20. 15, 16.)
If any man or woeman shall lye with any beaste or bruite creature by Carnall Copulation, They shall surely be put to death. And the beast shall be slaine, and buried and not eaten.

(Lev. 20. 13.)
If any man lyeth with mankinde as he lyeth with a woeman, both of them have committed abhomination, they both shall surely be put to death.

Lev. 20. 19. and 18, 20. Dut. 22. 23, 24.)
If any person committeth Adultery with a maried or espoused wife, the Adulterer and Adulteresse shall surely be put to death.

(Ex. 21. 16.)
If any man stealeth a man or mankinde, he shall surely be put to death.

(Deut. 19. 16, 18, 19.)
If any man rise up by false witnes, wittingly and of purpose to take away any mans life, he shall be put to death.

If any man shall conspire and attempt any invasion, insurrection, or publique rebellion against our commonwealth, or shall indeavour to surprize any Towne or Townes, fort or forts therein, or shall treacherously and perfediouslie attempt the alteration and subversion of our frame of politie or Government fundamentallie, he shall be put to death.

95. *A Declaration of the Liberties the Lord Jesus hath given to the Churches.*

All the people of god within this Jurisdiction who are not in a church way, and be orthodox in Judgement, and not scandalous in life, shall have full libertie to gather themselves into a Church Estaite. Provided they doe it in a Christian way, with due observation of the rules of Christ revealed in his word.

Every Church hath full libertie to exercise all the ordinances of god, according to the rules of scripture.

Every Church hath free libertie of Election and ordination of all their officers from time to time, provided they be able, pious and orthodox.

Every Church hath free libertie of Admission, Recommendation, Dismission, and Expulsion, or deposall of their officers, and members, upon due cause, with free exercise of the Discipline and Censures of Christ according to the rules of his word.

No Injunctions are to be put upon any Church, Church officers or member in point of Doctrine, worship or Discipline, whether for substance or cercumstance besides the Institutions of the lord.

Every Church of Christ hath freedome to celebrate dayes of fasting and prayer, and of thanksgiveing according to the word of god.

The Elders of Churches have free libertie to meete monthly, Quarterly, or otherwise, in convenient numbers and places, for conferences, and consultations about Christian and Church questions and occasions.

All Churches have libertie to deale with any of their members in a church way that are in the hand of Justice. So it be not to retard or hinder the course thereof.

Every Church hath libertie to deale with any magestrate, Deputie of Court or other officer what soe ever that is a member in a church way in case of apparent and just offence given in their places, so it be done with due observance and respect.

Wee allowe private meetings for edification in religion amongst Christians of all sortes of people. So it be without just offence for number, time, place, and other cercumstances.

For the preventing and removeing of errour and offence that may grow and spread in any of the Churches in this Jurisdiction, And for the preserveing of trueith and peace in the severall churches within themselves, and for the maintenance and exercise of brotherly communion, amongst all the churches in the Countrie, It is allowed and ratified, by the Authoritie of this Generall Court as a lawfull libertie of the Churches of Christ. That once in every month of the yeare (when the season will beare it) It shall be lawfull for the minesters and Elders, of the Churches neere adjoyneing together, with any other of the breetheren with the consent of the churches to assemble by course in each severall Church one after an other. To the intent after the preaching of the word by such a minister as shall be requested thereto by the Elders of the church where the Assembly is held, The rest of the day may be spent in publique Christian Conference about the discussing and resolveing of any such doubts and cases of conscience concerning matter of doctrine or worship or government of the church as shall be propounded by any of the Breetheren of that church, will leave also to any other Brother to propound his objections or answeres for further satisfaction according to the word of god. Provided that the whole action be guided and moderated by the Elders of the Church where the Assemblie is helde, or by such others as they shall appoint. And that no thing be concluded and imposed by way of Authoritie from one or more churches upon an other, but onely by way of Brotherly conference and consultations. That the trueth may be searched out to the satisfying of every mans conscience in the sight of god according his worde. And because such an Assembly and the worke thereof can not be duely attended to if other lectures be held in the same weeke. It is therefore agreed with the consent of the Churches. That in that weeke when such an Assembly is held, All the lectures in all the neighbouring Churches for that weeke shall be forborne. That so the publique service of Christ in this more solemne Assembly may be transacted with greater deligence and attention.

96. Howsoever these above specified rites, freedomes Immunities, Authorites and priveledges, both Civill and Ecclesiastical are expressed onely under the name and title of Liberties, and not in the exact forme of Laws or Statutes, yet we do with one consent fullie Authorise, and earnestly intreate all that are and shall be in Authoritie to consider them as laws, and not to faile to inflict condigne and proportionable punishments upon every man impartiallie, that shall infringe or violate any of them.

97. Wee likewise give full power and libertie to any person that shall at any time be denyed or deprived of any of them, to commence and prosecute their suite, Complaint or action against any man that shall so doe in any Court that hath proper Cognizance or judicature thereof.

98. Lastly because our dutie and desire is to do nothing suddainlie which fundamentally concerne us, we decree that these rites and liberties, shall be Audably read and deliberately weighed at every Generall Court that shall be held, within three yeares next insueing, And such of them as shall not be altered or repealed they shall stand so ratified, That no man shall infringe them without due punishment.

And if any Generall Court within these next thre yeares shall faile or forget to reade and consider them as abovesaid. The Governor and Deputy Governor for the time being, and every Assistant present at such Courts, shall forfeite 20sh. a man, and everie Deputie 10sh. a man for each neglect, which shall be paid out of their proper estate, and not by the Country or the Townes which choose them, and whensoever there shall arise any question in any Court amonge the Assistants and Associates thereof about the explanation of these Rites and liberties, The Generall Court onely shall have power to interprett them.

Source: William H. Whitmore, *The Colonial Laws of Massachusetts*. Boston: Rockwell and Churchill, 1890.

3. Action of Virginia General Court against Convict Transportation, 1670

The increase in the numbers of convicts transported to the colonies in the wake of the Restoration of the Crown in 1660 led to the following proclamation of the General Court of Virginia in April 1670.

APRIL the 20th, 1670—The complaints of severall of the councell and others gent. Inhabitants in the counties of Yorke, Gloster, and Middlesex representing their apprehensions and feares, least the honor of his majestic and the peace of this collony be too much hazarded and endangered by the great nombers of fellons and other desperate villaines sent hither from the several prisons in England, being this day read in councell, we have, upon most serious and carefull consideration of the same, thought fit to order and doe hereby accordingly order, that for prevention and avoiding the danger which apparently threatens us, from the barbarous designes and felonious practices of such wicked villaines, that it shall not be permitted to any person tradeing hither to bring in and land any jaile birds or such others, who for notorious offences have deserved to dye in England, from and after the twentyeth day of January next, upon paine of being forced to keepe them on board, and carry them to some other country, where they may be better secured. And we have been the more induced to make this order, by the horror yet remaineing amongst us, of the barbarous designe of those villaines in September 1663[, servants] who attempted at once the subversion of our religion lawes libertyes, rights and proprietyes, the sad effect of which desperate conspiracy we had undoubtedly felt, had not God of his infinite mercy prevented it, by a tymely and wonderfull discovery of the same; nor hath it been a small motive to us to hinder and prohibite the importation of such dangerous and scandalous people, since thereby we apparently loose our reputation, whilest we are believed to be a place onely fit to receive such base and lewd persons. It is therefore resolved that this order remaine in force untill his majestie shall siguifye his pleasure to the contrary, or that it be reversed by an order from his most honourable privy councell, and that it be forthwith published that all persons concerned therein may take notice of it accordingly.

Source: The Statues at Large; Being a Collection of All the Laws of Virginia from the First Session of the Legislature, in the year 1619, vol. 2, ed. William W. Hening. New York: Bartow, 1823, 509–510.

4. An Indenture Binding a Servant to Labor

Servants arriving in America from such places as Amsterdam, to pay their passage, had to bind themselves to a master to labor for a certain period. Below is an indenture from early 19th- century Philadelphia.

This Indenture Witnesseth That Peter Smith of his own free will (and consent of his Father, John Smith) for and in consideration as well of the Sum of $100 paid by Edwin Valette of the N. L. of the City of Philadelphia, Ship Brohen, to Jacob Sperry, for his passage from Amsterdam, as also for other causes and considerations he the said Peter Smith Hath bound and put himself, and by these Presents Doth bind and put himself Servant to the sd Edwin Vallette to Serve him his Executors Administrators and Assigns from the day of the date hereof for and during the full term of Three years from thence next ensuing—During all which said term the said Servant his Said Masters his Executors Administrators and Assigns faithfully Shall serve, and that honestly and obediently in All things, as a good and faithful servant ought to do. And the said Edwin Vallette his Executors Administrators and Assigns during the said term shall find and provide for the sd Servant sufficient Meat Drink Apparel Washing and Lodging—and also to give him 18 weeks' Schooling—And at the expiration of his term the said Servant to have two complete Suits of Clothes, one whereof to be new—And for the true performance the Covenants and Agreements aforesaid the Said Parties bind themselves unto each other firmly by these Presents. In Witness Whereof the Said Parties have interchangeably set their Hands and Seals hereunto.

Source: Karl Frederick Geiser. *Redemptioners and Indentured Servants in the Colony and Commonwealth of Pennsylvania*. New Haven, CT: The Tuttle, Morehouse, and Taylor Company, 1901.

5. An Indenture Binding an Apprentice to a Master

Parents bound children to masters to learn a craft or trade. Unlike indentured servants and redemptioners, apprentice indentures typically indicated what precisely the master would teach the apprentice.

This Indenture Wittnesseth that I, William Mathews, the son of Marrat of the City of New York, Widdow, hath put himself and by these Presents doth voluntarily and of his own free Will and Accord and by the Consent of his said Mother put himself Apprentice to Thomas Windover of the City aforesaid Cordwiner with him to live and (after the Manner of an Apprentice) to serve from the fifteenth day of August last Anno Dom one thousand seven hundred and Eighteen untill the full Term of seven years be Compleat and Ended. During all which Term the said Apprentice his said Master Thomas Windover faithfully shall serve his secrets keep, his lawfull Commands gladly every where Obey, he shall do no damage to his said Master nor see to be done by Others without letting or giving Notice to his said Master, he shall not waste his said Masters Goods, nor lend them unlawfully to any, he shall not Committ fornication nor Contract Matrimony within the said Term. At Cards, Dice or any Other unlawfull Game he shall not play whereby his said Master may have Damage with his Own Goods or the Goods of those during the said Term without Lycense from his said Master he shall neither buy or sell. He shall not absent himself day or night from his Masters service without his leave, nor haunt Alehouses, Taverns or Playhouses, but in all things as a faithfull apprentice he shall behave himself towards his said Master and all his during the said Term. And the said Master during the said Term shall, by the best means or Method that he can Teach or Cause the said Apprentice to be taught the Art or Mystery of a Cordwiner, and shall find and provide unto the said Apprentice sufficient Meat, Drink, Apparel, Lodging and washing fitting for an Apprentice, and shall during the said Term every winter at Nights give him one Quarters schooling, and at the Expiration of the said

Term to provide for the said Apprentice a sufficient New Suit of Apparell four shirts and two Necletts, for the true Performance of all and every the said Covenants and agreements Either of the said parties bind themselves unto the Other by these Presents.

In witness whereof they have hereunto Interchangeably put their hands and seals this twenty fifth day of September in the fifth year of his Majesties Reign, Anno Domini One thousand seven hundred and Eighteen. The Marke of William Mathews [seal] sealed and delivered in the Presence of John Rushton, H. D. Meyer, New York Sept 26th A° 1718 then appeared before me Jacobus Kip one of his Majties Justis of the Peace for the City and County of New York the within Named Apprentice and acknowledge the signing and sealing of this Indenture to be his Voluntary Act and Deed.

Source: "Indentures of Apprentices, 1718–1727." *Collections of the New-York Historical Society for the Year 1909.* New York: New York Historical Society, 1910, 113–114.

6. Runaway Indentured Servants in Pennsylvania

Colonial American newspapers in the 18th century frequently ran advertisements by masters seeking help in, and offering a reward for, the recapture of escaped servants.

"Runaway last Night, from on board the Dianna, of Dublin, Richard McCarty, Master, a Servant Man, named Valentine Handlin, aged about 30 Years, a lusty rawbon'd Fellow small round Visaged, is of a dark Complexion with short Black Hair, Had on when he went away, a brown bob Wig, Old Felt Hat, an old lightish colour'd cloth grear Coat, a blue grey Waistcoat, old leather Breeches, yarn Stockings, broad square toe'd Shoes; and perhaps may have taken some other clothes with him. He is remarkably hollow Footed and seems crump footed when his Shoes are off. Whoever secures the said Servant so he may be had again, shall have Twenty Shillings Reward, paid by William Blair."

—*Pennsylvania Gazette,* Dec. 11, 1740.

"Run away from Cornwall iron works, in Lancaster County, an English Servant Man, named Mathew Williams, belonging to William Keepers, of Baltimore County, in Maryland, a short well set fellow, about 25 years of age: Had on when he went away a castor hat, silk cap, a blue broad-cloth coat, and black damask Jacket, red plush breeches and a pair of boots. Whoever takes up the said servant and brings him to Amos Garrett, at said works shall receive 5 Pounds as a reward paid by Amos Garrett."

—*Pennsylvania Gazette,* May 16, 1751.

"Run away from Henry Caldwell, of Newton, in Chester County, an Irish Servant-man, named John Hamilton, about 22 years of age, of a middle stature, well set, fresh complexion, and speaks good English: Had on when he went away, a brown colour'd coat, white damask vest, very much broke, old felt hat, cotton cap, good leather breeches, Light coloured stockings, and old shoes; he has been a servant before, and is supposed to have his old indenture with him. Whoever takes up said servant, so that his master may have him again, shall have 30s. reward, and reasonable charges paid by Henry Caldwell."

—*Pennsylvania Gazette,* March 17, 1752.

"Run away on the 18th inst. at night from on board the ship Friendship, Hugh Wright, Commander, now lying at William Allen Esquire's wharff, James Dowdall, a servant man, a laborer, lately come in, but has been in many parts of this continent before; he is about 5 ft. 4 inches high, has short hair, but neither cap nor hat: Has on a blue frize coat and Jacket, a Check shirt, leather breeches, and blue yarn hose: speaks as a native of this Province; he is at present greatly infected with the itch, and not able to travel far. Whoever secures the said James Dowdall so that he be brought to the said Commander, or to Wallace and Bryan on Market Street Wharf, shall have 40s. reward and reasonable charges paid by Wallace and Bryan."

—*Pennsylvania Gazette,* Sept. 28, 1752.

"Run away the 20 ult. from Philip Moser: A Servant Man named Nicholas Wolfe five feet five inches high, having lost the little finger of his left hand, black hair'd; had on when he went away, a light grey cloth coat, blue Jacket new shoes with yellow buckles in them. Whoever takes up and secures him so that his master may have him again, shall have *Five Pounds* and all reasonable charges paid by Philip Moser."

Pa. Journal and Weekly Advertiser, Jan. 26, 1763.

Source: Karl Frederick Geiser. *Redemptioners and Indentured Servants in the Colony and Commonwealth of Pennsylvania.* New Haven, CT: The Tuttle, Morehouse, and Taylor Company, 1901.

7. Thomas Jefferson on Indentured Servitude

In a 1786 letter to Monsieur de Meunier, Jefferson outlined his understanding of indentured servitude in 18th-century America.

Indentured servants formed a considerable supply. These were poor Europeans, who went to America to settle themselves. If they could pay their passage, it was well. If not, they must find means of paying it. They were at liberty, therefore, to make an agreement with any person they chose, to serve him such a length of time as they agreed on, upon condition that he would repay to the master of the vessel the expenses of their passage. If, being foreigners, unable to speak the language, they did not know how to make a bargain for themselves, the captain of the vessel contracted for them with such persons as he could. This contract was by deed indented, which occasioned them to be called indented servants. . . . They could redeem themselves from his power by paying their passage, which they frequently effected by hiring themselves on their arrival. In some States I know that these people had a right of marrying themselves without their masters' leave, and I did suppose they had that right everywhere. I did not know that in any of the States they demanded so much as a week for every day's absence without leave. I suspect this must have been at a very early period, while the governments were in the hands of the first emigrants, who, being mostly laborers, were narrow-minded and severe. I know that in Virginia the laws allowed their servitude to be protracted only two days for every one they were absent without leave. So mild was this kind of servitude, that it was very frequent for foreigners, who carried to America money enough, not only to pay their passage, but to buy themselves a farm, it was common I say for them to indent themselves to a master for three years, for a certain sum of money with a view to learn the husbandry of the country. I will here make a general observation. So desirous are the poor of Europe to get to America, where they may better their condition, that being unable to pay their passage, they will agree to serve two or three years on their arrival there, rather than not go.

Source: The Jefferson Cyclopedia. Edited by John P. Foley. New York: Funk and Wagnalls, 1900.

8. George Washington and the Free-Willers

In a letter from 1774, George Washington, planter and land speculator, wrote a merchant to ascertain the prospects for importing Palatines, that is, free-willers or redemptioners, from Europe, to settle his lands in the Ohio valley. Washington proposed to pay for their passage and indenture the immigrants accordingly for reimbursement.

George Washington to Henry Riddell, Mount Vernon, 22 February, 1774.

SIR,

Mr. Young, hearing me express a desire of importing Palatines to settle on my lands on the Ohio, tells me, that, in discoursing of this matter in your company, you suggested an expedient, which might probably be attended with success; and that if I inclined to adopt it, you wished to be informed before the sailing of your ship.

The desire of seating and improving my lands on the Ohio, is founded on interested as well as political views. But the intention of importing Palatines for the purpose was more the effect of sudden thought, than mature consideration, because I am totally unacquainted with the manner, as well as the expense of doing it; and I was led into the notion principally from a report of either this or some other ship of yours being blamed, for not taking an offered freight of these Germans at forty shillings sterling. I was thus induced to think if this charge was not much accumulated by other expenses, that I could fall on no better expedient to settle my lands with industrious people, than by such an importation. The terms upon which I have thought of importing Palatines, or people from Ireland, or Scotland, are these; to import them at my expense, where they are unable to transport themselves, into the Potomac River, and from hence to the Ohio; to have them, in the first case, engaged to me under indenture; in the second, by some other contract equally valid, to become tenants upon the terms hereafter mentioned; as without these securities, I would not encounter the expense, trouble, and hazard of such an importation. But to make matters as easy and agreeable as possible to these emigrants, I will engage, on my part, that the indentures shall be considered in no other light, than as a security for reimbursing to me every expense I am under, with interest, in importing them, removing them to the land, and supporting them there, till they can raise a crop for their own subsistence; giving up the said indentures, and considering them altogether as freemen and tenants, so soon as this shall happen; not to each person or family respectively, but when the whole accumulated expense shall be discharged; as I must, for my own safety, consider them as jointly bound for this payment, till the expiration of the indented terms, otherwise I must be an inevitable loser by every death or other accident; whilst they cannot, in the worst light, be considered as more than servants at large during the indented term. I can also engage to set them down upon as good land as any in that country; and where there is neither house built, nor land cleared, I will allow them an exemption of rent four years; and where there is a house erected, and five acres of land cleared and fit for cultivation, two years. They shall have the land upon lease for twenty-one years, under the usual covenants. . . .

Having thus exhibited a general view of my design, I shall now be obliged to you, Sir, to inform me with as much precision as you can, what certainty there is that your ship will go to Holland; what probability there is of her getting Palatines, if she does go; when they may be expected in this country; what would be the freight; and as near as you can judge, the whole incidental expense attending each person delivered at Alexandria; and, moreover, whether it would be expected, that the whole of these charges, including freight, should be paid down immediately on the arrival of the ship here, as it must appear rather hard to make a certain provision for an uncertain event. It may not be amiss further to observe, that I see no prospect of these people being restrained in the smallest degree, either in their civil or religious principles; which I take notice of, because these are privileges, which mankind are solicitous to enjoy, and upon which emigrants must be anxious to be informed. I wrote to Philadelphia by the last post for full information of the manner and charge of importing these people from Holland; and, if your account in answer to this letter should prove agreeable to my wishes, I will send a more particular description of the lands, which I wish to settle, as well as copies of the plots, and do any other matter which may be judged necessary to further the design. I am, &c.

Source: *The Writings of George Washington*. Jared Sparks, ed. Vol. 2. Boston: Little, Brown, 1847, 383–387.

Sources Consulted

Contemporary Sources

An Account of the Proceedings against the Rebels, and Other Prisoners, Tried before the Lord Chief Justice Jefferies, and Other Judges in the West of England, in 1685, for Taking Arms under the Duke of Monmouth. 3rd ed. London: Andrew Bell, 1716. http://quod.lib.umich.edu/e/ecco/004840465.0001.000?rgn=main;view=fulltext

Autobiography of Benjamin Franklin. Edited by John Bigelow. Philadelphia: Lippincott, 1868.

Bacon, Francis. *Essays and New Atlantis.* New York: Walter J. Black, 1942.

Belknap, Jeremy. *The History of New-Hampshire.* Vol. 1. Dover, NH: Stevens, and Ela and Wadleigh, 1831.

Belknap Papers. *Collections of the Massachusetts Historical Society.* Ser. 5. Vol. 2. Boston: Massachusetts Historical Society, 1877.

Belknap Papers. New Hampshire Historical Society.

Blue Laws of Connecticut. The Code of 1650; Being a Compilation of the Earliest Laws and Orders of the General Court of Connecticut. Cincinnati: U. P. James, n. d.

Book of Common Prayer. London, 1604.

Boswell, James. *The Life of Samuel Johnson, LL.D.* Vol. 1. London: J. Davis. n.d.

"A Brief Account of the Causes That Have Retarded the Progress of the Colony of Georgia in America" (London, 1743). In *Collections of the Georgia Historical Society.* Vol. 2. Savannah: Georgia Historical Society, 1842.

Brown, Alexander. *The Genesis of the United States.* Vol. 1. Boston: Houghton Mifflin, 1890.

Bullock, William. *Virginia Impartially Examined, and Left to Publick View, to Be Considered by All Judicious and Honest Men.* London: John Hammond, 1649.

Burn, Richard. *The History of the Poor Laws with Observations.* London: Woodfall and Strahan, 1764.

Burroughs, Charles. *Discourse Delivered in the Chapel of the New Almshouse.* Portsmouth, NH: Foster, 1835.

Byles Family Papers. Massachusetts Historical Society.

Calendar of State Papers, Colonial Series, America and West Indies, 1661–1668. Edited by W. Noel Sainsbury. London: Longman, 1880.

A Collection of Acts Passed in the Parliament of Great Britain, Particularly Applying to the Province of Upper Canada. York, Ontario: R. C. Horne, 1818.

Colonial Records of the State of Georgia. Vol. 8. Atlanta: Franklin-Turner, 1907.

Colonial Records of the State of Georgia. Vol. 23. Atlanta: Chas. P. Byrd, 1914.

Colquhoun, Patrick. *A New and Appropriate System of Education for the Labouring People.* London: Savage and Easingwood, 1806.

Colquhoun, Patrick. *A Treatise on the Police of the Metropolis.* 7th ed. London: Bye and Law, 1806.

Crevecoeur, J. Hector St. John de. *Letters from an American Farmer and Sketches of Eighteenth-Century America.* London: Davies, 1782. Reprint edition: New York: Penguin Books, 1981.

Defoe, Daniel. *Giving Alms No Charity.* London, 1704. Reprint edition: *The Works of Daniel Defoe.* Edited by John S. Keltie. Edinburgh: William Nimmo, 1870.

Defoe, Daniel. *Life of Colonel Jack.* 2 vols. Edinburgh: James Ballantyne, 1810.

Defoe, Daniel. *The Fortunes and Misfortunes of Moll Flanders.* 1722. Reprint edition: *The Works of Daniel Defoe.* Edited by John S. Keltie. Edinburgh: William Nimmo, 1870.

Defoe, Daniel. *The History of the Life and Adventures of Mr. Duncan Campbell.* London: E. Curll, 1720.

De Vries, David Pietersz. *Voyages from Holland to America.* Translated by Henry C. Murphy. New York: Billin and Brothers, 1853.

"Diary of John Harrower, 1773–1776." *American Historical Review* 6 (1900): 65–107.

Diary of Thomas Burton, Esq. Member in the Parliaments of Oliver and Richard Cromwell, from 1656 to 1659. Vol. 4. London: Henry Colburn, 1828.

Documents Relating to the Towns in New Hampshire, New London to Wolfeborough. Vol. 13. Concord, NH: Cogswell, 1884.

Early Records of the Town of Portsmouth. Portsmouth, RI: E. L. Freeman and Sons, 1901.

The Early Records of the Town of Providence. Vol. 4. Edited by Horatio Rogers, George M. Carpenter, and Edward Field. Providence: Snow and Farnham, 1893.

Eddis, William. *Letters from America, Historical and Descriptive.* London: privately printed, 1792.

Eden, Frederic. *The State of the Poor.* 3 vols. London: Davis, 1797.

Eliot, John. *The Day-Breaking if Not the Sun-Rising of the Gospell with the Indians in New-England.* London: Fulk Clinton, 1647.

Eliot, John. *The Indian Grammar Begun: Or, an Essay to Bring the Indian Language into Rules.* Cambridge: Marmaduke Johnson, 1666; revised ed., Boston: Phelps and Farnham, 1822.

Eliot, John. *The Indian Primer, or, the Way of Training up of our Indian Youth in the Good Knowledge of God, in the Knowledge of the Scriptures, and in an Ability to Reade.* 1669. Reprint edition: Edinburgh, Scotland: Andrew Elliot, 1880.

Ellis, George W., and John E. Morris. *King Philip's War: Based on the Archives and Records of Massachusetts, Plymouth, Rhode Island and Connecticut, and Contemporary Letters and Accounts.* New York: Grafton Press, 1906.

English Economic History: Select Documents. Compiled and Edited by A. E. Bland, P. A. Brown, and R. H. Tawney. New York: Macmillan, 1919.

"Felons and Rattlesnakes, 9 May 1751." *Founders Online.* National Archives, last modified October 5, 2016. http://founders.archives.gov/documents/Franklin/01 -04-02-0040

"Against ffornication," 1662, reprinted in Encyclopedia of Virginia: https://www .encyclopediavirginia.org/_Against_ffornication_1661–1662

Fielding, Henry. *An Enquiry into the Causes of the Late Increase of Robbers, &c.* 2nd ed. London: Millar, 1751.

Gee, Joshua. *The Trade and Navigation of Great-Britain Considered.* London: Buckley, 1730.

"A German Indentured Servant in Barbados in 1652: The Account of Heinrich Von Uchteritz." Edited and Translated by Alexander Gunkel and Jerome S. Handler. *Journal of the Barbados Museum and Historical Society* 33 (1970): 91–93. http://jeromehandler.org/1970/01/a-german-indentured-servant-in-barbados-in-1652-the-account-of-heinrich-von-uchteritz/

Gottlieb Mittelberger's Journey to Pennsylvania in the Year 1750 . . . Translated by Carl Eben. Philadelphia: McVey, 1898.

Gyles, John. *Memoirs of the Odd Adventures, Strange Deliverances, &c. in the Captivity of John Gyles, Esq., Commander of the Garrison on St. George's River.* Boston: Kneeland and Green, 1736.

Hammond, John. *Leah and Rachel, or the Two Fruitfull Sisters, Virginia and Maryland.* London: T. Mabb, 1656. Reprint ed. Edited by Peter Force. *Tracts and Other Papers.* 4 Vols. Washington: Force, 1846.

Harrison, William. *The Description of Britain.* London: John Harrison, 1577.

Howard, John. *The State of the Prisons in England and Wales.* Warrington: William Eyres, 1777.

"Indentures of Apprentices, 1718–1727." *Collections of the New-York Historical Society for the Year 1909.* New York: New York Historical Society, 1910.

The Jefferson Cyclopedia. Edited by John P. Foley. New York: Funk and Wagnalls, 1900.

Laws of New Hampshire, 1702–1745. Vol. 2. Concord, NH: Rumford Printing, 1913.

Laws of New Hampshire, 1745–1774. Vol. 3. Bristol, NH: Musgrave Printing, 1915.

Lawson, John. *A New Voyage to Carolina; Containing the Exact Description and Natural History of That Country.* London: N.P., 1709.

The Life and Curious Adventures of Peter Williamson. Abderdeen: privately printed, 1826.

Martyn, Benjamin. *Reason's for Establishing the Colony of Georgia, with Regard to the Trade of Great Britain, the Increase of Our People, and the Employment and Support It Will Afford to Great Numbers of Our Own Poor.* London: Meadows, 1733.

Maverick, Samuel. "Maverick's Description of New England." *New England Historical and Genealogical Register* 39 (1885).

Moraley, William. *The Infortunate: The Voyage and Adventures of William Moraley, an Indentured Servant.* Edited by Susan E. Klepp and Billy G. Smith. 2nd ed. University Park: The Pennsylvania State University Press, 2005.

Morris, Richard B., ed. *Select Cases from the Mayor's Court of New York City, 1674–1784.* New York: American Historical Association, 1935.

"Narrative of Alexander Stewart." *Maryland Historical Magazine* 1 (1906): 349–352.

New Hampshire Laws, 1679–1702, Province Period. Vol. 1. Manchester, NH: John Clarke, 1904.

O'Callaghan, E. B., ed. *A Calendar of Historical Manuscripts in the Office of the Secretary of State.* Albany: Weed, Parsons, 1865.

O'Callaghan, E. B., ed. *Laws and Ordinances of New Netherland 1638–1674.* Albany: Weed, Parsons, 1868.

Orr, Charles, ed. *History of the Pequot War: The Contemporary Accounts of Mason, Underhill, Vincent and Gardener.* Cleveland: Helman-Taylor, 1897.

Paine, Thomas. *Common Sense; Addressed to the Inhabitants of America.* Philadelphia: Bradford, 1776.

Paine, Thomas. *The American Crisis.* London: Carlile, 1819.

Pearson, Jonathan, trans. *Early Records of the City and County of Albany and Colony of Rensselaerswyck.* Vol. 3. Albany: The University of the State of New York, 1918.

Pittman, Henry. *A Relation of the Great Sufferings and Strange Adventures of Henry Pitman, Chyrurgion to the late Duck of Monmouth.* London: Andrew Sowle, 1689.

Portsmouth Records, 1645–1656: A Transcript of the First Thirty-Five Pages of the Earliest Town Book, Portsmouth New Hampshire. Portsmouth, NH: By the author, 1886.

Portsmouth Town Records. Typescript, Portsmouth Library, Portsmouth, New Hampshire.

Purry, John Peter. *A Description of the Province of South Carolina, Drawn Up at Charles Town, in September, 1731.* Washington: Peter Force, 1837.

Revel, James. *The Poor Unhappy Felon's Sorrowful Account of the Fourteen Years Transportation at Virginia, in America.* York: Croshaw, n.d.

"Rev. John Eliot's Records of the First Church in Roxbury, Mass." *The New England Historical and Genealogical Register.* Vol. 33. Boston: Clapp and Son, 1879.

"Against Runaway Servants," 1658, reprinted in Encyclopedia of Virginia: http://www.encyclopediavirginia.org/_Against_Runaway_Servants_1657–1658

"Sales Contract between Thomas Jefferson and James Madison for an Indentured Servant's Remaining Term, 19 April 1809." Carter G. Woodson Collection, Library of Congress. http://memory.loc.gov/cgi-bin/query/h?ammem /mcc:@field(DOCID+@lit(mcc/060))

"Servants and Apprentices Bound and Assigned before James Hamilton Mayor of Philadelphia, 1745." *Pennsylvania Magazine of History and Biography* 30 (1906).

Smith, John. *Description of New England*. London: Robert Clerke, 1616. Reprint edition: *Works: 1608–1631*. Edited by Edward Arber. 2 vols. Birmingham: printed by author, 1884.

Smith, John. *The General History of Virginia*. 1624. Reprint edition: *Works: 1608–1631*. Edited by Edward Arber. 2 vols. Birmingham: printed by author, 1884.

Smith, John. *The Proceedings of the English Colonie in Virginia*. Oxford: J. Barnes, 1612. Reprint edition: *Works: 1608–1631*. Edited by Edward Arber. 2 vols. Birmingham: printed by author, 1884.

Smollett, Tobias. *The History of England from the Revolution to the Death of George the Second*. Vol. 3. London: Cadell and Baldwin, 1785.

Sparks, Jared, ed. *The Writings of George Washington*. Vol. 2. Boston: Little, Brown, 1847.

Sprague's Journal of Maine History 3 (1915–1916), 7 (1919–1920), 8 (1920–1921).

The Statues at Large; Being a Collection of All the Laws of Virginia from the First Session of the Legislature, in the Year 1619. Vol. 2. Edited by William W. Hening. New York: Bartow, 1823.

Supplement to the Boston Evening Post. November 30, 1772.

Thomas, Gabriel. *A Historical and Geographical Account of the Province and Country of Pensilvania; and of West-New-Jersey, in America*. London: Baldwin, 1698.

Toqueville, Alexis de. *Democracy in America*. Translated by Henry Reeve. Third Edition. 2 vols. New York: Adlard and Langley, 1839 and 1840.

Town Minutes of Newtown, 1653–1734. 4 vols. New York: The Historical Records Survey, 1941.

A True and Historical Narrative of the Colony of Georgia in America, from the First Settlement Thereof until This Present Period: Containing the Most Authentick Facts, Matters and Transactions Therein; Together with His Majesty's Charter, Representations of the People, Letters, &c. and a Dedication to His Excellency General Oglethorpe. http://quod.lib.umich.edu/e/evans/N03913.0001.001/1:4?rgn=div1;view=fulltext

Van der Donck, Adriaen. *A Description of New Netherlands*. 2nd ed. Amsterdam: Evert Nieuenhof, 1656.

Van Laer, A. J. F., ed. *Correspondence of Jeremias Van Rensselaer 1651–1674*. Albany: The University of the State of New York, 1932.

Van Laer, A. J. F., ed. *Early Records of the City and County of Albany and Colony of Rensselaerswyck*. Vol. 3. Albany: The University of the State of New York, 1918.

Van Laer, A. J. F., trans. *Minutes of the Court of Albany, Rensselaerswyck and Schenectady, 1668–1673, 1675–1680, 1680–1685*. 3 vols. Albany: The University of the State of New York, 1926–1932.

Van Laer, A. J. F., trans. *Minutes of the Court of Fort Orange and Beverwyck 1652–1656*. Vol. 1. Albany: The University of the State of New York, 1920.

Van Laer, A. J. F., trans. *Minutes of the Court of Fort Orange and Beverwyck, 1657–1660*. Vol. 2. Albany: The University of the State of New York, 1923.

Van Laer, A. J. F., ed. *Minutes of the Court of Rensselaerswyck 1648–1652*. Albany: The University of the State of New York, 1922.

Ward, Ned. *The London Spy Compleat*. 1703. http://grubstreetproject.net/works /T119938?image=338

Waugh, John. *A Sermon Preach'd at the Parish Church of St. Bridget, alias Bride, August 24, 1713, Being the Festival of St. Bartholomew; At a Meeting of about 1400 Persons of Both Sexes*. London: Strahan and Downing, 1713.

Whipple, Joseph. *A Geographical View of the District of Maine*. Bangor, ME: Edes, 1816.

Whitemore, William H. The Colonial Laws of Massachusetts. Boston: Rockwell and Churchill, 1890.

Williams, Roger. *A Key into the Language of North America*. 1643. Reprint ed. Bedford MA: Applewood Books, 1987.

"Witness to an Indenture, 9 October, 1721." *Miscellaneous Manuscripts*. Massachusetts Historical Society.

Secondary Sources

Adams, Nathaniel. *Annals of Portsmouth*. Portsmouth, NH: printed by author, 1825.

Alderman, Clifford L. *Colonists for Sale: The Story of Indentured Servants in America*. New York: Macmillian, 1975.

Allison, Hugh G. *Culloden Tales: Stories from Scotland's Most Famous Battlefield*. Edinburgh: Mainstream Publishing, 2007.

Bahadur, Gaiutra. *Coolie Woman: The Odyssey of Indenture*. Chicago: University of Chicago Press, 2014.

Ballagh, James C. *White Servitude in the Colony of Virginia: A Study of the System of Indentured Labor in the American Colonies*. Baltimore: Johns Hopkins, 1895.

Bartlett, John R., ed. *The Colony of Rhode Island and Providence Plantations, in New England: 1636–1663*. Providence: A. C. Greene, 1856.

Baseler, Marilyn C. *"Asylum for Mankind": America, 1607–1800*. Ithaca, NY: Cornell University Press, 1998.

Bassett, J. S. *Slavery and Servitude in North Carolina*. Baltimore: The John Hopkins Press, 1896.

Beer, George Louis. *The Old Colonial System: 1660–1754*. 2 vols. New York: Macmillan, 1912, 1913.

Benton, Josiah H. *Warning Out in New England*. Boston: W. B. Clarke, 1911.

Beverley, Robert. *The History of Virginia: In Four Parts*. London, 1722; revised ed., Richmond, VA: Randolph, 1855.

Blumenthal, Walter H. *Brides from Bridewell: Female Felons Sent to Colonial America*. Rutland, VT: C. E. Tuttle, 1962.

Bodge, John M. *Soldiers in King Philip's War: Being a Critical Account of That War, with a Concise History of the Indian Wars of New England, 1620–1677*. Boston: printed by author, 1906.

Brace, Charles Loring. *The Dangerous Classes of New York, and Twenty Years' Work among Them.* New York: Wynkoop and Hallenbeck, 1872.

Bridenbaugh, Carl. *Cities in the Wilderness: The First Century of Urban Life in America.* New York: Oxford University Press, 1938.

Bridenbaugh, Carl. *Jamestown, 1544–1699.* New York: Oxford University Press, 1980.

Bridenbaugh, Carl. *Vexed and Troubled Englishmen.* New York: Oxford University Press, 1968.

Bruce, Philip A. *Economic History of Virginia in the Seventeenth Century.* New York: Macmillan, 1907.

Buffalo Medical Journal and Monthly Review of Medical and Surgical Science. Edited by Austin Flint and S. B. Hunt. Buffalo, NY: Thomas and Lathrops, 1855.

Bushman, Richard L. *From Puritan to Yankee: Character and Social Order in Connecticut, 1690–1765.* Cambridge: Harvard University Press, 1967.

Butler, J. D. "British Convicts Shipped to American Colonies." *American Historical Review* 2 (1896): 12–33.

Campey, Lucille H. *The Scottish Pioneers of Upper Canada, 1784–1855: Glengarry and Beyond.* Toronto: Natural Heritage Books, 2005.

Candee, Richard. *Merchant and Millwright: The Water Powered Mills of the Piscataqua.* New England Bulletin of the Society for the Preservation of New England Antiquities. 1968.

Carnochan, Janet. *History of Niagara (in Part).* Toronto: Briggs, 1914.

Clarkson, L. A. *The Pre-Industrial Economy in England, 1500–1750.* London: B. T. Batsford, 1971.

Coldham, Peter W. *The Complete Book of Emigrants, 1607–1660.* Baltimore: Genealogical Publishing, 1987.

Coldham, Peter W. *English Adventurers and Emigrants, 1609–1660: Abstracts of Examinations in the High Court of Admiralty with Reference to Colonial America.* Baltimore: Clearfield, 1984.

Cole, Donald B. *Jacksonian Democracy in New Hampshire, 1800–1851.* Cambridge: Harvard University Press, 1970.

Coleman, Peter J. *Debtors and Creditors in America: Insolvency, Imprisonment for Debt, and Bankruptcy, 1607–1900.* Washington: Beard Books, 1999.

The Constitution and By-Laws of the Scots' Charitable Society of Boston. Cambridge: Wilson, 1878.

Craik, George L. and Charles Macfarlane, *The Pictorial History of England.* Vol. 3. London: Charles Knight, 1840.

Crane, Stephen. *Maggie: A Girl of the Streets.* New York: D. Appleton, 1896.

Crew, Albert. *London Prisons of Today and Yesterday.* London: Ivor Nicholson and Watson, 1933.

Cross, A. L. "English Criminal Law and the Benefit of the Clergy during the Eighteenth and Early Nineteenth Centuries." *American Historical Review* 22 (1917): 544–565.

Daniels, Bruce E. "Long Range Trends of Wealth Distribution in Eighteenth-Century New England." *Explorations in Economic History* 11 (1973–1974).

Dobson, David. *Scottish Emigration to Colonial America, 1607–1785*. Athens: University of Georgia Press, 1994.

Earle, Alice Morse. *Margaret Winthrop*. New York: Charles Scribner's Sons, 1895.

Flick, A. C., ed. *History of the State of New York*. Vols. 7–8. Port Washington: New York State Historical Association, 1962.

Fogel, Robert W., and Stanley L. Engerman. *Time on the Cross: The Economics of Negro Slavery*. Boston: Little, Brown, 1974.

Ford, Worthington C. *Washington as Employer and Importer of Labor*. Brooklyn: privately printed, 1889.

"Forensic Analysis of 17th-Century Human Remains at Jamestown, VA., Reveals Evidence of Survival Cannibalism." *Smithsonian Insider*. May 2013. http://smithsonianscience.si.edu/2013/05/forensic-analysis-of-17th-century-human-remains-at-jamestown-va-reveal-evidence-of-cannibalism/

Foxcroft, George A. *A Genealogy of the Descendants of Hugh Gunnison of Boston, Mass*. Boston: printed by author, 1880.

Galenson, David W. "The Rise and Fall of Indentured Servitude in the Americas: An Economic Analysis." *The Journal of Economic History* 44 (1984): 1–26.

Gallay, Alan, ed. *Indian Slavery in Colonial America*. Lincoln: University of Nebraska Press, 2009.

Gallay, Alan, ed. *Voice of the Old South: Eyewitness Accounts, 1528–1861*. Athens: University of Georgia Press, 1994.

Games, Alison. *Migration and the Origins of the English Atlantic World*. Cambridge: Harvard University Press, 2001.

Geiser, Karl F. *Redemptioners and Indentured Servants in the Colony and Commonwealth of Pennsylvania*. New Haven, CT: The Tuttle, Morehouse, and Taylor Company, 1901.

Gillian, Charles F. "Jail Bird Immigrants to Virginia." *Virginia Historical Magazine* 52 (1944): 180–182.

Goodrich, Charles A. *Lives of the Signers to the Declaration of Independence*. New York: Thomas Mather, 1837.

Gookin, Frederick W. *Daniel Gookin, 1612–1687: Assistant and Major General of the Massachusetts Bay Colony*. Chicago: printed by author, 1912.

Greer, Allan. *The People of New France*. Toronto: University of Toronto Press, 1997.

Greer, George C. *Early Virginia Immigrants*. Richmond: W. C. Hill Printing Company, 1913.

Guasco, Michael. *Slaves and Englishmen: Human Bondage in the Early Modern Atlantic World*. Philadelphia: University of Pennsylvania Press, 2014.

Haar, Charles. "White Indentured Servants in Colonial New York." *Americana* 34 (1940) 370–392.

Handlin, Oscar, and Mary Handlin. *Origins of the Southern Labor System*. Indianapolis: Bobbs-Merrill, 1957.

Harley, Lewis. *The Life of Charles Thomson: Secretary to the Continental Congress and Translator of the Bible from the Greek*. Philadelphia: George W. Jacobs, 1900.

Harris, Thaddeus M. *Biographical Memorials of James Oglethorpe: Founder of the Colony of Georgia.* Boston: printed by author, 1841.

Hasbach, Wilhelm. *A History of the English Agricultural Labourer.* London: P. S. King, 1908.

Herrick, Cheesman A. *White Servitude in Pennsylvania: Indentured and Redemption Labor in Colony and Commonwealth.* Philadelphia: J. J. McVey, 1926.

Hill, Jackie. "Case Studies in Indentured Servitude in Colonial America." *Constructing the Past* 9, no. 1 (2008): Article 9.

Hofstadter, Richard. *America at 1750: A Social Portrait.* New York: Random House, 1971.

Hopkins, Charles. *The Home Lots of Early Settlers of the Providence Plantation.* Baltimore: Clearfield, 2009.

Hume, Robert. *Early Child Immigrants to Virginia, 1618–1642.* Baltimore: Magna Carta Book Company, 1986.

Iceland, John. *Poverty in America.* 2nd ed. Berkeley: University of California Press, 2006.

"Indenture of David Thomson." *Proceedings of the Massachusetts Historical Society.* Boston: Massachusetts Historical Society, 1875–1876.

Innes, Stephen. *Labor in a New Land: Economy and Society in Seventeenth Century Springfield.* Princeton, NJ: Princeton University Press, 1983.

Jackson, Gaines B. *Indentured Servitude Revisited.* Bloomington, IN: Xlibris, 2014.

Janney, Samuel M. *The Life of William Penn: With Selections from His Correspondence and Autobiography.* 2nd ed. Philadelphia: Lippincott, 1852.

Jernegan, Marcus W. *Laboring and Dependent Classes in Colonial America, 1607–1783.* New York: Frederick Ungar, 1965.

Jordan, Don, and Michael Walsh. *White Cargo: The Forgotten History of Britain's White Slaves in America.* New York: New York University Press, 2008.

Kellaway, William. *The New England Company, 1649–1776: Missionary Society to the American Indians.* New York: Barnes and Noble, 1961.

Knorr, Klaus. *British Colonial Theories, 1570–1850.* Toronto: University of Toronto Press, 1944.

Knowles, James D. *Memoir of Roger Williams: The Founder of the State of Rhode-Island.* Boston: Lincoln, Edmands, 1834.

Lauber, Almon W. *Indian Slavery in the Colonial Times within the Present Limits of the United States.* PhD dissertation, Columbia University, 1913.

Lawson, Russell M. "The English Poor Laws in the Age of Mercantilism." *Oklahoma State Historical Review* 2 (1981).

Lawson, Russell M. *Passaconaway's Realm: Captain John Evans and the Exploration of Mount Washington.* Hanover, NH: University Press of New England, 2002.

Lawson, Russell M. *Portsmouth: An Old Town by the Sea.* Charlestown, SC: Arcadia Publishing, 2003.

Lawson, Russell M. *The Sea Mark: Captain John Smith's Journey to New England.* Hanover, NH: University Press of New England, 2015.

Lawson, Russell M., and Benjamin A. Lawson. *Poverty in America: An Encyclopedia.* Westport, CT: Greenwood Press, 2008.

Leavitt, Emily W. *Palmer Groups: John Melvin of Charlestown, and Concord, Mass. and His Descendants.* Boston: David Clapp and Son, 1901–1905.

Leonard. E. M. *The Early History of English Poor Law Relief.* Cambridge: University Press, 1900.

Lepore, Jill. *In the Name of War: King Philip's War and the Origins of American Identity.* New York: Knopf Doubleday, 2009.

Lewis, Alonzo, and James R. Newhall. *History of Lynn, Essex County, Massachusetts.* Boston: Shorey, 1865.

Lindert, Peter H. *Fertility and Scarcity in America.* Princeton, NJ: Princeton University Press, 1978.

Litwack, Leon. *North of Slavery: The Negro in the Free States, 1790–1860.* Chicago: University of Chicago Press, 1971.

Lockley, Timothy J. *Lines in the Sand: Race and Class in Lowcountry Georgia, 1750–1860.* Athens: University of Georgia Press, 2001.

Lunn, Alice J. E. *Economic Development in New France, 1713–1760.* PhD dissertation, McGill University, 1942.

MacKay, Thomas. *The English Poor: A Sketch of Their Social and Economic History.* London: Murray, 1889.

McCormac, Eugene I. *White Servitude in Maryland, 1634–1820.* Baltimore: Johns Hopkins Press, 1904.

McKee Jr., Samuel. *Labor in Colonial New York, 1664–1776.* New York: Columbia University Press, 1935.

McLaughlin, James F. *Matthew Lyon, the Hampden of Congress: A Biography.* New York: Wynkoop Hallenbeck Crawford, 1900.

Main, Gloria L. *Tobacco Colony: Life in Early Maryland, 1650–1720.* Princeton, NJ: Princeton University Press, 1982.

Main, Jackson T. *The Social Structure of Revolutionary America.* Princeton, NJ: Princeton University Press, 1965.

Marcou, Jane Belknap. *Life of Jeremy Belknap, D. D. The Historian of New Hampshire.* New York: Harper, 1847.

Marin, Richard B. *Runaways of Colonial New Jersey: Indentured Servants, Slaves, Deserters, and Prisoners, 1720–1781.* Berwyn Heights: Heritage Books, 2007.

Marshall, Dorothy. *English People in the 18th Century.* London: Longmans, 1965.

"Master John Sullivan, Margery Sullivan, and Their Remarkable Family, Berwick, Maine." http://www.oldberwick.org/index.php?option=com_content&view=article&id=518&Itemid=285

Middleton, Stephen. *The Black Laws in the Old Northwest: A Documentary History.* Westport, CT: Greenwood Press, 1993.

Middleton, Stephen. *The Black Laws: Race and the Legal Process in Early Ohio.* Athens: Ohio University Press, 2005.

Montaigne, Michel de. *Essays.* Translated by Donald M. Frame. Stanford: Stanford University Press, 1958.

Morgan, Edmund S. *American Slavery, American Freedom.* New York: W. W. Norton, 2003.

Morgan, Kenneth. *Slavery and Servitude in Colonial North America: A Short History.* New York: New York University Press, 2001.

Morris, Richard B. *Government and Labor in Early America.* New York: Harper and Row, 1946.

Mortimer, Ian. *The Time Traveler's Guide to Elizabethan England.* New York: Penguin, 2012.

Murray, David. *Colonial Justice: Justice, Morality, and Crime in the Niagara District, 1791–1849.* Toronto: University of Toronto Press, 2002.

Neill, Edward D. *History of the Virginia Company of London, with Letters to and from the First Colony Never before Printed.* Albany: Joel Munsell, 1869.

Newell, Margaret Ellen. *Brethren by Nature: New England Indians, Colonists, and the Origins of American Slavery.* Ithaca, NY: Cornell University Press, 2015.

New England Historical and Genealogical Register. Vol. 46. Boston: New-England Historic Genealogical Society, 1892.

New Georgia Encyclopedia. "James Oglethorpe, 1696–1785." http://www.georgi aencyclopedia.org/articles/history-archaeology/james-oglethorpe -1696-1785

Nicholls, George. *A History of the English Poor Law.* 2 vols. London: Murray, 1854.

O'Callaghan, E. B. *History of New Netherland; or, New York under the Dutch.* Vol. 2. 2nd ed. New York: D. Appleton, 1855.

Pelling, Margaret. *The Common Lot: Sickness, Medical Occupations and the Urban Poor in Early Modern England.* New York: Routledge, 2014.

Pentland, H. Clare. *Labour and Capital in Canada, 1650–1860.* Toronto: James Lorimer, 1981.

The Popham Colony: A Discussion of Its Historical Claims. Boston: K. Wiggin and Lunt, 1866.

Porter, Bill. "Lawson, William—A Scottish Rebel." http://www.electricscotland .com/webclans/minibios/l/lawson_william.htm

Radzinowicz, Leon. *A History of English Criminal Law: And Its Administration to 1750.* London: Stevens, 1948.

Reese, Peter. *Cromwell's Masterstroke: The Battle of Dunbar, 1650.* South Yorkshire: Pen and Sword Books, 2006.

Ribton-Turner, C. J. *A History of Vagrants and Vagrancy, and Beggars and Begging.* London: Chapman and Hall, 1887.

Riis, Jacob A. *How the Other Half Lives: Studies among the Tenements of New York.* New York: Charles Scribner's Sons, 1890.

Rodriguez, Junius P., ed. *The Historical Encyclopedia of World Slavery.* Vol. 1. Santa Barbara, CA: ABC-CLIO, 1997.

Rushton, Peter. "'Barbados'd'—The Transportation of Convicts," in *Convict Voyages: A Global History of Convicts and Penal Colonies.* http://convictvoyages .org/expert-essays/caribbean

Russell, David L. *Oglethorpe and Colonial Georgia: A History, 1733–1783.* Jefferson: McFarland and Company, 2006.

Rutkow, Ira. *Seeking the Cure: A History of Medicine in America.* New York: Scribner, 2010.

"Scots Prisoners and Their Relocation to the Colonies, 1650–1654." https://www
.geni.com/projects/Scots-Prisoners-and-their-Relocation-to-the-Colonies
-1650-1654/3465

"The Scottish Prisoners of 1650." Old Berwick Historical Society. http://oldber
wick.org/index.php?option=com_content&view=article&id=261:the
-scottish-prisoners-of-1650&catid=53:historical-events&Itemid=72

Seybolt, Robert F. *Apprenticeship & Apprenticeship Education in Colonial New England & New York.* New York: Columbia University, 1917.

Shaw, A. G. L. *Convicts and the Colonies: A Study of Penal Transportation from Great Britain and Ireland to Australia and Other Parts of the British Empire.* London: Faber, 1966.

Simcox, Alison C., and Douglas L Heath. *Breakheart Reservation.* Charleston, SC: Arcadia Publishing, 2013.

Sinclair, Upton. *The Jungle.* Printed by author, 1920.

Smith, Abbot E. *Colonists in Bondage: White Servitude and Convict Labor in America, 1607–1776.* New York: W. W. Norton, 1947.

Smith, Abbot E. "Indentured Servants: New Light on Some of America's First Families." *Journal of Economic History* 2 (1942): 40–53.

Smith, Warren B. *White Servitude in Colonial South Carolina.* Columbia: University of South Carolina Press, 1961.

Stackpole, Everett S. *Old Kittery and Her Families.* Kittery, ME: Lewiston Journal Company, 1903.

Steinfeld, Robert J. *The Invention of Free Labor: The Employment Relation in English and American Law and Culture, 1350–1870.* Chapel Hill: University of North Carolina Press, 2014.

Tepper, Michael, ed. *New World Immigrants: A Consolidation of Ship Passenger Lists and Associated Data from Periodical Literature.* Vol. 1. Baltimore: Genealogical Publishing, 1979.

Thompson, Ralph E., and Matthew R. Thompson. *David Thomson 1592–1628, First Yankee.* Portsmouth, NH: Peter E. Randall Publisher, 1997.

Tomlins, Christopher L. *Freedom Bound: Law, Labor, and Civic Identity in Colonizing English America, 1580–1865.* New York: Cambridge University Press, 2010.

Tomlins, Christopher L. *Law, Labor, and Ideology in the Early American Republic.* New York: Cambridge University Press, 1993.

Tooker, William W. *John Eliot's First Indian Teacher and Interpreter: Cockenoe-de-Long Island and the Story of His Career from the Early Records.* New York: Francis P. Harper, 1896.

Towner, Lawrence W. *A Good Master Well Served: Masters and Servants in Colonial Massachusetts.* New York: Taylor and Francis, 1998.

Ulrich, Laurel T. *Good Wives: Image and Reality in the Lives of Women in Northern New England, 1650–1750.* New York: Alfred A. Knopf, 1982.

Vaughan, Alden T., and Edward W. Clark, eds. *Puritans among the Indians: Accounts of Captivity and Redemption, 1676–1724.* Cambridge: Harvard University Press, 2009.

Wareing, John. *Emigrants to America: Indentured Servants Recruited in London, 1718–1733.* Baltimore: Genealogical Publishing, 1985.

Webb, Sidney, and Beatrice Webb. *English Prisons under Local Government.* London: Longmans Green, 1922.

White, George. *Historical Collections of Georgia.* New York: Pudney and Russell, 1855.

Whittemore, Henry. *Genealogical Guide to the Early Settlers of America.* Baltimore: Genealogical Publishing, 1967.

Williamson, Jeffrey G., and Peter H. Lindert. *American Inequality: A Macroeconomic History.* New York: Academic Press, 1980.

Winsor, Justin. *The Memorial History of Boston.* Vol. 1. Boston: Osgood, 1881.

Wright, Louis B. *The Cultural Life of the American Colonies.* New York: Harper and Row, 1957.

Index

Adams, John, 147–149
Aitken, Robert, 140–143
Albany, New York. *See* Fort Orange
Almshouse, 6, 48–49, 52, 74
America, promise of, 3–4, 13–14,
    71–73, 85, 94, 96–97, 100,
    103–106, 120, 145–147
American-Indians, 2, 12, 19–28,
    31–40, 43, 49, 62–64, 97, 119,
    136–137, 149–150, 152–153;
    Abenakis, 26, 31, 36–38;
    Algonquians, 2, 11, 19, 21, 23, 26,
    62; Iroquois, 22, 62–64; Mashpees,
    26; Massabesics, 26; Massachusetts,
    21–22, 26; Mi'kmaqs, 26, 37–38;
    Mohegans, 26; Mohicans, 64;
    Montauks, 19–20; Narragansetts,
    21, 24–25; Nausets, 26; Nipmucs,
    24, 26; Norridgewocks, 26, 39;
    Passamaquoddys, 26; Penacooks,
    22, 26, 28, 31; Penobscots, 26–28,
    38; Pequawkets, 26, 28; Pequods,
    26; Pequots, 19–20, 26;
    Piscataquas, 26; Sokokis, 26;
    Wampanoags, 24
American Revolution. *See* War for
    American Independence
Andriesz, Claes, 59
Anglican Church. *See* Church of
    England
Anguish, Thomas, 7–8

Antigua, 115
Apprentices. *See* Servants
Atkinson, John, 48

Bacon, Francis, 41
Bacon's Rebellion, 127, 153
Baker, Thomas, 33
Barbados, 104, 114–115, 118–119
Belknap, Jeremy, 33, 140–143; *History
    of New-Hampshire,* 28, 140
Belknap, Joseph, 140–143
Belknap, Ruth, 141–142
Benefit of the clergy, 76–77
Beverley, Robert, 127–128
Birkenhead (rebellion), 117
Bondage. *See* Bound labor
Book of Common Prayer, 4–5
Boston, Massachusetts, 29, 31, 43,
    47–48, 51, 52, 88, 93, 117, 131,
    136, 138, 140–143
Bothwell Bridge, Battle of, 115
Bound labor, 9, 12, 14–15, 19–20,
    25–26, 32, 40–42, 90, 105,
    113–114, 119, 143, 145, 150–153
Boyle, Robert, 22–23, 31
Breckenridge, Maria, 39
Bridewell, 1, 6, 7, 9, 10, 13, 68,
    75–76
British colonial policy, 14, 104
Bullock, William, 14
Byles, Mather, Jr., 138

Callicott, Richard, 20–21
Caribbean, 20, 29, 114, 116
Champernowne, Francis, 45–46
Chanco, 12
Charles River, 22
Charter of Freedoms and Exemptions, 55
Chesapeake Bay, 2, 119, 127
Church of England, 4–5, 57, 77, 130
Cochecho River, 31, 35, 43, 140
Cockenoe, 20–23
Colquhoun, Patrick, 72–75
Commonwealth, 70, 75, 87–88, 115–116, 119
Connecticut River, 19, 56
Constitution, U.S., 148, 151
Convicts. *See* Felons
Convict transportation. *See* Servants, transported
Council of New England, 42–43
Council of Virginia, 10
Craigie, James, 123, 130–131
Crevecoeur, J. Hector St. John de, 145–146, 150, 153, 155
Cromwell, Oliver, 88, 116–119, 127
Culloden, Battle of, 113–114, 119

Daingerfield, William, 129–133
Davis, Richard, 48
Debt imprisonment, 61, 76, 103, 106, 151
Declaration of Independence, 145–147, 152, 154
Deerfield, Massachusetts, 33
Defoe, Daniel, 68–77, 93, 103, 153; *Colonel Jack,* 69, 71–74, 77; *Giving Alms No Charity,* 73–74; *Life and Adventures of Duncan Campbell,* 68; *Moll Flanders,* 68–69, 72, 77, 93, 154
Delaware River, 82, 93–98
Democracy, 146–147
De Tocqueville, Alexis, 146
De Vries, David Pietersz, 12
Dircksz, Adriaen, 58

Dispossession, 106, 120, 152–153
Dover, New Hampshire, 28, 31, 33, 140–141
Dunbar, Battle of, 116–119
Dutch East India Company, 51
Dutch West India Company, 51, 57

Eddis, William, 72, 85, 88–90
Eden, Frederic, 7
Eliot, John, 21–23, 31
Enclosure movement, 8
Endicott, John, 19
Engagés, 32
Enlightenment, 149–150
Ewen, William, 109–110

Felons, 9, 10, 15, 32, 41, 59, 68–78, 89, 103, 127–128, 150
Fielding, Henry, 68–69, 73–74
Fleet, 103
Fort Orange (Fort Nassau), 55, 57, 59, 61–63
France, 22, 26–28, 31–32, 34, 36, 38, 113, 116
Franklin, Benjamin, 77–78, 88, 93, 143
Freedom, ideas of, 6, 104, 107, 110, 143, 145–150, 153–155
Freedom dues, 58, 84, 87, 98–100, 128, 151
Freeman, John, 151
Free Willers. *See* Redemptioners

Gee, Joshua, 7, 72
Gerrish, Sarah, 32–33
Gibbons, Ambrose, 43–44, 116
Glen, Jacob Sandersz, 61
Glorious Revolution, 26, 69, 113, 115, 145
Gookin, Daniel, 23
Gorges, Ferdinando, 41–43, 45
Great Commission, 12
Gunnison, Hugh, 45
Gyles, John, 33–38; *Memoirs of Odd Adventures, Strange Deliverances, &c. in the Captivity of John Gyles, Esq.,*

Commander of the Garrison on St. George's River, 33, 36, 38
Gyles, Thomas, 34

Hanover Dynasty: George I, 75–76; George II, 103–104, 106
Harrison, William, 7
Harrower, Annie, 123, 125, 129, 130, 131, 133
Harrower, John, 13, 123–133, 153
Hawkins, Margaret (Harwood), 24
Hawkins, William, 24–25
Hawley, Gideon, 26
Hazard, Ebenezer, 140–142
Headrights, 11, 86
Henricksz, Dirck, 59
Hobson, Mary, 136
Hole, John, 46
Hospital, 3, 6, 7, 74
House of correction, 3, 6–7, 51, 74–76
How, Millicent, 104
Hudson, Henry, 55
Hudson River, 55–56, 62

Immigrants, 12–13, 45, 79, 86, 96, 98–100, 104, 120, 145–146, 150–152
Isles of Shoals, 46

Jamaica, 115
James River, 1, 11–12, 127
Jamestown, 1–3, 41, 70; children in, 1–2, 14–15
Jefferson, Thomas, 147–154
Jesus of Nazareth, 145
Johnson, Samuel, 155
Jones, Thomas, 46
Just war, 20

Kennebec River, 34, 39, 41, 43
Kidnapping, 8, 14, 26, 68, 87
King, John, 87
King James Bible, 5
Kittery, Maine, 43, 45–46, 117
Knight, Nathan, 136–137
Knight, Roger, 44–45

Labor. *See* Bound labor
Latham, William, 42
Laws: against the criminal poor, 49, 74, 76; against kidnapping the poor, 14; regulating servant interaction with Indians, 63; regulating servitude, 58, 72, 128, 135, 137–138; in relief of the poor, 5–6, 8, 48, 50, 74, 76; transporting felons to America, 69, 75–76, 127
Lawson, William, 114
Leader, Richard, 116–117
London, 1, 6, 7, 8–10, 42, 67–71, 73–77, 93–94, 103–105, 116–117, 124–127, 131
London Company, 1, 10, 11, 12
Lord Mayor of London, 9, 10, 94
Lyon, Matthew, 153–154

Madison, James, 151
Maine, 3, 27–28, 31, 33–34, 37–38, 41, 43, 116–117
Manorial system, 6–7
Marshalsea, 7
Martyn, Benjamin, 105–106
Mason, John, 43–45, 116
Massachusetts Body of Liberties, 20
Maverick, Samuel, 46
Mercantilism. *See* British colonial policy
Merrimack River, 22, 28, 43
Middle colonies: New Jersey, 95–96, 99; New York, 19–20, 23, 27, 51, 55, 57–62, 64, 86, 93, 98, 131, 151–152, 154; Pennsylvania, 26, 27, 81–82, 84–88, 94, 96–97
Midland Revolt, 8
Missionaries, 21–23
Mittelberger, Gottlieb, 81–86, 89
Monmouth Rebellion, 115
Montaigne, Michel de, 149–150
Moore, Jasper, 42
Moraley, William, 94–98, 100
Morgan, Edmund S., 153
Mycall, John, 143

Nesutan, Job, 23
Netherlands, the, 55–57, 124, 131
Neulander, 85–86, 89
New Amsterdam, 57
New England colonies: Connecticut, 19–20, 24, 26–27, 64, 137–138; Massachusetts, 19–24, 26–28, 38, 45, 51, 116, 137–138, 143; New Hampshire, 28, 31, 42–43, 50, 116, 136, 140, 143; Plymouth, 24, 42, 137; Rhode Island, 19–20, 24–25, 136
New England Company, 23, 31
New France, 31–34, 39
Newgate, 7, 13, 68–69, 71–72, 75–76, 78, 95
Newichawannock River, 43–45, 116
New Netherland, 55–61, 64
Nolden, Evert, 58–59
Norwich Children's Hospital, 7–8

Oglethorpe, James, 103–109
Old Bailey, 68, 76–77
Ontario, 39, 120
Opechancanough, 11
Otis, Margaret, 33
Overseers of the poor, 6, 48–51, 99

Paine, Thomas, 114, 147–148, 153
Palatine (Palatinate), 79, 81, 84, 86, 95
Parliament, 14, 39, 51, 75–78, 90, 103, 109, 116, 129–130
Passaconaway, 22
Patroon, 55–56, 59, 64
Pearson, Isaac, 95, 98
Pels, Evert, 57, 60–61
Pemaquid, Maine, 33–34
Penn, William, 85–87
Penobscot River, 27, 34, 37–39
Penruddock Uprising, 115
Philadelphia, 77, 86–88, 90, 93–94, 98–100, 140–143, 151, 154
Phips, Spencer, 27
Piscataqua River, 28–29, 31, 42–47, 51, 116, 141
Pitman, Henry, 115

Plymouth Company, 42
Poor: children, 1, 3–10, 12, 14, 42, 48, 50, 67–69, 87, 106, 152; disabled, 7, 49; in England, 1–10, 12–14, 16, 42, 67–77, 94, 103–106, 125; insane, 7, 49; orphans, 7, 8, 51, 67, 69, 103; sturdy, 3, 6–7, 47–48, 70–71, 75, 106; vagrants and vagabonds, 6, 8–9, 49, 71, 74–76; widows, 51, 71
Popham, John, 41
Portsmouth, New Hampshire, 45–51, 136, 141
Portsmouth, Rhode Island, 25, 136
Pring, Martin, 42
Providence, Rhode Island, 24–25
Purry, John Peter, 105
Pynchon, John, 117–118

Quakers, 25, 95, 104
Quebec, 31, 33, 38–39

Rappahannock River, 70, 127, 129
Redemptioners, 26, 79, 82–87, 89, 105, 150–151, 153
Reed, John, 47
Renaissance, 149
Rensselaerswyck, 56–61
Restoration (1660), 20, 34, 70, 104, 127
Revel, James, 69–70
Revolution, 147–150, 152
Rhine River, 81–82, 84, 86
Rogers, Christopher, 46

Saco River, 28, 37, 43
Sagadahoc, 41–43
Sandys, Edwin, 10
Sassamon, John, 23
Saugus ironworks, 117
Savannah River, 105, 107–110
Scotland, 44, 70–71, 87, 99, 100, 113–117, 120, 123–125, 133, 143
Scotland, Maine, 117
Scots' Charitable Society, 117
Seasoning, 12

Servants: African-American, 15, 32, 39, 49, 57, 60, 63, 138, 150–151, 153; American-Indian, 12, 15, 19–26, 28–29, 32, 52, 54, 57, 64, 136, 138, 150, 153; apprentices, 5–6, 10, 11, 32, 42, 48, 50, 70, 93–94, 97, 99–100, 135–143, 151; children, 1, 5–6, 10–11, 15, 45, 48–50, 68, 76, 83–85, 87, 135–143; Dutch, 56–64, 87; English, 5, 9, 11, 13, 14, 25, 32, 33–40, 42–44, 47–48, 68, 70–71, 85, 87, 94–100, 104–106, 108–109, 125, 127–129, 138–143, 153; French, 11, 32, 38, 64; German, 26, 83–87, 95, 107, 118–119, 127; indentured, 32, 45, 49–50, 56–57, 73, 78–79, 86, 93–99, 104, 117, 126–129, 131, 135–138, 151, 153–154; Irish, 87–88, 93–94, 99–100, 153–154; relationship to masters, 5–6, 13, 48, 57–64, 70, 88–89, 135–143; runaways, 49, 70, 84, 88–89, 93–96, 128, 137–138; Scandinavian, 44–45; Scots, 39, 44, 87, 99–100, 107, 114–118, 125–133, 153; suffering in America, 12–13, 64, 83–86, 88–89, 115–116, 118–119; Swiss, 105; transported, 9–11, 14, 19, 32, 41, 43, 55–56, 68–78, 89, 103, 114–116, 127, 150; voyage across the Atlantic, 12, 64, 82–83, 94, 100, 107, 115, 126–127; Welsh, 87
Servitude. *See* Servants
Shetland Islands, 123–127, 130
Slavery, 14–15, 19–21, 25, 26, 28–29, 39, 52, 70–72, 77, 88–89, 95–97, 104–105, 107–110, 113, 118, 127–129, 143, 149–150, 153
Small, Elizabeth, 46
Smith, Captain John, 2–4, 11–12, 20, 42; *Description of New England* and, 2–4, 42
Smollett, Tobias, 114

Society for Propagating the Gospel, 107
Society for Propagation of the Gospel in New England. *See* New England Company
Southern colonies: Georgia, 103–110; Maryland, 72–73, 77, 89, 104, 114, 125, 131, 151; North Carolina, 104–106, 123–124; South Carolina, 104–107, 115; Virginia, 9–14, 41, 70, 72, 77, 104, 114–116, 125, 127–131
Spain, 107–108
Spirits (crimps), 14, 67–68, 71, 85, 94
Statute of Artificers, 5, 135
Stewart, Alexander, 119–120
Stewart, Duncan, 118
Stewart, John, 117
St. John's River, 31, 35, 37–39
St. Lawrence River, 22, 31
Strawberry Banke, 43, 46–47
Stuart, Charles (Bonnie Prince Charlie), 113–114
Stuart, James, 114
Stuart Dynasty: Charles I, 14, 42, 116–118; Charles II, 14, 70, 75, 86, 104, 115–11, 127; James I, 3–5, 8, 10, 41–43; James II, 34, 113
Stubbes, Phillip, 7
Sullivan, James, 153–154
Sullivan, John, 51, 153–154
Swarton, Hannah, 38

Taylor, George, 154
Thomson, Charles, 153–154
Thomson, David, 42
Thorpe, George, 13
Tudor, Elizabeth (I), 1–2, 5–6, 8, 48, 74
Turner, William, 23–34
Tyburn, 13, 68–69, 76

United Colonies of New England, 23
Upper Canada. *See* Ontario

Van der Donck, Adriaen, 56–57, 65; *A Description of New Netherlands,* 56
Van der Ripe, Mary, 61–62

Van Rensselaer, Killian, 56, 61
Van Slichtenhorst, Brant, 57–59
Vines, Richard, 42–43
Virginia Company. *See* London
    Company
Von Uchteritz, Heinrich, 118–119

Waaubon, 22
Wahunsenacawh (Powhatan), 11
Waldron, Richard, 28–29, 31–32,
    35
Wannalancet, 22, 29
Wannerton, Thomas, 44–45
War: Dummer's War, 26, 33, 38;
    English Civil War, 116, 118;
    French-Indian War, 26–27, 38–39;
    King George's, 26, 38; King Philip's,
    20, 23–26, 28, 34, 47, 114; King
    William's (War of the League of
    Augsburg), 26, 31, 33–34, 38, 47,
    81; Pequot, 19–20, 24, 114; Queen
    Anne's (War of the Spanish

Succession), 26, 38, 75, 81; Thirty
    Years, 56, 81; War for American
    Independence, 39, 51, 72, 77, 90,
    110, 114, 120, 131–133, 143, 145,
    147–148, 151, 153–154
War captives, 19–20, 26–29, 32–40,
    114–119
Ward, Ned, 67–68
Warning out, 46
Washington, George, 78–79, 129,
    148, 153
Waugh, John, 138–140
Webb, George, 94
Wesley, John, 107
Whitney, Samuel, 38–39
Williams, Roger, 21, 24–25
Williamson, Peter, 87
Winthrop, John, 21
Winthrop, John, Jr., 21, 117
Worcester, Battle of, 116, 118
Workhouse, 3, 6–7, 48–51, 74–75,
    88, 106

About the Author

Russell M. Lawson is professor of history at Bacone College, a Fulbright Scholar, and author of over a dozen books. He has a BA and a MA from Oklahoma State University and a PhD from the University of New Hampshire. In 2010, Dr. Lawson was Fulbright Visiting Research Chair in Transnational Studies at Brock University. In December 2011, Fulbright Canada awarded him a grant to establish a traditional organic garden for teaching purposes at Bacone College. Dr. Lawson teaches and writes on scientists and explorers; the history of America, Europe, and the world; the history of ideas; and social history. His works include four books published by ABC-CLIO/Greenwood/Praeger: *Encyclopedia of American Indian Issues Today* (2013); *Poverty in America: An Encyclopedia* (2008); *Science in the Ancient World: An Encyclopedia* (2004); and *The American Plutarch: Jeremy Belknap and the Historian's Dialogue with the Past* (1998).